PRAISE FOR
THE FIRE OUTSIDE MY WINDOW

"The Cedar fire was a landmark event in American and Californian fire history. It continues to be a valuable case study for fire-line leaders and emergency responders. *The Fire Outside My Window* captures the epic scale, drama, and impact of today's recurring megafires better than any other book I know, and Sandra Younger's harrowing account of her own brush with death should be required reading for all emergency responders and anyone who lives in the wildland-urban interface. *The Fire Outside My Window* has become a classic account of a historic wildfire."

Tom Boatner
Chief, Bureau of Land Management (BLM)
Fire Operations (retired)

"Sandra Millers Younger has brilliantly documented what is now a sadly recurring tragedy. But she doesn't stop there—she tells how she survived and leads us into ways we can better live in this world of nature and neighbors. She's more than a survivor. She's a trustworthy guide."

Dean Nelson, Ph.D., author of *Talk to Me, God Hides in Plain Sight* and two other books
Director, Journalism Program
Director, Writer's Symposium by the Sea
Point Loma Nazarene University, San Diego, California

"As we in the fire service battle what has become a year-round fire season—from megafires burning across cactus-covered landscapes to wind-driven blazes raging through once-safe coastal zones—we aim to seek out and widely share resources that have the power to shift perspectives, educate the public, and bolster support for first responders. Sandra Younger's book is such a resource, and in my half-century of fighting California's biggest wildfires, few case studies have inspired the resilience or cultivated the information necessary to truly transform and elevate wildfire suppression as much as *The Fire Outside My Window*."

Brian Fennessy
Fire chief, Orange County [California] Fire Authority
2023 International Association of Fire Chiefs (IAFC)
Chief of the Year

"Sandra Younger's book should be required reading for those who live where homes and wildlands—and wildfire—meet. Younger has done a splendid, literate job of reporting her own near-death experience with Southern California's catastrophic Cedar Fire and expanding the account into a broader tale of what it's like for everyone, from firefighters to homeowners, to experience one of these howling monsters, which destroy dreams, landscapes, and sometimes lives."

John N. Maclean
Author, *Home Waters*, *River of Fire*, and four other
acclaimed books about wildfire

"The roughest assignment of many bad fires that I ever commanded as a CAL FIRE incident commander was the 2003 Cedar Fire. I thought I knew everything about the fire until I read Sandra Younger's book, *The Fire Outside My Window*. Critical details added to my framework of thoughts, enabling me to better understand not just what firefighters faced at that fate-testing fire, which killed fifteen people, but the serious situation citizens faced. They awoke during the night to find rapidly spreading fire enveloping communities and their own properties. The element of panic encased the moments of real threat. I highly recommend *The Fire Outside My Window*. This book should be mandatory reading for all fire officers, commanders and emergency managers. Thank you, Sandra Younger."

John R. Hawkins
Incident commander, Cedar Fire
CAL FIRE unit chief and Riverside County
[California] fire chief (retired)

"Sandra Younger's depiction of her family's harrowing escape from a catastrophic fire will have you sitting on the edge of your seat from start to finish. Her personal story of survival is masterfully interwoven with that of a larger tapestry of tales—of families torn apart by death and injury, of valiant firefighters, even that of the lost hunter who ignited the tragic blaze. Younger's memoir gains special relevance in this era of epic wildfires, not just in California but the rest of the world. This book should be required reading for those who live in harm's way, for firefighters, and for anyone who enjoys a well-told, suspenseful story."

Marivi Soliven Blanco
Author, *The Mango Bride*

"*The Fire Outside My Window* brings readers directly into the flames of tragedy, heroic resilience and community spirit experienced during and after the Cedar and Paradise fires as written from the personal experience of Sandra Millers Younger. As a fire chief with the responsibility to protect over 23,000 residents who live within 85 square miles of a beautiful but dangerous backcountry community, I use Sandra's amazing story to educate people who live, work, and play in our community. She helps us understand that megafires are a force of nature that will continue to occur. And when they do, we will all be better prepared from the personal experiences and lessons shared in *The Fire Outside My Window.*"

Joe Napier
Fire chief, Valley Center [California] Fire Protection District

"The Cedar Fire ushered in the megafire era, and people around the world continue to learn the same hard lessons described in Sandra's book after the fact. Sandra's reporting is comprehensive and extremely unbiased given her experience as a survivor. Emergency responder, elected official or resident of the wildland-urban interface, *The Fire Outside My Window* will provide you a compelling experience that you will be moved by and learn from."

Mark Smith
Emergency response trainer and consultant
Mission-Centered Solutions

"*The Fire Outside My Window* provides a riveting, firsthand look into the sheer terror and life-altering decision-making that author Sandra Millers Younger and so many other unsuspecting backcountry residents like her faced the night the Cedar Fire roared into their communities. It also delivers fascinating personal accounts of the fire and the challenges faced by firefighters in command of a wildfire the likes of which they'd never faced before."

Carlton Joseph
Cedar Fire initial attack incident commander
Forest fire chief, USDA Forest Service,
Cleveland National Forest (retired)

"From a hotshot with a chainsaw in hand to an incident commander with thousands of resources to direct and be responsible for, my firefighting career has given me a front-row seat for many of the worst natural and human-caused disasters of the past four decades. With experience, this comes easy, but what's hard is to look back and see how actions or inactions affected the lives of those we serve. Twenty years after the tragic Cedar Fire, Sandra's compelling story of what happened and why remains a relevant reminder for responders on why the work they do is important. But that's not the only reason I applaud this book. I live in Chico, California, in the shadow of the 2018 Camp Fire that devastated the town of Paradise, and I've given copies of *The Fire Outside My Window* to several survivors as a 'must read' for anyone who has lost their home to a disaster and found themselves in Sandra's shoes."

Tony Doty
Emergency management officer, All-Hazards Incident
Management Program (retired)
US Department of the Interior

"As fire commanders, we looked at wildfires strategically and as a thing we needed to defeat. This book taught me to remember that there are real people with real lives whose futures are about to change. And that they were the real reason I did what I did and always felt I needed to try even harder. The Fire Outside My Window also marks the moment when the megafires began. In 2003, faced with a siege of unprecedented monstrous wildfires burning throughout Southern California, fire commanders could see into the future and the kind of incidents that would challenge them year after year. This is the story of those who died and those who survived, whose lives were forever changed by California's historic Cedar Fire—firefighters, regular people who simply lived in the way, and one man lost in the wildlands of Southern California. We all need to learn from them."

Robert Lewin
Principal, Resolute Associates, LLC
Former director, Santa Barbara [California]
County Office of Emergency Management
CAL FIRE unit chief/San Luis Obispo County [California]
fire chief (retired)

"The Fire Outside My Window is relevant to everyone living in the wildland fire environment. It shares firsthand author Sandra Younger's experience of escaping an out-of-control wildland fire. This reality of fire burning into the wildland-urban interface will continue to exist, and human actions and reactions can change the outcomes. Sandra's experience allows others to reflect on their readiness for a similar incident and their capacity for resilience afterwards. Her message is timeless. What occurred then continues to occur today."

Paige R. Boyer
Assistant director, Operations, Northern California (retired)
USDA Forest Service, Pacific Southwest Region

"After twenty years, the Cedar Fire continues to have a significant impact on both the fire service and local communities. *The Fire Outside My Window* captures the moments during the Cedar Fire when the world of fire and people collided head-on. Sandra Younger does an excellent job of telling the story, not only from the survivors' view, but also from the perspective of firefighters battling the flames. Each spring, the San Diego County Fire Training Association hosts the Cedar Fire/Steven Rucker Staff Ride. As part of their pre-study, to help students understand the events that led up to the Rucker fatality, they're required to read *The Fire Outside My Window*."

Douglas Elliott
Captain, El Cajon [California] Fire (retired)

"The Fire Outside My Window is a look into the first megafire to affect California. The 2003 Cedar fire caused the California fire service to rethink how we responded to and managed fires. These lessons have provided tremendous benefit in an age of modern megafires."

Tony Mecham
CALFIRE unit chief, San Diego [California]

20TH ANNIVERSARY EDITION

THE FIRE OUTSIDE MY WINDOW

A SURVIVOR TELLS THE TRUE STORY OF
CALIFORNIA'S EPIC CEDAR FIRE

SANDRA MILLERS YOUNGER

Cover photograph: © USO/Dave Gatley
Map credit: Melissa Baker © Morris Book Publishing, LLC
Author photo: Jennifer Curry Wingrove, Wingrove Studios

ISBN Paperback: # 979-8-9891540-1-2
ISBN Electronic: # 979-8-9891540-0-5

Library of Congress Control Number: #2023917948

Publishing Consultant: PRESStinely, PRESStinely.com

Printed in the United States of America

Second Edition: October 2023
10 9 8 7 6 5 4 3 2

Sandra Millers Younger
Terra Nova Ink
SandraYounger.com

*For my father, Art Millers, who understood
why I live in wildfire country.*

*And in memory of those who died in the Cedar
and Paradise fires, San Diego County,
California, October 2003:
Galen Blacklidge, Gary Edward Downs, Nancy Morphew,
John Leonard Pack, Quynh Yen Chau Pack,
Mary Lynne Peace, Ashleigh Roach, Steven Rucker,
Christy-Anne Seiler-Davis, Stephen Shacklett Sr.,
James Shohara, Randy Shohara, Solange Shohara,
Jennifer Sloan, Robin Sloan, Ralph Marshall Westly,
and one unidentified man*

Barn's burnt down.
Now I can see the moon.

—Mizuta Masahide (1657—1723)

Contents

INTRODUCTION TO THE
CEDAR FIRE 20TH ANNIVERSARY EDITION

TWENTY YEARS LATER, I STILL worry when the wind blows. Especially on those hot, dry autumn nights when Southern California's storied Santa Anas, midwives to catastrophic wildfires, rip through the mountains from the northeast and funnel down Wildcat Canyon, bending every twig of chaparral to their will.

At times like that, I live by the weather reports—the temperature, the humidity, the projected wind speeds, the emergence and expected duration of red-flag conditions. I tune the scanner, check media feeds and emergency apps. I email my neighbors, urge them to stay alert and ready to evacuate if necessary. I post online: Be smart, San Diego. Be ready. Be safe.

By day, I watch for plumes of smoke. At night, I go outside, sniff the air and search the horizon in every direction for any hint of an orange glow. I am like a meerkat scout on duty, scanning obsessively for danger.

In Santa Ana weather, I bring in my outdoor furniture cushions, my porch decorations and welcome mat—anything and everything that could burn. I position my go bag and laptop by the door, dog leashes and cat carrier beside them. I keep my car fueled. I make a point of always knowing where my keys and purse are.

At bedtime when the wind is high, I leave clothes at the end of the mattress and shoes on the floor below. Then I burrow deep into the covers, reach out and touch my husband for comfort. He takes my hand, and we lie there together without speaking, listening to the wind and trying to focus on the present moment, the only moment we ever really have. In the present moment, all is well. In the present moment, we are safe.

But on Santa Ana nights, I don't sleep. I don't want to let my guard down, even for a moment. Because I don't want to wake up to the sight of fire outside my window. Not ever again. So I lie awake in the darkness, hour after hour, as the wind moans and the house creaks. Everything in me is poised at the edge of action, like a runner in the block, waiting for the jolt of the starting gun.

I did not always feel this way about wildfires. Until that unforgettable October night in 2003, when California's epic Cedar Fire took our home, the lives of twelve neighbors and nearly our own, Bob and I paid little attention to red-flag warnings. Though we were newbies in fire country, only seven months removed from our former home in a placid San Diego suburb, we thought we were prepared for life in the backcountry. We'd done our homework, followed fire agency recommendations, cleared a generous swath of defensible space all around. The house itself had been built to resist flames and embers—tile roof, stucco walls, sealed eaves and soffits. It seemed as solid as a fortress. I knew it could still burn. I just never thought it actually would. But once the unthinkable happens, you know it can. And so, after twenty years, I still worry when the wind blows.

People sometimes ask, why did you go back? Why did you rebuild your house in the same precarious spot? I could give them a million reasons why Bob and I chose to return to Terra Nova, our "new land" in the canyon, why we love it so much despite the danger. But they all boil down to one, so my answer is always the same: Because it's home.

You may understand all too well what I'm talking about, because you also may have lost your home to wildfire or some other natural disaster. Indeed, perhaps the most painful aftershock of my own fire experience is knowing so many other unsuspecting people will suffer the same enormous loss, some this year, some further down the line. The timing is uncertain, but the reality is inescapable. Wildfire is coming. It has always come and always will, a key component of Earth's natural systems.

For centuries, perhaps millennia, fires came in broadly predictable cycles and behaved in broadly predictable ways. Today, all bets are off. Worldwide and year-round, twenty-first-century wildfires are confounding all expectations, burning across entire mountain ranges, leaving whole towns in ashes, devastating suburbs miles from the wildland-urban interface (WUI), and killing untold numbers of humans and animals, all while polluting distant skies and scorching vast expanses of Earth.

In 2003, the Cedar Fire commanded international head-lines on its way to becoming the biggest wildfire in California's recorded history, a dubious distinction that lasted fourteen years. Today, that infamous incident barely makes the state's top ten list. You'd think it would soon disappear into the foot-notes of fire history.

Yet the Cedar Fire is more relevant today than ever. Its lessons still resonate, for both emergency professionals and the public. In fact, the Cedar Fire now serves as a case study in crisis response, reviewed in university classrooms, fire line training, and elite incident management programs. At least two of these courses currently use *The Fire Outside My Window* as a text.

Looking back at fire history over the past two decades, the Cedar Fire also stands out as a significant benchmark. Since 2011, it's been documented among the first of a new, more virulent breed of wildfires dubbed the megafires. These enormous and extreme fires of the early twenty-first century foretold the extraordinary climate-driven fire regimes we're now seeing globally. No place beyond our shrinking ice caps is immune. Today's fires are destroying fragile desert ecosystems, devastating lush tropical islands, and burning well inside the Arctic Circle. Firefighters deployed to the Cedar Fire sensed this fundamental shift at the time. As one veteran chief told me: "2003 was the year we all looked at each other and said, 'Things are changing.'"

In 2004, when I began researching and writing this book, it seemed clear to me that a major shift in weather patterns had helped create the record drought and unseasonable heat that transformed Southern California's backcountry into a vast sea of tinder, vulnerable to any wind-driven spark. But at the time, the specter of adverse climate change had yet to permeate public awareness, and some people advised me not to mention it. Too controversial, they said. Don't introduce anything that might detract from the story.

Twenty years later, climate change *is* the story, and the Cedar Fire stands as a clear signal of our entrance into an unprecedented era many experts are calling "the new abnormal."

The notorious fire I first saw outside my bedroom window I now see as a powerful mandate to do all we can as fast as we can to heal our shared planet, our only home, and safeguard the future for our children, grandchildren and generations to come.

The emergence of climate-fueled megafires has prompted vigorous response among researchers, emergency leaders, and related sectors. Today's firefighters benefit from robust coordination among agencies, advanced fire monitoring technology, and phenomenal air power. Many major utilities have begun implementing public-safety power shut-offs during dangerous winds to prevent fire starts from downed power lines. Meanwhile, foresters, scientists, and other experts are working to improve wildland management methods, from AI-assisted forest-growth modeling to reintroduction of indigenous fire practices.

The lessons of the Cedar Fire apply to those of us in the public, too. Though today's fires skew bigger and gnarlier than before, the experiences on the ground during a wildfire crisis remain essentially the same. Despite better warning systems, far too many people fleeing from fires make the same mistakes we did—not being prepared or aware, underestimating fire speed and behavior, not trusting their own sense of danger, and waiting too long to leave. Meanwhile, others have learned from past fire survivors and taken proactive action that may well have saved their lives. What could be more gratifying to an author than hearing, as I have, from readers who escaped when fire rolled through their neighborhoods because they'd read my book and knew what to do (or not do)?

It's often been my privilege over the past decade since this book's initial publication to speak about the Cedar Fire's lasting legacy—in the media, to community groups, and at fire and emergency management training programs and conferences. They all want to know what I learned from my research, my personal fire experience, and the process of rebuilding our home and lives. Over the years, I've found the biggest takeaways apply to all: Think bigger, far beyond past expectations. Plan and partner well in advance. Exercise your innate personal resilience.

This last lesson unfolded as all of us affected by the fire faced our losses and began the long, slow process of recovery. What I saw then is still true. Charity handouts, FEMA housing, even full-replacement insurance policies (for those lucky enough to have them) aren't enough to heal traumatized minds and hearts. But faith, caring support and a few simple yet profound practices (like gratitude, optimism, and perseverance) can make a big difference in how well disaster survivors—and overstressed emergency professionals—recover from catastrophic experiences.

Sharing these comeback concepts has become the core of my work as a writer, speaker and coach. It's crucial for those whose worlds have fallen apart to know that they *can* come back, often in new ways, because they are more resilient and resourceful than they can imagine.

Life is a paradox. Twenty years ago, the Cedar Fire destroyed my home, cracked me open, and sent me reeling in a new direction. Yet that great upheaval led to great opportunities, and my life is richer today than before. It's clear to me now that the universe works in this fundamental cycle. Summer, winter, spring. Birth, death, rebirth. Order, disorder, reorder. It's a certainty I hold onto in this era of great uncertainty. A certainty I hope you gain from the Cedar Fire story, too.

Sandra Millers Younger
Lakeside, California
September 2023

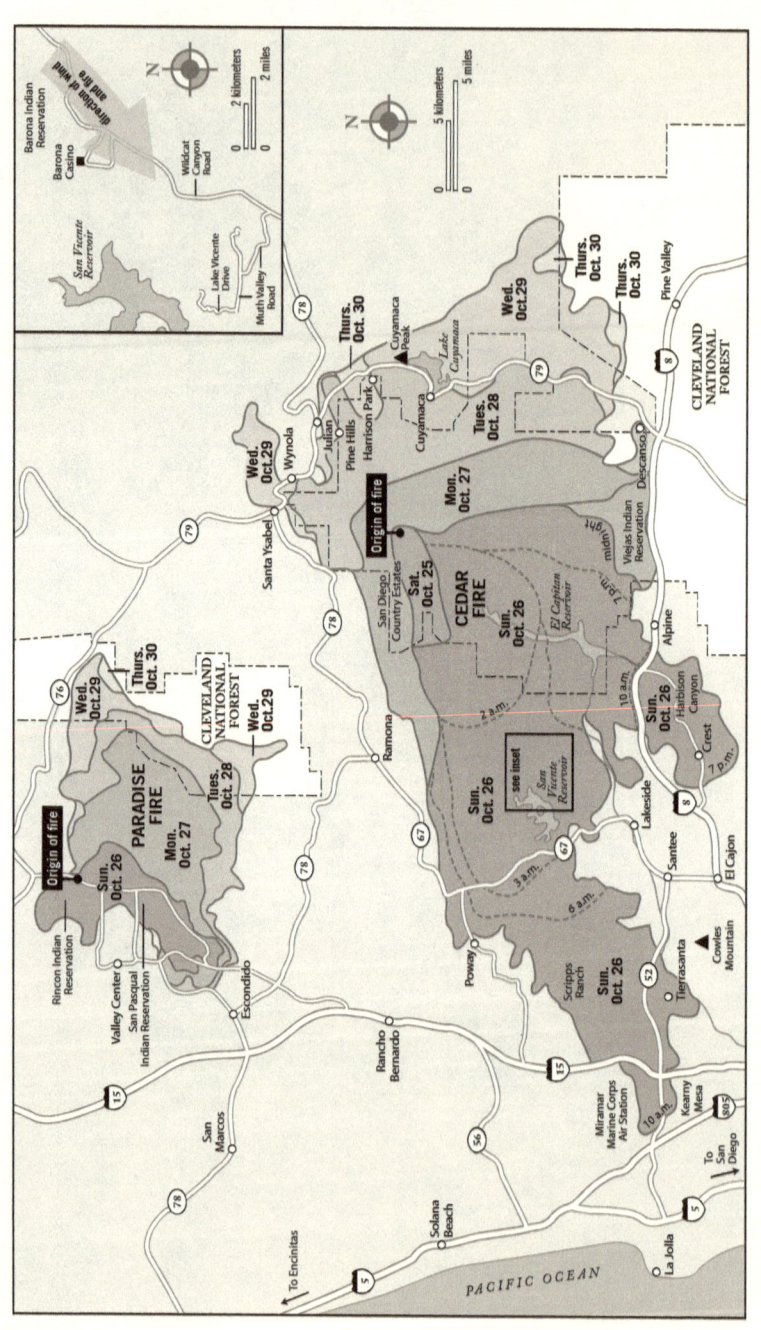

N

0 2 kilometers
0 2 miles

Barona Indian Reservation

Barona Casino

direction of wind and fire

Wildcat Canyon Road

San Vicente Reservoir

Lake Vicente Drive

Murth Valley Road

N

0 5 kilometers
0 5 miles

Thurs., Oct. 30

Wed. Oct. 29

Thurs., Oct. 30

Pine Valley

Cuyamaca Peak

Lake Cuyamaca

CLEVELAND NATIONAL FOREST

8

Thurs., Oct. 30

Cuyamaca

79

Harrison Park

Pine Hills

Indian

Tues. Oct. 28

Mon. Oct. 27

Descanso

Wed. Oct.29

Santa Ysabel

Wynola

Origin of fire

San Diego Country Estates

Sat. Oct. 25

CEDAR FIRE

Sun. Oct. 26

El Capitan Reservoir

14b

Viejas Indian Reservation

79

79

78

Ramona

2 a.m.

10 a.m.

Alpine

Sun. Oct. 26

Harbison Canyon

Crest

7 p.m.

Thurs., Oct. 30

Wed. Oct.29

CLEVELAND NATIONAL FOREST

Wed. Oct.29

76

PARADISE FIRE

Tues. Oct. 28

Mon. Oct. 27

Sun. Oct. 26

Origin of fire

Rincon Indian Reservation

Valley Center

San Pasqual Indian Reservation

Escondido

67

Sun. Oct. 26

San Vicente Reservoir

see inset

3 a.m.

6 a.m.

8

Lakeside

Santee

El Cajon

Poway

67

Scripps Ranch Sun. Oct. 26

52

Cowles Mountain

Tierrasanta

Rancho Bernardo

15

Miramar Marine Corps Air Station

Kearny Mesa

10 a.m.

805

San Marcos

56

15

78

5

To San Diego

5

To Encinitas

Solana Beach

La Jolla

PACIFIC OCEAN

PROLOGUE

Sergio Martinez didn't set out to cause a catastrophe. He only wanted to have a good time with a friend, drink some beer, smoke some weed, maybe shoot a buck. It didn't turn out that way. He'd never once hunted deer before that Saturday, October 25, 2003. But despite anything else he might have done in his thirty-three years, despite anything else he might do in the future, from that day on, Sergio Martinez would be known as the lost hunter who started the Cedar Fire, for fourteen years the biggest wildfire in California's recorded history.

Under normal circumstances, Martinez and I wouldn't have had much in common. He was a young construction worker in Los Angeles. I was a fifty-year-old university magazine editor in San Diego. If not for the spark that jumped from his hand and took off running straight toward my home in a canyon fourteen miles away, Martinez and I never would have met.

But then there was nothing normal, or so it seemed at the time, about what happened after Sergio Martinez got lost in the Cleveland National Forest and made a desperate decision to light a signal fire amid critical wildfire conditions. Spurred by a rare confluence of ominous circumstances, Martinez's spark took hold in a patch of desiccated native brush and exploded into a perfect firestorm. Timing, location, and weather conspired against air tankers, fire engines, and bull-dozers, giving the flames a chance to gather strength.

And then, almost at the stroke of midnight, the Cedar Fire broke away on a swelling wind and galloped west toward the Pacific Ocean. Moving faster than firefighters had ever seen a wildfire move before, it devoured two, three, sometimes four acres a second, spitting brands and embers miles ahead of itself, rearing up into hundred-foot towers of flames. In the course of its weeklong rampage, unstoppable waves of fire took the lives of fifteen people, incinerated 2,232 homes, and ravaged a chunk of San Diego County nearly twenty times the size of Manhattan.

When the Cedar Fire first flickered to life, a faraway circle of flames, neither my husband nor I could have imagined it would touch us. And when it rose and thundered in our direction, we did not perceive its coming. Instead, like every other creature living in our backcountry canyon, including the bobcat that would save our lives, we carried on unaware, lingering in our dreams until flames began to light the sky and devour the land outside our windows.

CHAPTER 1

A SINISTER BRILLIANCE

Aᴛ ꜰɪʀꜱᴛ, I ʀᴇꜱᴇɴᴛᴇᴅ ᴛʜᴇ alarm in my husband's voice. "Whoa! It's time to get out of here."

I was so asleep. Why was he waking me? What could possibly be so important? I opened my eyes to a strange yellow light that cast his naked figure into relief against our broad bedroom windows. What was going on? In another instant I understood. The canyon was on fire. Perfectly framed by our open draperies, a huge swath of flames stretched across the mountain opposite us. At its edges, fountains of fire shot high above the ground, surging and swaying in a ragged dance, vivid orange against surrounding darkness.

"Oh my god!" I reached for a pair of jeans thrown across the foot of the bed and pulled them on. "What do we do?"

"Don't panic," Bob said, but his voice sounded thin and forced. "We do what we need to do. First get some clothes. We don't know when we'll be able to come back."

He turned on the lights and disappeared into the bathroom. I opened a dresser drawer, grabbed some underwear, put on a pair of socks, and then dashed into the closet and stood for a moment looking at the line of hanging clothes. What should I take? My mind couldn't focus. Fire. There was fire outside the windows. I ran back and looked out again, as if to make sure. This time I noticed an orange glow deep below us, near the entrance to our neighborhood road. A spike of electricity surged through me as I pieced it all together. The flames on the mountain across from us must be only part of a bigger fire, a massive beast closing in.

"Bob, it's on our side!" I said, my throat closing around the words.

He was standing by the bed over an open suitcase but rushed to join me.

"It's on our side," he repeated, almost in a whisper.

At that moment, something shifted inside me. A distinct sensation. Bob felt it, too. We talked about it later, how thinking and doing slammed together in an instant, in a rush of adrenaline. From then on, we were caught up in a current of pure instinct, obeying without question some kind of primitive knowing that moved us step by step toward safety, kept us from lingering too long on any one task. Above all, we knew we had to leave. We should have left already.

We'd both managed to throw on jeans and T-shirts. Next, I needed some usable shoes—sneakers or boots—but all I could see in my closet were heels. And on the top shelf, beyond my reach, an almost empty plastic laundry basket.

"Give me that," I said to Bob.

"What?"

I couldn't think of the word.

"That!" I pointed toward the closet shelf.

Bob understood then and tossed me the basket, and I started filling it with framed photographs snatched off the walls and dresser. My grandfather in his Sunday best, a favorite dog at the beach, and our two daughters—in ruffled pink baby dresses, blonde pigtails and giant hair bows, tasseled caps and graduation gowns. At the same time, my mind jumped ahead, trying to visualize our escape. Judging from the glow below us, the fire had reached the intersection between our private neighborhood drive and Wildcat Canyon Road, the only way out. For all we knew, we were trapped.

"What if we can't get to Wildcat Canyon Road?"

"We'll get to Wildcat Canyon Road," Bob said.

His voice suddenly sounded so normal, so reassuring, that I simply believed him and turned my full attention to the task of filling the laundry basket. I noticed my favorite silver bracelet lying on the dresser, but decided not to take it, thinking I didn't have time, and that it would still be there when we returned. Yet I squandered precious seconds running downstairs to look for shoes. Opening the closet by the garage door, hoping to find my hiking boots, I looked right at them, saw them as Bob's instead, and then ran back upstairs to check the bedroom closet one more time.

In a way it all seemed so normal, the house as quiet and secure as any other night, my rushing about no more significant than if I were leaving for work or some routine appointment. It didn't seem possible that outside the world could be ending. Finally, I gave up on finding shoes, picked up the laundry basket, and headed downstairs again, shod only in white gym socks.

"I'll take care of the dogs," I told Bob. "You get your negatives."

He'd had a Nikon slung around his neck thirty years before when I met him—a chiseled college sophomore with mahogany eyes and dark hair cropped military short. His body had thickened since then, his hair had silvered, and his passion for photography had deepened.

I looked over at our two big black Newfoundlands, snoozing on the floor by the bed like a pair of shaggy hibernating bears, oblivious to our chaos. Perhaps if it hadn't been so hot outside—so hot that even in late October we'd closed the windows and resorted to air conditioning—they (or we) might have smelled smoke, might have heard the wind—hot, wild, and shrieking—and sensed danger. As it was, I had to wake them.

"Terra! Charter!" I tried to sound normal, even cheerful. "Let's go!"

Both dogs hopped up right away, all bright eyes and waving tails, excited by the prospect of a middle-of-the-night adventure. We rushed down the stairs together, the Newfs jostling me at every step. To them it was always a race. At the bottom, I stopped to pull one last family portrait off the wall. Only a few steps more, into the next room, and I could have collected my laptop, my mother's wedding portrait, family photo albums and videos, little gifts the girls had made for us in school. But none of that entered my mind. I had time only to grab what lay directly in my path—my purse hanging on the coat rack in the living room, dog collars and leashes dangling from hooks beside the door to the garage.

Bob was still upstairs. I could hear him now, yelling something, his voice charged with urgency.

"Call Sean," he said. "Call Sean."

Sean? To this point, I'd thought only about us. I hadn't remembered that our neighbors Sue and Randy Fritz were out of town, that they'd left their twenty-three-year-old son behind to house-sit.

"I don't have the number," I shouted back.

We had it somewhere. But I had no idea where, and I didn't have time to look it up. Without my reading glasses, I couldn't have deciphered it anyway. In a sobering flash, I realized I couldn't call Sean. I just had to keep moving. At the door to the garage, I slammed slip collars over Newfy heads, not noticing I'd put both collars on the same dog.

"Get your negatives!" I screamed over my shoulder toward Bob. "Get your negatives!"

I opened the door to the garage, flicked on the lights, and both Newfs burst through ahead of me. Just then Bob arrived carrying an armload of boxes filled with transparencies, the best of his life's work.

I held out the laundry basket. At that moment, all the lights in the house sputtered and died, throwing us into darkness. Somewhere outside I heard a loud crack, like a lightning strike in a rainstorm. I imagined power poles falling into flames, and a single thought thundered through me: *We have to get out. We have to get out now.*

"How are we going to open the garage door without electricity?" My voice sounded shrill.

"I can open it," Bob said. "That part is easy."

He dumped the transparencies into the basket and disappeared again into the lightless house. Some of the smaller boxes missed the mark and fell to the floor. I dropped to my knees and felt around until I found them. Then Bob's voice, tight with anxiety, came from the kitchen.

"I can't find my glasses!"

"Forget them!"

The basket felt heavy as I pushed into the garage. Despite the blackout I had no trouble seeing. A flood of sulfurous light poured through a window on the east wall, as if a downtown streetlight had switched on outside. I heard Bob shout again.

"I can't find my car keys!"

"We'll take my car!"

He drove a Chevy Suburban, an enormous sport utility vehicle. I drove a white Acura coupe.

When I opened my trunk to set the basket inside, I discovered a pair of old black flats, my rain shoes. I snatched them up, dropped them to the concrete, and slipped them on before closing the trunk again. As awful as they looked over white sweat socks, I felt intensely grateful to have them. My thoughts next turned to Chelsea, our cockatiel. We kept a small traveling cage in the garage. I scanned my surroundings until I spied it on a high shelf, fished it down with a piece of PVC pipe, and spun around to find Bob behind me.

"Get Chelsea," I said, thrusting the cage toward him.

He disappeared again into the house, while I opened the driver's door of the Acura and flipped the seat back forward. Terra, small for a Newfoundland at ninety pounds and pathologically eager to please, jumped in right away. But Charter, all 140 pounds of him, balked at the idea.

"Charter, go," I said, pushing against his rump.

Over the top of the car, I could see the light from the east window growing brighter and changing colors, from orange to yellow. *Oh god,* I thought, *this fire must be getting closer.* Still Charter stood resolute, refusing to move.

"Go, Charter," I kept urging. "Go, go."

Finally, he lifted one enormous paw and stepped slowly into the footwell of the backseat. The other front foot followed at glacial speed, and then I shoved the rest of him in. When Bob returned with Chelsea, I expected him to leap into the passenger seat, birdcage and all. Instead he shouted at me to pop the trunk. As I watched in the rearview mirror, he reached up and pulled the dangling red emergency handle that released the garage door, and then raised it easily. Red and orange embers gusted past through a smoky haze behind him as he worked to fit the cage in alongside the laundry basket. He seemed to be taking forever. Meanwhile, the light through the window had gone white. We were out of time. I started the car.

"Bob!"

I don't remember hearing the bellow of approaching flames chewing through shrubs and trees, but I had to scream to be heard.

"We have to go. We have to go now!"

He gave the birdcage a last hard push before slamming the trunk lid and leaping into the front seat beside me, and I started backing the car into the eerie light and blowing embers.

"Wait!" Bob shouted.

We were only halfway out of the garage, but I hit the brakes, and he cracked his door just enough to reach out and retrieve a big Nikon he'd picked up on his last pass through the house, and then set on the hood against the windshield. The moment he pulled the car door shut, I punched the gas, and the Acura shot up the long, steep driveway in reverse as if by reflex. I never thought about stopping again, even for the few seconds it would have taken one of us to get out of the car and close the garage door. Perhaps I should have. Such a quick, simple thing might have saved our home. Or proved a fatal error on a night when every moment mattered. I will always wonder.

At the top of the driveway, amid a meteor shower of embers, I paused just long enough to shift gears and turn the car's wheels toward the road. In that instant it seemed the whole world had split in two—undisturbed night on one side, brightest day on the other. We had lived in Wildcat Canyon only seven months, seven months of idyllic, post-suburban life in a wildland nirvana hewn from mountain and sky. Now fire loomed over this new land of ours, leaping toward us in a towering arc of yellow-white light, spitting red, swirling foam into a poisoned sky. In the midst of it, our darkened house cut a defiant silhouette against a surging, sinister brilliance.

"Where is the fire department?"

The agony in Bob's voice spoke for both of us, and for nearly everyone caught in the fire, those who lived and those who died. Yet in that briefest of moments, before we drove away into the night, it was clear no help was coming.

CHAPTER 2

BLACK SMOKE RISING

To tell the whole story of the Cedar Fire—to really do it right—I must take you back in time to an Earth still hot and heaving. We'd need to find a vantage point somewhere in space where we could see the entire planet spinning below, and then fast-forward through millennia as the world cooled, shifted, and settled into continents, regions, and ecosystems. If we watched long enough, we'd see the arrival of plants, animals, and humans. And all the while, on almost every part of the planet, we'd see fire. Fires flickering to life, then sputtering out, sometimes a mere hiccup—a match flare followed by a puff of smoke—and sometimes burning for weeks, reddening vast chunks of ground, streaking the atmosphere with long tails of smoke.

After a few millennia of this, we'd conclude, and rightly so, that ours is a planet shaped by fire. It's a reality we've lost sight of, perhaps because space exploration has given us an image of Earth unseen by previous generations—a luminous blue ball, suspended in the inky vacuum of space. Looking at that floating globe, so cool and serene, it's easy to forget that the heart of Mother Earth is molten, that in the beginning, there was fire and plenty of it.

It's still with us, of course, crackling across the dark face of a storm, bubbling just below the surface. Sometimes it stabs down from the sky all the way to the ground, splintering trees that can smolder for hours or days before flickering into spreading flames. Sometimes it boils through dark tunnels, looking for a fissure in the planet's bones and then spewing upward into sunlight, or dripping red into the ocean. It has always been this way, a cycle as fundamental as day and night, sun and rain, summer and winter.

Ron Serabia stands tall and solid as a redwood and talks easily in a voice deep enough to draw water. It doesn't take much of a conversation to discover what's most important to him: his Christian faith; his wife, Kathy; and fighting fire. Even as a kid, living across the alley from a volunteer fire station in his hometown of Ramona, California, Serabia envied his father and the other men who came running when the siren sounded, and then roared off aboard wailing engines, their veins thumping with adrenaline and idealism. Serabia had seen plenty of fire over thirty-six years with the California Department of Forestry and Fire Protection (CDF),[1] most recently from the shotgun seat of an OV-10A Bronco spotter plane. As a CDF captain and one of three officers in command of the agency's Ramona Air Attack Base, he coordinated air tankers and helicopters that dropped water and fire retardant on wildfires.

On Saturday, October 25, 2003, Serabia had just gotten back from ten days of decompression therapy—elk hunting

---

[1] The California Department of Forestry and Fire Protection is now known as CAL FIRE.

in Colorado—and was looking forward to another week of vacation at home before returning to work. It was a brilliant fall day, surprisingly hot, but by late afternoon, the temperature had dropped enough to invite a leisurely drive, one of Ron and Kathy Serabia's favorite pastimes. They especially liked to check on the progress of new houses under construction in nearby neighborhoods and collect ideas for the retirement home they planned to build. Still topped by a shock of dark hair, Serabia hardly looked old enough to hang up his boots, but he'd already submitted the paperwork. His long career with the CDF would end on December 31, 2003, right there in Ramona where it began.

Usually, the couple's afternoon drives took them into San Diego Country Estates, a manicured suburban island carved into the chaparral southeast of Ramona, but on this particular Saturday they wandered beyond the Country Estates and farther south into Barona Mesa, a more rural community sprinkled with a mixture of old homesteads and new mini-mansions. Suddenly, on a street blessed with panoramic views of the Cuyamaca mountain range rising against a clear, azure sky, Ron Serabia hit the brakes, stopping the car dead in the middle of the road.

"What's wrong?" his wife asked.

"Look at that," he said, peering straight ahead.

Kathy Serabia followed his gaze. This was so like her husband, always on the lookout for the unusual, the out-of-place, the significant details others missed. After so many years flying air attack, he could probably see a match strike from a mile up.

"What is it?"

"Black smoke coming up, right there in the upper end of Cedar Creek. Just a puff. Looks like a small plane might've crashed."

"There are no houses in there that could be burning," Kathy said.

"No. It's too rugged and remote."

Ron Serabia knew the place as well as anyone. And he knew its history. He was only seven in 1956, when the infamous Inaja Fire exploded in a canyon near Cedar Creek and roared west past Ramona, but he still remembered. It had been fall then, too, late November, and crazy windy. He remembered how smoke and fire washed over his world, how the sun shrank to a purple dot, and darkness fell by noon. He remembered that night, watching lines of flames push over the hills and run far, far into the distance. And he remembered eleven firefighters had died in the blaze.

If you could see the Inaja Indian Reservation where fifteen-year-old Gilbert Paipa lived in 1956—852 acres of backcountry San Diego County so rugged, so remote, that no one lives there on a permanent basis anymore—you could believe a teenage boy might get bored enough to do something stupid. Canyons a thousand feet deep, defined by nearly vertical walls, blanketed by tall, dense thickets of brush and scrub oaks, broken only by enormous boulders and sheer rock cliffs.

It was a Saturday morning late in the year—November 24 to be exact—a time when winter rains already should have ended the fire season. But in 1956, drought, low humidity, and Santa Ana winds had converged to create extreme fire danger. All in all, Gilbert Paipa could hardly have picked a worse place or time to run out of things to do. The official after-action report on the incident, titled "The Inaja Forest Fire Disaster," tells what happened next.

"I just got a mad, crazy idea to do it," Paipa reportedly confessed when apprehended. "I threw a match in the grass to see if it would burn."

It did.

By 9:15 a.m., just five minutes after Paipa acted on his mad, crazy idea, two Forest Service lookouts had spotted and reported the blaze. Ten minutes later, a three-man firefighting crew arrived at the scene. But already it was too late. By 9:25 a.m., the fire had spread beyond their ability to control it. Firefighters worked for five days to rein in the Inaja Fire, five days of throwing everything they had against it. More than 2,000 men battled the flames, supported by ninety trucks, twenty-seven bulldozers, two scouting planes, three helicopters, and—in an experimental role—four air tankers dropping chemical fire retardant. Yet despite the immediate response and an army of resources, the Inaja Fire devoured nearly 44,000 acres—seventy square miles—along a path almost identical to the route the Cedar Fire would take forty-seven years later. The Inaja blaze burned only five homes, scattered across pristine backcountry still largely uncluttered by structures. But the deaths of eleven firefighters caught in a sudden flare-up during the fire appalled the public and prompted a highly publicized federal investigation.

The victims all worked on a hand crew cutting a fire line deep in the San Diego River Gorge, hundreds of feet below the canyon rim. Armed only with picks and shovels, chain saws, and specialized ax-and-mattock tools called Pulaskis, hand crews are the backbone of every wildland fire attack. Theirs is the grueling but essential work of cutting trees and vegetation to clear long lines of bare earth broad enough to stop a line of oncoming flames. No matter how many helicopters or air tankers may be deployed against a wildfire, history confirms it is always boots on the ground that put out a blaze.

This particular hand crew included several trained minimum-security inmates, a practice that began in California during World War II. While the Forest Service later switched to all-professional hand crews, called hotshots, the CDF continued to depend on inmates in this critical firefighting role. By the time of the Cedar Fire in 2003, the agency operated almost forty "conservation camps," which housed and trained some 4,300 full-time wildland firefighters. Distinguishable from regular CDF personnel only by their bright orange jumpsuits, inmate firefighters worked the same fire lines and took the same risks—all for a few dollars a day plus time off their sentences.[2]

That Sunday afternoon in November 1956, the second day of the Inaja Fire, the crew leader sent one of his team, twenty-one-year-old Forest Service employee Kenneth Joseph, back upslope to check on the progress of bulldozers clearing a major firebreak along the ridgeline. Just shy of the top, Joseph paused and looked back at the fire, burning deep in the gorge, well below his crewmates. At that moment, flames suddenly flared in their direction. Joseph shouted a warning, and the men immediately stopped working and started up the long, steep trail back to the rim. They couldn't yet see the fire surging toward them, but Joseph could. He yelled again, urging them to hurry. At that, the men picked up the pace, and most dropped their tools.

The two men working closest to the ridgeline held a slight advantage and made it to the top first. The next two stopped to rest, giving five men lower down enough time to catch up and pass them. Nine more followed just behind. Suddenly, the fire jumped and crossed the trail higher up, cutting off their escape. The group of five scaled a sheer rock bluff and sprinted the final seventy-five feet to the rim, fire chasing them all the way. Safe at the top with Joseph and the dozer crew, they watched helplessly as flames devoured a huge swath of the canyon in a single gulp, an event firefighters call a "flashover." Caught in the midst of an inferno, the eleven firefighters still struggling toward the ridge had no chance of survival.

---

[2] California Department of Corrections and Rehabilitation

The Inaja victims were honored in a public memorial service marked by stirring eulogies, and later with a roadside stone monument near Santa Ysabel, close to where the crewmates died. Surrounded now by picnic tables and parking spaces, the Inaja Fire Memorial still stands "in honor of the men who lost their lives fighting the Inaja Forest Fire on November 25, 1956."

Firefighters Killed in the Inaja Forest Fire
November 25, 1956

Forest service employees Albert W. Anderson, 45; Carlton Ray Lingo, 19; and Forrest B. Maxwell, 30; Viejas Honor Camp correctional officer LeRoy "Jack" Wehrung, 41; and camp inmates Miles Daniels, 33; William D. Fallin, 22; George A. Garcia, 41; Joseph P. O'Hara, 45; Lonnie L. Shepherd, 26; and Joe Tibbits, 34.

The Inaja Fire marked a turning point in wildland firefighting. From that time forward, the study of fire behavior evolved into a sophisticated science. Today, when fire commanders confront dicey decisions, with lives and property on the line, they can draw not only from their own collective fire experiences, but also from academic research and computer-aided projections. Just as important, the findings and recommendations of the Inaja Fire investigators were codified into a set of ten directives intended to safeguard firefighters from the dangerous lapses that contributed to the Inaja tragedy and other deadly fires. Adopted by every wildland firefighting organization in the nation, the 10 Standard Firefighting Orders have remained essentially unchanged ever since.

The 10 Standard Firefighting Orders

Fire Behavior
1. *Keep informed on weather conditions and forecasts.*
2. *Know what your fire is doing at all times.*
3. *Base all actions on current and expected behavior of the fire.*

Fire Line Safety
4. *Identify escape routes and make them known.*
5. *Post lookouts when there is possible danger.*
6. *Be alert. Keep calm. Think clearly. Act decisively.*

Organizational Control
7. *Maintain prompt communication with your forces, your supervisor, and adjoining forces.*
8. *Give clear instructions and ensure they are understood.*
9. *Maintain control of your forces at all times.*
10. *Fight fire aggressively, having provided for safety first.*

After the fire, young Kenneth Joseph had good reason to feel grateful—or at least lucky. He had escaped the flashover and saved seven crew members. But Joseph had also seen three of his fellow Forest Service employees, including his best friend, nineteen-year-old Carlton Lingo, swallowed by flames. The next year, when Joseph and his wife welcomed twin sons, they named the first one Carlton, in tribute to their fallen friend. Not long after that, Kenneth Joseph got out of firefighting and took up police work. But the twins, Carlton and Kevin, who grew up listening to their father's tales of woods and wildfires, found it difficult to imagine a more exciting life than the one he had left behind. Both signed up with the Forest Service as seasonal firefighters while still in high school. By 2003, they'd both advanced to the rank of division chief, Kevin in Colorado and Carlton in San Diego, where nearly half a century after the historic Inaja incident, he would lead the initial attack against the Cedar Fire.

I was three years old at the time of the Inaja tragedy, growing up across the continent in a small North Carolina town and spending weekends at my grandparents' farm an hour's drive away. One fall morning when I was eight or nine, I woke up in my grandmother's guest room aware of a crackling sound coming from somewhere outside. Such a curious noise, and yet somehow familiar. Then it came to me.

Fire. It was the sound of a fire burning.

I struggled out from under the weight of multiple handmade quilts, slid off the big, tall bed, and ran barefoot to the window. The dirt yard outside the farmhouse, bare and dusty all summer long, at this time of year became a mosaic of brown, yellow, orange, and red leaves, the surest sign of autumn in North Carolina. On this particular morning, the leaves were on fire.

My eyes widened in surprise but not fear, because in the midst of the smoke stood my grandfather, a man I all but worshiped, dressed in his everyday overalls and plain shirt, leaning on a rake and puffing on a White Owl cigar. He did this every year, this burning of the leaves. It was his way of dealing with the detritus of another summer gone, perhaps even his way of marking the changing seasons.

If my sister, Karen, and I were available, Grandpa usually talked us into doing the raking. We'd work for hours, making a long, mounded pile of leaves that stretched from one side of the yard to the other. Then he'd light a cigar, puff it up hot as a poker, and touch it to one end of our raked row. Karen and I stood astonished, watching the flames catch hold and snake down the line. If we weren't around to rake for him, Grandpa would simply light some random patch of ground and let the fire go, cutting a ragged path of ashes across the leafy carpet. The rake was to keep things under control. But my grandfather had a looser concept of control than most people. His way was more slapdash—a lick and a promise, as we said in the South. So it didn't surprise anyone that he would let a leaf fire creep across the yard and lick at the dry, clapboard walls outside the room where his beloved granddaughters lay sleeping.

I can't remember now who sounded the alarm or how, but someone must have informed Grandpa that he was about to burn the house down. I suppose he finally put his rake to use, or else the leaves smoldered out on their own against the mossy brick underpinning of the place (as he no doubt knew they would), because the house did not burn; it's still standing today, a simple farmhouse planted amid the red clay and green fields of rural North Carolina. I trace many of my best memories to that place and time, but waking up to flames outside my window is not one of them.

Ron Serabia would never forget that day the sun shrank, and smoke shrouded his hometown; he grew up endlessly fascinated by the Inaja Fire story. Sitting in his car with his wife all those years later, eyeing the narrow column of smoke ascending so close to the origin of the Inaja blaze, Serabia wanted to prevent a repeat of that catastrophe. He and his colleagues had to put this new fire out before it could get any bigger. Serabia reached for his cell phone to call 911, but it couldn't pick up a signal. Neither could Kathy's. He started driving again, searching for a connection. His phone was the first to find one. He handed it to his wife.

"Call 911."

She did but couldn't get through.

"It's busy," she said.

She kept trying, over and over, each time with the same results.

Man! Ron Serabia thought. Every minute counted.

At least this fire didn't seem to be getting much bigger. And the smoke was rising straight up—no wind yet near the ground. But this late in the day, a time when every pebble cast a shadow and visibility deteriorated at low altitudes, Serabia knew it had to be nearly "cutoff." The exact time changed with the calendar, but CDF regulations held firm. Half an hour before sunset marked the end of the day for pilots flying below 1,000 feet—where water- and retardant-dropping aircraft must maneuver to ensure accurate drops. Firefighters say the cutoff rule was "written in the blood of pilots," and in fact, just two years before, a 2001 mid-air collision in Northern California had killed two CDF air tanker pilots, a sober reminder of the dangers inherent to aerial firefighting.[3] No one knew better than Ron Serabia that CDF would have to get air tankers or water-dropping helicopters in the air before cutoff or wait until morning. And 911 still hadn't answered.

Suddenly Serabia remembered he had a direct number for the Monte Vista Interagency Command Center in El Cajon, where 911 calls ended up. He took his phone back from Kathy and dialed. Monte Vista records show his call as one of the very first reports of the Cedar Fire, coming in at 5:39 p.m. Serabia then made another critical call. Firefighter Shari Lee, a savvy twenty-year CDF veteran, answered at the Ramona Air Attack Base.

"Shari, I'm out here driving around Barona Mesa, and I just reported this fire."

"Yeah, they're dispatching now. Where exactly is it?"

"It's at the upper end of Cedar Creek, way up at the top above Cedar Falls, near Eagle Peak Road. It's not very big.

---

[3] National Transportation Safety Board

Looks like a plane might've crashed because it's just the one column, and it's not really getting any bigger."

And then Serabia asked the top question on his mind.

"Are there any airplanes on base?"

He braced himself for the answer. He'd come home from Colorado to news of multiple fires burning all across Southern California. The aircraft stationed in Ramona might well be deployed elsewhere. He was right. Both Ramona-based air tankers had worked in San Bernardino that day. The lighter lead plane that served as Serabia's air attack command post, parked outside the Ramona control tower, might have been some help in scouting the fire, but it was after cutoff, Lee reported, and the pilot had left for the day.

"When was cutoff?" Serabia asked.

"5:36."

Three minutes before he'd reported the fire to Monte Vista.

"Wait," Lee said. "We've got a helicopter landing."

CDF pilot Ted Smith had just flown in from the Roblar 2 Fire, burning for four days at Camp Pendleton, the vast US Marine Corps training base that fronts the ocean along San Diego County's northern border. Maybe he could take a quick high-altitude look at the situation. But no, Lee reported after checking. Smith had already flown his allotted seven hours for the day. In keeping with safety regulations, he was done until morning.

As soon as Serabia hung up, his phone rang again. The duty chief at Monte Vista wanted an update on the fire. "Well, it looks like it's a little bit bigger based on the smoke," Serabia reported, "but there's no wind on it; the smoke's still going straight up in the air."

He took a long breath.

"You know it's going to be hard to get to," he told the chief. "It's rugged country."

"Well, we've got a full dispatch going from both CDF and the Forest Service," the chief said. "But there's no aircraft available."

The records confirm that Monte Vista did try to dispatch aircraft as part of the initial attack, but the Ramona Air Base couldn't comply because of cutoff. No one questioned this response; it was simply a matter of policy. Fires often started after cutoff, and firefighters were accustomed to attacking without air support. Still, the location of this fire was so remote, some at Monte Vista worried it could be trouble.

"Ron, based on your experience," the duty chief asked, "what's the potential for this thing?"

Serabia had been working on the same question, his mind churning through the ominous convergence of factors: the remote location and rugged terrain, making it difficult to insert personnel and equipment; the dry, heavy fuel load; the single-digit humidity and strong seasonal winds—California's storied Santa Anas—forecast to blow in overnight from the northeast. He thought about the way the canyons surrounding Cedar Creek ran east/northeast, perfectly aligned to channel those winds. And the way moving air acts just like water, taking the path of least resistance, following the natural folds and funnels of the land. He thought about how the wind gathers speed as it pushes through narrow passages, sometimes creating such a jumble it even changes directions on itself. Still, the results of his calculations seemed so extreme, so improbable, that he hesitated before answering the chief's question.

"Well, if the east winds come up, as they're forecast to, by daylight we'll probably have fire down to the San Diego River bottom. Or even across on this side if it blows hard enough."

"What are you saying in acres?"

"Fifteen to twenty thousand."

Kathy Serabia reached over and grabbed her husband's arm. "Don't exaggerate," she scolded.

CHAPTER 3

THE LOST HUNTER

KESSLER FLAT IS A BROAD, grassy break in the corrugated expanse of peaks and canyons that distinguish backcountry San Diego County. It's a beautiful spot, even after a hot, dry summer has bleached the grass into a rippling, golden lake studded by enormous dusty green oaks. Some maps show a bit of trail at Kessler Flat, just a line from one point to another near the pale gravel of Eagle Peak Road, the only way in and out of the place. On the ground, there's no path at all, only a hint of tire tracks that peter out fairly soon. It's strictly a cross-country trek across the grass and into the brush, as Bob and I discovered one brilliant June morning long after the Cedar Fire had come and gone, when we hiked to the spot where Sergio Martinez lit his infamous signal fire.

The drive from Wildcat Canyon took us through the old-time ranching town of Ramona, past farms, horse ranches, and even a camel dairy as we followed California Highway 78's winding ascent into the Cuyamaca Mountains. About a mile past the crossroads at Santa Ysabel, we stopped to pay our respects at a local historic site—the Inaja Fire Memorial.

Only a short distance farther, just outside the old gold-mining town of Julian, we turned south into the rural neighborhood of Pine Hills, where some 350 firefighters waited out the Cedar Fire's first hours while their chiefs drove one dirt road after another, searching for access to the flames. Eagle Peak Road came closest. Cutting southeast from Pine Hills, it transitions quickly from asphalt to gravel and dirt as it bores deep into the Cleveland National Forest. To Bob and me, the four slow, bumpy miles through scrub brush and meadows along Eagle Peak Road to Kessler Flat seemed endless. But finally we arrived at the point where Martinez had left his truck and taken off on foot with his hunting buddy, Ron Adkins, in search of deer. Bob parked alongside the road, and we set out to retrace the lost hunter's footsteps.

We'd made a point of coming better prepared than Sergio Martinez. We wore backpacks loaded with water, and we'd armored ourselves against the elements with sunscreen, sunglasses, caps, and snake boots. We'd brought a sheaf of topographical maps, and we each carried a GPS unit programmed with coordinates from the sheriff's report on the Martinez rescue. Bob even strapped on a pistol, just in case some hungry mountain lion thought we looked tasty. Kessler Flat is that far out in the backcountry.

Beyond the spreading grass and oaks, the terrain drops away for at least a hundred feet and then levels out again in a meadow bordered on the far side by a narrow creek, a line of leafy young trees, and a short rise to the next ridgeline. Tall weeds hide a scattering of rusted household belongings—a bedstead, a farm implement, a wagon wheel. Relics from another time. The creek had shriveled enough since the rainy season for us to step over. We climbed the bank and hiked a bit farther through waist-high scrub until we found the jumble of rocks where a sheriff's helicopter crew had first spotted Sergio Martinez, a short, heavy figure in camouflage hunting clothes, and nearby, a patch of flames about half the size of a football field.

Point to point, it's only about four miles west from Martinez's rock pile to San Diego Country Estates, where the Cedar Fire claimed its first homes. But Martinez couldn't have seen the Country Estates from his seat on the rocks. For that Bob and I had to hike farther uphill, to the top of a knoll where the flames first began to descend out of the Cleveland National Forest. From that vantage point we could see the entire community—3,100 homes and a brown water tank on the eastern edge where California Department of Forestry and Fire Protection Battalion Chief Kelly Zombro and USDA Forest Service Division Chief Hal Mortier met on the day Sergio Martinez got lost, to size up a just-reported fire burning near Cedar Creek.[4] From the rock pile where he was found, Martinez would have been looking east across a deep canyon toward the soaring profiles of the Cuyamaca Mountains, forested by 400-year-old conifers that towered over the cool green quiet of Cuyamaca Rancho State Park. Generations of San Diegans and hundreds of generations of indigenous Kumeyaay people had considered Cuyamaca a sort of natural cathedral, sacred and irreplaceable. The Cedar Fire would turn it into a ghost forest, charred and skeletal.

Two US presidents deserve credit for preserving the Cleveland National Forest as open space. In 1897, Grover Cleveland set aside an expansive tract of land stretching from the San Gorgonio Pass between San Bernardino and Palm Springs all the way to the Mexican border. Named after the highest peak in the area, this protected territory was christened the San

---

4 2000 US Census, US Census Bureau.

Jacinto Forest Reserve. In 1908, Theodore Roosevelt combined the reserve with other protected land to create a single national forest, which he named after his predecessor.

"It seemed to me eminently fitting," Roosevelt wrote in a letter to Cleveland's widow, "that one of the forests which he created should bear his name throughout all time."

The test of eternity remains open, of course, but nearly a hundred years later, when Sergio Martinez headed into the dry brush of the Cleveland National Forest, it remained as when Roosevelt named it, an amalgam of three discontinuous islands in San Diego, Riverside, and Orange Counties, adding up to 438,000 acres—nearly 700 square miles—of increasingly rare undeveloped Southern California land.[5]

From the start, park administrators wrestled to balance three mandates: resource conservation, public access, and fire prevention. Nearly all of the Cleveland is covered in chaparral, a dense assortment of scrub oaks and native shrubs sometimes called "the elfin forest." With their woody stems and drought-adapted oily leaves, plus accumulated dead branches and underlying leaf litter, most chaparral species are notoriously flammable. Even before significant residential development came to San Diego's backcountry, chaparral's innate propensity to burn posed a threat to the scattered houses and cabins built on inholdings of private land within the forest's borders.

At the time of the Cedar Fire, extended drought and a related bark-beetle infestation had killed hundreds of thousands of trees across Southern California, filling forested land with massive stores of standing firewood primed to burn. In 2002, the situation became so critical that Forest Service supervisors, including Cleveland Forest Supervisor Anne Fege, closed all of the region's national forests during "red-flag warnings," periods of critical fire danger declared by the

---

[5] Mike Lee, "Forest Marks 100 Years," *The San Diego Union-Tribune*, June 29, 2008.

National Weather Service. The following spring, California Governor Gray Davis responded to the threat of "catastrophic wildfire, injury, and property damage" by proclaiming a state of emergency in Riverside, San Bernardino, and San Diego Counties. The governor's action authorized landowners and private contractors to cut unlimited numbers of dead trees in an effort to reduce the fire threat.[6] In June 2003, citing extreme fire danger, Davis allotted extra funds to beef up CDF staffing and equipment in Southern California. The Forest Service also braced for a bad fire season, investing $15 million in "fire severity funding" to add personnel, engines, bulldozers, and helicopters to its firefighting forces.[7]

Despite the extreme danger, heavy public demand complicated the forest administrators' management challenge. In 2003, the Cleveland National Forest averaged roughly 850,000 visits per year. After the Cedar Fire, people asked— some in a class-action lawsuit—why the Cleveland had not been closed to hunters like Sergio Martinez on a red-flag day. The reason was simple, Fege told me. Too many park visitors had complained about the previous year's closures. National forests are public lands, they said, and should be accessible to the public at all times.

Sergio Martinez lived with his parents in the house where he'd grown up in West Covina, a modest neighborhood near Los Angeles. Early Friday afternoon, October 24, 2003, he and Ron Adkins, a fellow construction worker, took off in Martinez's

---

[6] Public Utilities Commission of the State of California. *Energy Division Resolution E-3824*, April 3, 2003.

[7] California Department of Forestry and Fire Protection, California Governor's Office of Emergency Services and USDA Forest Service, *California Fire Siege 2003: The Story*, 11.

truck to bag a deer or two. Unlike his buddy, Adkins was an experienced hunter, and when deer season opened Saturday morning, he wanted to be in a spot where he'd had good luck before, a place in the Cleveland National Forest east of San Diego called Kessler Flat.

They arrived late in the day Friday, Martinez testified in court during his sentencing hearing, but the two men still managed to squeeze in a short reconnaissance jaunt before dark.

"I was really excited," the first-time deer hunter recalled.

Afterward, the hunters backtracked an hour's drive to Escondido, where they checked into a motel, shared a six-pack of beer, and Martinez took out his marijuana pipe for a smoke. By five o'clock Saturday morning, the two men were back at Kessler Flat. On the way, a deer had jumped across Eagle Peak Road ahead of them—a good omen.

On paper, everything about Martinez's hunting trip looked in order. The Cleveland was open for hunting, deer season had begun, and both men held valid hunting licenses. But at some point that morning, things took a wrong turn. To be precise, it was Martinez who took a wrong turn—and ended up hopelessly lost. The original plan, he testified, was to hunt for three hours at most, and then return to the truck for food and water. Adkins led the way through the predawn darkness up to a ridge overlooking a flat open field—perhaps the meadow Bob and I crossed on our way to the rock pile. Martinez followed, lighting his steps with a flashlight until the sky brightened enough to see without it. At the ridgetop, the hunters spaced themselves about 400 yards apart and then sat quietly for the next few hours, watching and waiting for deer that never came.

"It was pretty boring looking down at the flats," Martinez testified.

Even with the cheap binoculars he'd brought along, there was nothing to see. Finally, around 10:30 a.m., the hunters decided it was time to hike back to the truck. Martinez felt relieved.

"I was hungry," he said. "I'd had no food since five o'clock the day before."

As the two men converged toward the truck, Adkins easily outpaced his hunting partner. Adkins was lighter and faster on his feet than Martinez, who measured five feet seven and weighed 250 pounds. Looking back, the lost hunter wondered why he hadn't shouted at Adkins to slow down, wait up.

"Ron was getting farther ahead," Martinez testified, "but I didn't yell because all day he'd wanted us to stay quiet, not risk scaring the deer."

Soon Martinez realized he'd lost Adkins, and his bearings too. He'd expected the truck to be only a hundred yards or so away, but when he couldn't find it he figured he must've gotten turned around.

"I don't know which direction I went," he told the court. "After about forty-five minutes, when I wasn't hitting no roads, I realized I was getting into trouble. I told myself not to panic, and I tried to find the ridge [closest to the truck], but they all looked the same."

As the sun climbed farther into the sky, the temperature crept up steadily, ultimately reaching a high of 84 degrees Fahrenheit in nearby Julian. Typical late-October highs in the mountain community seldom hit 70.[8] All week, Southern California had been baking in unseasonable heat; several inland communities had hit 100 degrees or more. At home, Bob and I had been forced to keep the dogs inside and run the air conditioner almost nonstop. And there'd been no rain to break the siege, no rain at all in San Diego for six months. Such an extended dry spell was typical for our Mediterranean climate, characterized by long, hot, dry summers and short, mild, rainy winters. But San Diego hadn't seen its typical rainfall—just shy of eleven inches—for five years. Despite natural adaptations for

---

[8] National Weather Service

drought conditions, the native chaparral couldn't take much more. Everywhere the brush was crackling dry, half of it dead and the rest close to it.

Experienced outdoor enthusiasts know better than to venture into inhospitable terrain, especially under such extreme conditions, without plenty of water—at least a gallon (preferably two) per person per day. Many hikers limit their routes to flat land while the sun is high, saving more strenuous uphill treks for cooler morning or evening hours. Few set out without a cell phone, a map, and a compass—even better, a GPS unit or app. It's just too easy to get lost in wilderness areas, where one vista looks pretty much like the last. Or the next.

Sergio Martinez, who, to be fair, had expected a few hours' hunting sortie rather than an all-day hike, followed none of these safety guidelines. He left his phone in the truck and took along a single, partially filled canteen of water, probably no more than a quart, which didn't last long. So he just kept walking, looking for water in the bottoms of ravines.

"It was really hot, and there was no water," he said, "so I got worried I would dehydrate. I was trying to stay calm, trying to find a way out."

He fired five shots from his rifle, a .300 Winchester Magnum, but no one responded. (Three shots would have conveyed a universal SOS.) Sergio Martinez was alone and thoroughly lost.

"I thought if worse comes to worst, I could light a fire," he told the court. It was something he'd heard in a hunter safety course the year before.

By late afternoon, after seven hours of stumbling up and down hills in relentless heat and sun, Martinez was thirsty beyond experience or imagination. He tried sucking on cactus leaves, hoping they might contain enough moisture to revive him. They didn't.

"My ears were ringing," he told the court. "I had blurry vision because I'd lost my glasses. My tongue was thick. I had hundreds of cactus spines all over my hands. I'd sprained my ankle in some rocks. It took me fifteen or twenty minutes to chip my foot out."

He kept falling down, he said, sometimes on his face. His pants had gotten so loose he could barely keep them on, and lines of white salty residue marked the camouflage pattern of his shirt and waistband. Realizing his body was literally drying out terrified him, Martinez testified. He began to fear that he might die. As a last resort he tried drinking his own urine. Anything to keep going, stay conscious.

Adkins's side of the story came out in unsealed excerpts of federal grand jury testimony. He testified that he'd started to search for Martinez as soon as he realized the two had become separated, estimating they'd been within 400 yards of the truck at the time. Whereas Martinez claimed his hunting partner outpaced him, Adkins said Martinez simply disappeared. After waiting at the truck for a while, Adkins began to worry.

"I started to think he'd possibly had a heart attack," he testified. But he couldn't call for help. His phone was locked in the vehicle with Martinez's, and Martinez had the keys. So Adkins had to wait until late afternoon, when another couple of hunters happened by, to borrow a cell phone, find a signal, and call 911.

In the meantime, Sergio Martinez had reached his limit. He told the court he found a big rock, lay down next to it, and tried to sort out his options, such as they were. The sun was dropping. It would be dark soon. He was glad he'd reserved a few bullets to protect himself from mountain lions.

"I wasn't hungry anymore," he said. "Thirst was sucking the life out of me. I didn't think I was going to live."

All things considered, Martinez could think of only one thing that might save him.

"There was grass right next to me, and I made a little signal fire," he told the court. "I cuddled it so I could put it out. I didn't think I wasn't going to be able to control it."

No one can know how far Martinez actually wandered that day. When sheriff's deputies arrived by helicopter to rescue him, he pointed out the rugged canyon just east of his perch atop the rock pile and told them he'd hiked all the way down and back. The day Bob and I looked out over that fearsome territory, I found it hard to imagine how anyone could do such a thing. How could Martinez walk so far in the wrong direction, through terrain so much steeper than he'd crossed on his way in from the road, and possibly think he was retracing his steps rather than pushing farther off course? Then again, I didn't know how far extreme thirst might take a man looking for water. And I couldn't know what the land had looked like before fire cleared away the vegetation. I saw only grass and scattered low shrubs. But from the sheriff's report and the telltale black skeletons of once-mature scrub oak, Martinez had struggled in places through dense brush twelve to fifteen feet tall.

Two things did become perfectly clear to me that day as I stood where Sergio Martinez ended his long day's journey into exhaustion. First, I was surrounded by unbroken wilderness, a vintage version of Southern California seldom seen in our urbanized era. On the other hand, I could turn in a circle and see nearly every place the Cedar Fire had traveled. It seemed so very far away when Bob and I first heard of it. Miles and miles. But that was before I knew that miles don't matter to a wildfire running with the wind at its back.

CHAPTER 4

THE RESCUE

Sʜᴏʀᴛʟʏ ᴀꜰᴛᴇʀ 4:30 ᴏɴ Sᴀᴛᴜʀᴅᴀʏ afternoon, October 25, when Ron Adkins reported his hunting partner missing in the Cleveland National Forest, two San Diego County Sheriff's deputies took off in a helicopter to search for the lost man. Except for their helmets and olive drab flight suits, the pair looked a bit mismatched. At six-four, pilot Dave Weldon stood nearly a head taller than his elder, bulkier partner, Rocky Laws, a decorated former US Marine officer who'd flown choppers in Vietnam. But the two men shared a passion for aviation and police work, and they'd each seen more than their share of dicey situations. All good training for the night to come.

As Weldon eased the blue-and-white MD 500D off the tarmac at El Cajon's Gillespie Field, a second call came in. The Oceanside Police Department, about thirty-five miles up the coast from San Diego, needed help searching for a confused elderly man missing from his home. Weldon and Laws conferred and agreed: A lost hunter could more likely wait than somebody's missing grandpa. So Weldon pointed the copter, dubbed ASTREA3, toward Oceanside.[9]

Within an hour the deputies located the lost man wandering in a neighborhood park, and around 5:30 p.m., Weldon turned his aircraft back east toward Julian to look for Sergio Martinez. On the way they crossed directly over the Ramona Air Attack Base, where they could see a CDF helicopter below them on the tarmac, its rotors slowly turning. From there, looking ahead toward the mountains, Weldon and Laws saw a column of smoke.

"That's probably our guy lighting a signal fire," Weldon said over his helmet radio.

"Yeah, probably," Laws agreed. "I bet if we look around up there we'll find him."

Entering the mountains at an altitude of 500 to 800 feet, the deputies ran into a northeast wind. Weldon gauged it between twenty and thirty miles per hour, plenty strong enough, should it drop to the ground, to turbocharge a wildfire. *Better get some resources on this fire before then,* he thought. Weldon tried to reach the CDF helicopter they'd seen, using the Ramona Airport frequency, but he couldn't raise anyone. The pilot had timed out for the day and turned off his radio. Meanwhile, Laws contacted Gene Palos, a fellow deputy flying ASTREA1. His MD 530F was equipped with a Bambi bucket, a collapsible canvas bag used to scoop and drop water on fires. Given the day's critical fire danger, the CDF had asked Palos to load his gear and stand ready to fight fire.

"We have a vegetation fire out here," Laws advised Palos. "You might have to head this way."

---

[9] ASTREA is an acronym for Aerial Support to Regional Enforcement Agencies

Adding to their urgency, both deputies knew the current chop might well signal worse fire weather on the way. The forecast called for full-on Santa Ana conditions to develop overnight.

A fabled Southern California phenomenon, Santa Ana winds sweep in several times each year, spilling over the mountains and funneling through the passes that separate Los Angeles and San Diego from the vast deserts to the east. And when they come, they do not come gently.

Blowing hot, dry, and strong, sometimes for days at a time, Santa Anas are known for raising both temperatures and tempers. Typically, they reach at least thirty miles an hour in velocity, gusting to fifty, sixty, or more in places, especially at night or early in the morning when competing ocean breezes subside. Santa Anas don't often bother to make an appearance during the summer, preferring instead to warm up the cooler months of the year—as early as September, as late as May, but most often October through February.

Because these so-called "devil winds" bring such sweltering weather, most people think they originate in the deserts. Actually, they begin at least 500 miles to the northeast as a high-pressure center over the Great Basin, that vast watershed stretching between the Sierra Nevada and Rocky Mountain ranges. The contrast between this colder, denser air and warmer, low-pressure air over Southern California sets up a huge atmospheric pinwheel that feeds on itself as it falls west toward sea level.

With the drop in altitude, the cold air streaming from the Great Basin accelerates, warms up and dries out, boosting the contrast between the two air masses. Eventually, a river of cold, dense air pools and cascades over the mountains, reaching the ground as Santa Ana winds that surge through narrow passes and canyons on their way out to sea. Only when the colder, denser air fueling this atmospheric phenomenon begins to dissipate does a Santa Ana event die out.[10]

Such an episode inspired the memorable opening lines of mystery writer Raymond Chandler's novel, *Red Wind*: "There was a desert wind blowing that night. It was one of those hot dry Santa Anas that come down through the mountain passes and curl your hair and make your nerves jump and your skin itch. On nights like that every booze party ends in a fight. Meek little wives feel the edge of the carving knife and study their husbands' necks. Anything can happen."

Aside from prompting bar fights and domestic violence, Santa Anas can also damage structures and create dangerous travel conditions, triggering turbulence stiff enough to tip over RVs and tractor trailers caught in the natural wind tunnel of a mountain pass. But the devil winds are perhaps most notorious for feeding wildfires by lowering humidity, desiccating vegetation, and literally fanning the flames. Especially in October, before winter rains typically end Southern California's long, dry summer, a Santa Ana can whip any spark into a major conflagration. In fact, the majority of catastrophic wildfires in Southern California's known history can be linked to Santa Ana winds.

At 5:51 p.m., according to Dave Weldon's official report, he and Rocky Laws arrived at Kessler Flat and began circling the fire. Burning westward atop a small hill, it looked to be about fifty yards square. The deputies noted the GPS coordinates and the absence of roads or trails leading into the place. And then, some twenty yards upwind of the flames, they found their lost

---

[10] Thanks to wildfire meteorologists Brian DAgostino and Steven Vanderburg, who informed this simplified explanation of Santa Ana winds.

hunter—a short, heavyset Hispanic man dressed in camouflage, perched on a pile of rocks, waving frantically with a flashlight.

Weldon set the chopper down nearby on a slight slope, the only clear spot he could find, and idled the engine while Laws climbed out into gathering dusk and headed off through the chaparral toward Martinez, some fifty to seventy-five yards away across a shallow gully. The brush must've been at least thirty to fifty years old—up to fifteen feet tall and so thick in places Laws had to drop to his hands and knees and crawl through. Weldon kept seeing his partner disappear and then pop up again a little farther away. Finally, after about ten minutes, Laws reached the rock pile. The lost hunter seemed disoriented, so Laws slung the man's rifle over his own shoulder, took Martinez by the arm, and pushed him toward the helicopter.

In the meantime, Weldon had reported to headquarters on the fire's progress and requested assistance.

"We need to get Gene out here now," he told the dispatcher.

Gene Palos and his partner, fellow deputy Kevin Price, were staffing an event at Balboa Park in downtown San Diego, more than thirty miles to the west. But with a cruising speed of 155 miles per hour, ASTREA1 could reach Kessler Flat in less than fifteen minutes. After a decade flying for the sheriff's department, Palos knew the backcountry intimately. As he flew toward Cedar Creek, he could see in his mind's eye a couple of private ponds within a mile of the fire's reported location; he visualized setting down beside one of them, deploying the canvas bucket, and then loading up and dropping water. But as ASTREA1 approached the fire, about five minutes out, a new order came over the radio: "Stand down. Forest Service says you're too late; it's after cutoff."

Damn, Palos thought. *I'm practically on top of it.*

The sheriff's department had no cutoff rule of its own. ASTREA pilots routinely flew after dark, often with the help of night-vision goggles. But when fighting fire, interagency agreements obligated the sheriff's pilots to honor fire agency regulations. So Palos followed protocol and obeyed orders. Residents on the ground who saw a sheriff's helicopter turn back just short of an unchecked wildfire couldn't believe it. Neither could Palos. After the fire, angry citizens and politicians railed against the arbitrary cutoff rule, arguing that Palos could have prevented a catastrophe. Fire officials countered that the bucket aboard his chopper—holding 110 gallons, the equivalent of two barrels of water—could hardly have dented the blaze. Considering the distance of the fire from El Capitan Reservoir, they said, Palos could have made only two passes, three max, before dark—330 gallons of water versus an estimated twenty acres of burning chaparral.

Palos disagrees. It still galls him that he was called off before he had a chance to attack the flames or even size up the situation. If he could relive that moment, he told me, he would ignore the radio order to stand down, and just keep flying. To back his claim that he might well have made a difference, he cited an experiment he and his partner ran a couple of weeks after the fire. Flying back to Kessler Flat, they simulated the whole thing, deploying the bucket, filling it from the nearby ponds Palos had in mind, and then dropping on the fire zone. In forty minutes, the remaining daylight time Palos figured he could have flown, they made fourteen round trips. Fourteen 110-gallon buckets against a spreading hillside of fire. Would it have made a difference? No one can know. But Palos—along with a lot of other San Diegans—wishes he'd had the chance to find out.

Even so, the evidence of firefighting history is this: Aerial drops alone can't fully extinguish a wildfire. They can only slow it down, retard it. Short of complete saturation, fire will skunk its way through or around wet spots and pop up again on the other side, especially when fanned by a stiff wind. Any wildland firefighter from any agency anywhere in the world will tell you that it takes troops on the ground—driving bulldozers and hand-cutting firebreaks—to stop a line of flames. Inserting troops requires decent access, plenty of room to move lots of oversize vehicles in and out in a hurry. In other words, a place that accommodates the 10 Standard Fire Orders, the crucial safety commandments of wildland firefighting. Sergio Martinez's rock pile, deep in a hell of old-growth chaparral a half-mile from the closest road, didn't qualify as one of those places.

In the meantime, with Palos en route, Laws was having trouble getting Martinez back to the chopper. His legs kept cramping, a classic symptom of dehydration. Over the radio, Weldon could hear his partner urging the distressed hunter onward.

"Come on, son. Get your butt in gear. There's a fire going here. Do you want to get burned up?"

"I can't," Martinez kept saying. "My legs won't work."

Weldon took another look at the fire—a long fringe of orange rising above the native shrubs at its forward edge. Still headed mostly away from them, its smoke wafting straight up before bending slightly toward the sunset, the swelling patch of flames was moving laterally, too. Before long it would overtake his position.

"Do you need me to shut down and come help you?" he asked Laws over the radio.

"Yeah, I do."

"Then let's just hope the battery holds, and we can start up again before this fire gets much bigger."

It happened sometimes, an engine refusing to crank. Not often, but Weldon didn't want this to be one of those occasions. He grabbed his backpack canteen, filled with half a gallon of water, and fought his way through the pungent brush toward the other two men. Brittle branches cracked and gave way around him, smelling of sage and dry earth. When he punched through, he handed the canteen to a haggard-looking Martinez, who immediately drained it. The two deputies got on either side of the lost hunter and half dragged, half carried him toward the helicopter. Several times, Martinez told them he needed to stop and rest.

"We can't," Weldon said. "We've got fire moving this way, and we're running out of daylight."

More than once, Weldon reported, Martinez looked back at the flames and apologized. "I'm really sorry about this," he said.

"Did you start this fire?" Laws asked.

"No," Martinez answered, and then dropped his head and stole another look at the flames. "I'm sorry," he said again. "I'm really sorry about all of this."

He tried to show them where he'd wandered during the past hours—over a low ridge, he said, and then down into a precipitously steep canyon and back, hoping to find water at the bottom. It was a route that would have taken him farther away from his truck, Weldon noted.

"How did you start the fire?" he asked.

Still the lost hunter didn't answer. Flames had advanced to within twenty yards now. It was time to leave. When they reached the helicopter, the deputies shoved Martinez into the backseat, and Weldon asked him once more for an explanation.

"What did you use to start the fire? Matches or a lighter?"

Martinez said nothing.

"You know this thing's going to get big."

"I'm sorry," Martinez repeated. "I thought I was going to die out there. Thanks for saving my life."

He had a bit more to say as the copter got underway, a few further complaints about his aching legs and a few choice words directed at Adkins, whom he accused of deserting him. The engine caught as soon as Weldon hit the ignition; he felt a cool wave of relief as they lifted off at 6:21 p.m.

Responding to Weldon's radio call for medical assistance, an ambulance sat waiting when he touched down in San Diego Country Estates. By now, Martinez had consumed even more water—a few bottles stowed aboard the copter—and he kept guzzling it down while the paramedics checked him over. No doubt, they concluded, this guy had reached a point of severe dehydration.

Once rehydrated and revived, Martinez waived further treatment. He was transferred into the custody of a USDA Forest Service officer, who drove him to the Ramona sheriff's substation. Unsure whether or not she should detain Martinez, the officer consulted with her chain of command. Without any real evidence he'd set the fire, the Forest Service brass decided not to hold him. Besides, they told her, they had his contact information; they could find him again if they needed to. So the lost hunter was cited for carelessness and released.

In the aftermath of the Cedar Fire, Sergio Martinez became a celebrity of sorts, a household name in San Diego, and a footnote in California history. Some labeled him an outright murderer; others, an irresponsible stoner; still others, an unlucky idiot. Some demanded he serve maximum jail time; some said a lifetime of guilt should be punishment enough. But apart from anyone's opinion, Sergio Martinez was certainly this: a desperate man driven to a desperate act that would both save and ruin his own life, end fifteen others, and forever change thousands more, including mine.

Chapter 5

Terra Nova

I credit my father for my love of nature, a lifelong attraction that drew me to live in wildfire country just as surely as he played shining trout all the way to mossy stream banks. Art Millers's passion for the natural world, if not a dominant gene, at least proved contagious. My sister, Karen, and I caught a bad case of it hiking and fishing with him on Sunday afternoons at our grandparents' farm, and on summer Saturdays under leafy canopies alongside his favorite fishing streams in the nearby Blue Ridge Mountains.

Everything in my father's world fit together, ran in cycles, conformed to a preordained order. Tides rose and ebbed; seasons came and went and came again; trees grew in concentric circles that gave away their age and told what kind of weather they'd seen—a fat ring for a rainy year, a skinny ring for a dry one. Each kind of animal played a specific role within a delicate balance. And if ever that balance tipped, Daddy assured us, nature had ways of restoring her equilibrium.

What my father was really teaching us, of course, was how to live in harmony with the natural world. With time I got it. Like him I grew to sense the raw spirituality of nature, to respect the primordial ties that bind us as humans to every other piece of the planetary puzzle. Like him, I learned that wonder leads to worship, and worship makes us whole.

The night before my wedding to Bob, North Carolina lay in the path of a lunar eclipse. Daddy and I sat side by side on the back steps of the red brick house where I'd grown up and watched the earth's shadow steal away the moon, hold it hostage for a while, and then slowly give it back. I don't remember for certain now, so many years later, but I imagine my father slipped a sermon in there somewhere. Or maybe by then, my last night of living in his home, he didn't need to.

When I first met Bob Younger, he was a smart-ass twenty-year-old with dark eyes, darker hair, a condescending smirk, and that big, black camera hanging from his neck. We were sophomores at rival universities, and the minute a mutual friend introduced us, Bob found it necessary to make an insulting remark about my alma mater. I wrote him off as an obnoxious jerk and didn't waste another thought on him until he walked back into my life a year later.

By then, I'd decided to study journalism, which meant transferring to the University of North Carolina at Chapel Hill, Bob's campus. That's when I discovered Bob also was a journalism major, which eventually threw us together as classmates in a weekly news-editing lab, a six-hour marathon. As it turned out, Bob could be a lot more charming than he'd initially let on. He was intelligent, funny, thoughtful, occasionally given to philosophy—and very good-looking when he wasn't smirking. During our class supper break, we fell into the habit of walking over to Franklin Street, Chapel Hill's main drag, to share a quick pizza.

As the weeks went by, I found more and more to like about Bob Younger. He was confident and decisive; he got things done. He was a physical guy, a future Marine who ran ten miles at a clip and spent his summer vacations at boot camp. Yet the lens of his ever-present Nikon captured images best seen with the heart—a flower blooming in the crevice of a boulder; an old wino asleep on a wooden pier beside his empty bottle; a beggar draped in faded fabric, holding out an empty hand to strangers against the backdrop of a huge stone cathedral.

On May 10, 1975, the day we both collected our Carolina diplomas, Bob was commissioned as a second lieutenant in the US Marine Corps. The officer in charge was Admiral Elmo Zumwalt, the recently retired and highly decorated chief of naval operations. Zumwalt coached the midshipmen through the oath of office and declared them all commissioned officers. Next he presented individual honors, including a shining silver Marine officer's sword to recognize the newly commissioned Marine most likely to succeed in the Corps. In 1975, that sword went to Second Lieutenant Robert E. Younger.

It was a proud moment for a young bride-to-be, and as for Bob, the sword he received as a gift from the hands of a legendary admiral instantly became one of his most cherished possessions. Two weeks later, Bob and I ran through a hail of post-wedding rice, jumped into my tiny gold Dodge Colt, and drove away from North Carolina toward a lifetime of shared horizons.

After Bob completed his training as an artillery officer, we moved to California where he served with the Marines for three more years and eventually settled into a civil service career in San Diego. We spent the next two decades working, parenting, joining, contributing. By 2003, the year Bob and I both turned fifty, we felt ready for a change. We'd talked for years about loading up our two big black Newfoundland dogs and moving to the country. Now we were almost there. Our older daughter, Lauren, had finished her college degree and landed a great job in Seattle; her sister, Kendall, had just begun her final undergraduate semester. At last we could see the end of tuition payments approaching. So for Bob's birthday that January, I gave him a bathrobe. "It's just a token," I joked, "something to wear around the house I'm going to buy you."

I expected it would take a year or so to find just what we wanted, something a little different from the typical California stucco box, something with character and enough elbow room to accommodate friends and family. But only a couple of nights after Bob's birthday, as I sat on our family room sofa with my laptop, sifting through the usual boring parade of online real-estate listings, I found my needle in the haystack. A stunning house on five acres, a jaw-dropping view framed by mountains, boulders, and sky—and miraculously close to our price range.

The location was Wildcat Canyon, a long and largely undeveloped piece of backcountry wedged between two soaring ridgelines about twenty-five miles east of downtown San Diego. I knew the territory. A year or so before, a veterinarian who'd treated one of our Newfs had moved there.

"How do you like it?" I'd asked Peter Slusser.

"It's beautiful up there," he said.

So I went to see for myself—and completely agreed. The photos on my laptop confirmed that initial impression.

"Bob, look at this."

I turned the screen toward him and clicked through the photos, showing first the house itself, and then that unbelievable view.

"My gosh," Bob said. "Call Henry."

I'd met Henry Large a decade before in an extension course, where his studious demeanor, arcane questions, and brown polyester wardrobe quickly set him apart as the class geek. Gradually, however, I'd discovered in Henry not only a brilliant mind, but also surprising insight and a wicked sense of humor. He was in his mid-sixties now and just beginning a new career in real estate. Despite his rookie status, I knew I could trust Henry to help us. So the next day during my lunch hour, I climbed into his green pickup, and we set off under a cerulean sky to see the house in Wildcat Canyon.

From one end to the other, Wildcat Canyon Road makes for a scenic Sunday afternoon kind of drive, taking about half an hour, depending on traffic. Its two lanes twist northward some twelve miles from the country-western community of Lakeside, climbing a thousand feet in elevation before opening into a wide valley anchored by the old ranching town of Ramona. Everywhere you look in Wildcat Canyon, spectacular granite boulders poke up from the ground like gigantic stone statues, piercing through the dusty green blanket of shrubbery that covers mountains rising both right and left. On the canyon floor, along the roadbed, occasional clusters of gnarled coast live oaks spread green canopies against blue sky.

As the canyon rises, the vegetation changes, from grasses and scattered sagebrush to spreading thickets of native chaparral. California's predominant plant community is a vast and fragrant bouquet of wildland bushes—sumac, chamise, ceanothus, yucca, manzanita, and scrub oak, for starters. From a distance, mature chaparral looks soft, like dark green balls of cotton clinging to the mountains. But it's often so thick with branches it can be impossible to wade through, which explains why Old West cowboys wore leather "chaps," designed and named for brush busting.

Despite its scenic beauty, most people who have driven Wildcat Canyon Road complain about it. About five miles up from Lakeside, the road bisects the Barona Indian Reservation, home to a sovereign nation and the site of Barona Valley Ranch, a major hotel, casino, and golf complex. The Barona tribe's decision to build a full-fledged resort in the middle of Wildcat Canyon frustrated everyone who used the road on a regular basis. Traffic volume more than doubled after the casino opened. Collisions, injuries, and even fatalities became fairly commonplace, often stalling traffic for miles in both directions. There was nothing to do but wait for an accident to clear. Barona's success had turned remote Wildcat Canyon into a popular destination, and Wildcat Canyon Road was the only way in or out of the place.

Maybe all this should have bothered me that sunny day in January 2003, as Henry and I drove farther and farther into the backcountry, straining to read mailbox numbers in our search for the beautiful house I'd seen in the real estate listing. But it didn't. Growing up in the foothills of the Blue Ridge Mountains, I'd learned to drive on winding two-lane roads. I only hoped, for the Newfs' sake, that the place wasn't too near all that traffic. By the time Henry and I finally stumbled upon the right mailbox at the turnoff to the right dirt road, we'd explored half a dozen others and asked directions from a man on horseback. From there, we still had to drive about a half-mile to reach the house. At least, I thought, I could quit worrying about the dogs.

Two houses past the turnoff, a closed gate in a chain-link fence forced us into a sharp left turn, and then Henry stopped. We both stared up at what struck me as the steepest, skinniest sliver of asphalt this side of Nepal, cut high into the side of the mountain. Henry sized it up in a single word. "Hell-o," he said, and slipped the truck into low gear. As we reached what had looked like the top of this narrow road, it widened into a further stretch of crisp new blacktop. We climbed even farther, around a huge boulder and then over a crest. Suddenly, that incredible view from my computer screen opened up before us—mountains and boulders and sky all the way back down Wildcat Canyon and beyond into Mexico. Even Henry, who by his own admission harbored no unexpressed thought, fell speechless.

Sue and Randy Fritz, the sellers of the house we'd come to see, made their living building beautiful custom homes. This one they'd built for their own family, which accounted for the unique character and craftsmanship of the place—huge windows, hardwood floors, natural rock fireplaces, and high ceilings trimmed with thick crown molding—not to mention the positive energy I felt as soon as I set foot on the property. I couldn't wait to call Bob.

"So how was it?" he asked.

"It's a very nice house," I said, punching the word very. "You have to see it."

Bob got the message. But he was slammed at the office. It would be Saturday before he could make the trek to Wildcat Canyon. He paused for a moment.

"Is this the one you want?" he asked.

"Well, it's a lot of money. But, Bob, this place is unbelievable. You'll love it."

"Then tell Henry to go ahead and write up an offer so we don't lose it."

"Seriously? Are you sure?"

"Yeah, I am. You know what we're looking for. And I saw the pictures."

So by Saturday morning, when Bob finally saw our new home for himself, caught his first glimpse down Wildcat Canyon and fell in love just as I had, just as I'd known he would, Henry had already submitted our offer to the Fritzes, and they'd already drawn up a counteroffer. I felt a little light-headed. At Henry's recommendation, we'd put pretty much everything we had on the table from the start.

"Let's go in strong," he'd said. "Don't try any lowball nonsense. Let them know you're serious."

Now we wondered how much more serious the counteroffer would be.

The Fritzes weren't moving far, just next door where they owned another piece of land with a western view all the way to the Pacific. They'd already built a guesthouse there and planned to live in it while working on their next home. We were happy to hear that. We'd liked them both immediately. They must have felt a connection, too, or at least thought we'd make good neighbors. As we left them that Saturday morning, they were both all smiles. On our way back down the canyon, Bob drove, and Henry opened the envelope containing the Fritzes' counteroffer. It was more than reasonable, given their extraordinary property, but I wasn't sure Bob would go for it.

"What do you think?" I asked him.

"Let's get down this mountain to some place where we can sign that contract before these people change their minds," he said.

I once read about a man who traveled someplace new, someplace he'd never been before, and realized he'd belonged there all along. That's exactly what Bob and I experienced the moment we saw the house in Wildcat Canyon. We'd happened upon a truly special place; it raised our spirits just to be there. Never before, in twenty-eight years of marriage, had we lived anywhere we really loved, anywhere we'd felt deeply at home. But this place, this oasis in the canyon, felt different. It had an ambiance, a personality, all its own. So much so, we decided, that it needed a name. During the long weeks of escrow, we entertained several possibilities. But nothing quite fit. And then one day we stumbled over the obvious.

"How about Terra Nova?" Bob suggested. It was an old Latin term, meaning "new land," something we'd learned when we first fell in love with Newfoundland dogs. In Italy, "Terra Nova" is the literal name of the breed. Now the concept of "new land" struck us as the perfect metaphor for a promising next chapter of our lives.

The day escrow closed—a brilliant day in early April—Henry escorted me back to Wildcat Canyon. As we walked up to my new front door, he handed me the key and smiled.

"Welcome home," he said.

It was hard to believe, turning that key, walking into that beautiful house, its windows filled with mountains and sky, that it was actually ours. During our first few weeks at Terra Nova, Bob and I kept looking at each other, wide-eyed, asking, "Do we live here?" Gradually, as the reality settled in, our question turned into a statement, though still heavy with amazement.

"We live here," we said over and over, each time breathing a silent thank-you.

It wasn't just the house, so much more than we'd ever dreamed of. It was the place. Each day, we encountered some new delight. A species of bird we'd never seen before. A handsome gopher snake sliding by in the grasses just beyond our front deck. Hawks, ravens, and vultures sailing overhead. Lizards sunning on the rock outside our kitchen window, flashing neon blue bellies as they cranked out little lizard push-ups. One Saturday morning, while I was watering the plants outside our front door, a tiny tree frog hopped out from among the leaves. I scooped it up and carried it inside to show Bob. It was a wonderful and wiggly little thing that promptly escaped my fingers, flung itself hopefully into space, and landed on a kitchen window, where it stuck effortlessly until I recaptured it and returned it to the garden.

And then, early one morning on my way to work, I crested the ridge between our house and the main road and caught my first glimpse of a bobcat, sauntering right down the middle of the pavement. At first I thought it must be a coyote; it was about that size, and we'd heard coyotes singing at night somewhere in the canyon below. But this animal's shoulders slipped from side to side as it walked, a decidedly feline gait. In another instant, it sensed my presence and streaked into the chaparral. Watching it disappear in a gray and brown blur, I realized I hadn't seen a coyote's bushy tail. I hadn't seen a tail at all.

"I think I saw a bobcat this morning," I told Bob that evening. "On the road out, just over the hill."

"Oh yeah? I was going to tell you. I saw one the other day, a little farther down, on the flat."

Something so elusive, so mysterious. Almost a phantom, really. If only one of us had seen it, we might have dismissed the idea. It must have been a coyote, we might have said. But no, we both had seen it, at different times, and almost in the same spot—a real wildcat in Wildcat Canyon! What a magical place we'd found. So much of what we'd been searching for had come to us in that single key Henry dropped into my hand.

It's almost painful now to look back, to realize how naive we were, how unsuspecting of impending catastrophe. We would not have believed our newfound land could so quickly devolve into ashes and memories. We could not have imagined it would become not only a place, but also a state of mind, perhaps even a state of grace, sustaining us through the long and treacherous journey ahead. What we did know—and we knew it to our bones—was that Terra Nova was home. And despite everything that was to come, that was all we needed to know.

CHAPTER 6

FIRE IN THE FOREST

A FEW HOURS BEFORE THE CEDAR Fire started, CDF Battalion Chief Kelly Zombro looked east toward the mountains from the suburban streets of San Diego Country Estates and didn't like what he saw. The awesome, thousand-foot-deep San Diego River Gorge. Ridge after ridge of dry chaparral beyond. And nothing but a few chicken-scratch roads offering access to any of it. *If a fire got started out there,* Zombro thought, *unless it happened right alongside a road, there'd be no way to get to it.* Maybe he could safely squeeze in a single engine and a hand crew, but mounting a full wildland initial attack would take five strike teams—each comprising five engines—and two or three buses full of troops, plus bulldozers and water tenders. You can't send that many vehicles single file down a winding dirt road into unburned fuel. For sure, he figured, there'd be no place for them to park, no place to turn around—in short, no way to maintain the safety margins imposed by the 10 Standard Orders. Bottom line, as Zombro liked to put it, "It's not acceptable to kill firefighters."

Seeing the area from a helicopter, as he would after the fire, proved even more alarming. "You see it from the sky, and you realize: With an east wind, it's a giant, steep, rock-faced funnel right to the Country Estates and on into Wildcat Canyon," he told me later, his usually open and friendly face furrowed in dismay. "I never knew that before, but when you see it, it's daunting; it's oh my gosh."

After seven years as a CDF battalion chief, Kelly Zombro still missed the adrenaline rush of his early career. He'd started young, lean, and hungry for action, chasing his first fires as a sixteen-year-old volunteer reservist with the Poway Fire Department north of San Diego. Three weeks before the end of high school, that experience earned him a seasonal position with the CDF. He had to beg his teachers to let him take finals early, and then ask his new boss for a day off to attend graduation. But in the end it was worth it; Kelly Zombro was living his boyhood dream.

By twenty, he'd landed a permanent engineer's position in Riverside, where the CDF served as the county fire agency, covering structure fires as well as wildland incidents. Zombro loved the diversity of the work, the quick satisfaction of dousing a house fire versus days in the field corralling a wildland blaze. He pursued the promotion to battalion chief for the sake of his family. As a chief he could go home at night, spend time with his wife, see more of his kids' soccer games and school programs. Now thirty-eight, Zombro didn't regret the trade-off, but the paperwork that came with an administrative job jeopardized what little hair he had left and kept him in the office far more than he liked. It was a rare day he could hop in his truck and drive his territory. Occasionally, though, when the weather turned seriously hot and dry, he set the papers aside and took off. If and when something went down, he didn't want to be caught sitting behind a desk.

Saturday, October 25, was one of those red-flag days. Zombro was out checking his assigned territory, on the county's south side near the city of Chula Vista, when headquarters called to advise him of a change in plans. The battalion chief in Ramona had been deployed to a fire north of Los Angeles; Zombro now would be responsible for that battalion as well as his own. He didn't know the Ramona area too well, so he headed north to scout it out. Looking over the rugged wilderness stretching east of the Country Estates, Zombro tried to dismiss his concerns as overblown. Realistically, what was going to happen? Why would anyone start a fire way out there in the middle of nowhere? Why would anyone even be out there? He got back in his truck and headed home to grab a bite of supper, arriving sometime close to sunset. Within minutes his pager buzzed, and Kelly Zombro was on his way back to Ramona.

A battalion chief (BC for short) can specialize—in training, aviation, or law enforcement, for instance—but most juggle emergency response duties with day-to-day administrative oversight of two, three, or four fire stations. With that many resources available to each BC, rarely is more than one dispatched in an initial wildland fire response. But on October 25, when Zombro was ordered to Cedar Creek, so was his colleague and good friend, Ray Chaney, the battalion chief in the Campo area, east of Zombro's home territory.

Both men wondered about that but chalked it up to the day's red-flag conditions. Besides, with both of them on the fire, they could team up. Chaney and Zombro made good partners. They'd come from similar backgrounds and usually saw things eye to eye. The son of a one-time Forest Service firefighter, Chaney, like Zombro, was thirty-eight and had grown up in Poway. He'd acquired an early taste for firefighting as a young teenager invited to ride along in the engine with his dad and Bill Clayton, a good friend, fellow firefighter, and Ray Chaney's godfather. Straight out of high school, Chaney started working as a seasonal firefighter with the CDF; he even ditched school for a week to attend the required training. He and Zombro seemed to be living parallel lives. Way back in their rookie days, they both posed for the same group photograph— Zombro in the front row, tall with dark hair and a determined look; Chaney, shorter, blond, and square-jawed, popping up between faces behind him. Years later, when work brought the two men back together, they got a kick out of finding their kid faces in that old image.

En route now to the Cedar Fire, they talked by cell phone, coordinating their strategy as they drove. Chaney, coming from his home on the east side of the fire in the town of Alpine, would approach from that angle, while Zombro would come in from the west, through Ramona. Neither would be calling the shots at this point. The fire's location within the Cleveland National Forest gave the USDA Forest Service responsibility for managing the incident, meaning Chaney and Zombro would each play a supporting role, assisting the Forest Service chief in charge. Both the Forest Service and the CDF were responding with full wildland fire contingents, in keeping with a mutual-aid agreement between the San Diego area's state and federal firefighters. If things got out of hand and the fire became a threat to homes, or if it grew past Cleveland National Forest borders, the CDF would assume duplicative authority under a prescribed system known as "unified command."

Mutual aid had long been a way of life in San Diego County, the largest of a very few California counties with no fire department of its own. Once upon a time, the CDF had played that role by contract, as it still did in nearly forty of California's fifty-eight counties. But in the mid-1970s, in an effort to cut costs, San Diego County supervisors dropped the CDF contract. After that, a patchwork of some sixty fire agencies—Forest Service and CDF, the San Diego Fire- Rescue Department, and other municipal fire agencies, plus an assortment of tribal and volunteer organizations—shared responsibility for protecting one of the world's most fire-prone metropolitan regions.

About 6:30 p.m. on Saturday evening, as Zombro drove into the suburban center of the Country Estates, he came up behind a Forest Service passenger truck and realized he knew the driver, Forest Service Division Chief Hal Mortier. Although they worked for different agencies, the two men had covered a lot of fires together over the years. Both were headed now for the same vantage point—Thornbush Road at the far eastern end of the Country Estates. When they got there they parked at a high point, beside a community water tank, with the abyss of the San Diego River Gorge spread out before them. Beyond it, about four miles from their position, Zombro and Mortier could see a round patch of flames edging slowly down a knoll. Clearly a much smaller fire than the twenty acres dispatch had estimated, it looked to be completely unaffected by wind; the two chiefs could tell by the straight-up smoke column and the way the flames burned evenly on all sides. But the fire's location could hardly have been worse—exactly the remote, inaccessible chunk of wilderness Zombro had scoped out earlier that afternoon.

Some ten miles to the east, Chaney made slow progress toward Cedar Creek on graveled Boulder Creek Road. Finally, he crested a ridgeline and got his first look at the column of smoke rising from the newly reported fire. It was still a good way off—he guessed it would take him at least half an hour longer to reach it—but from what he could see, it didn't strike him as particularly menacing. In fact, he thought it looked almost like a "backing fire," meaning it seemed to be spreading slowly and evenly on all sides, making it easier to catch than a forward-driving head of flames.

A gentle plume, not much more than you'd expect from a campfire, rose straight up 1,000, maybe 1,500 feet or so before bending nonchalantly under a slight east wind. It was dusk now, too late for air tankers and water-dropping helicopters to fly. But even without the prospect of air support, Chaney wasn't worried about this fire. From the location dispatch had given, he figured it shouldn't be hard to access; they'd probably be able to drive the engines to within striking distance. "Mundane" was the word that came to mind as Chaney drove on toward the rising smoke. *I'll be home by midnight,* he thought.

As soon as Ron and Kathy Serabia returned from their Saturday afternoon drive, Kathy jumped on the phone, warning everyone she knew in the Country Estates and adjacent Barona Mesa about the growing fire to the east. Soon the Serabia house filled with evacuees. Behind their nervous conversation, the scanner kept up a steady squawking. By late evening, a time when wildfires often settle down a bit, the scanner chatter indicated that this one was starting to pick up, catching the slight forward edge of an east wind.

As Ron Serabia expected, fire crews couldn't get anywhere close to the flames. He listened as the radio spat out the details. Tough terrain, steep slopes, no access, no safety zones, no emergency escape routes. He thought about the spiderweb of rutted dirt roads and abandoned truck trails he'd seen all across the backcountry from his seat in the OV-10. So many were dead ends, trailing off into dense chaparral. A big vehicle could easily get stuck out there.

Those voices on the scanner belonged to men and women Serabia knew, coworkers and friends. He imagined them out there, probing the darkness, pushing down rough, uncertain trails. His mind jumped once again to the Inaja Fire of his childhood. He thought about the eleven men swallowed by a wind-driven flare-up near Cedar Creek, and how far the fire had run from there, stampeding through Ramona and beyond. Serabia picked up the phone and dialed the home number for Shari Lee, his long-time CDF colleague at the air attack base in Ramona.

"I'm coming in tomorrow, and I'll be there early," he told her. "Order me ten tankers and five helicopters."

The forces marshaling to fight the fire burning near Cedar Creek included not only CDF and Forest Service resources, but also various local departments in the area. Only one officer would lead this joint effort as incident commander, or IC. With the fire still burning entirely inside the Cleveland National Forest, that job fell to the senior Forest Service fire manager on duty. On October 25, 2003, that person happened to be Division Chief Carlton Joseph.

Joseph was supposed to have Saturday off. But in his three decades as a firefighter, he'd seldom seen the fire danger so critical. Something was bound to jump off somewhere before nightfall; he could feel it. Much of the rest of Southern California was already burning. A hundred miles to the north, the Grand Prix blaze threatened a string of cities between San Bernardino and Los Angeles. At least, Joseph thought, the Roblar 2 Fire at Camp Pendleton finally seemed to be winding down, after four days.

Looking almost professorial with his gold wire-rimmed glasses, thick brown hair, and mustache, Joseph had barely settled into his desk chair at the Cleveland's San Diego headquarters when he got word that a new fire had exploded in the mountains just north of San Bernardino, showing every sign of yet another massive blaze in the making. Time to pack a bag, Joseph figured. Besides his regular duties in the Cleveland National Forest, he belonged to an elite Type 1 incident management team that specialized in coordinating attacks on big fires. Joseph's fellow Forest Service division chief, Hal Mortier, led the group, one of only sixteen such teams nationwide, and the next up in rotation for assignment.

Soon Mortier phoned Joseph to confirm that he'd be taking command of the San Bernardino blaze, dubbed the Old Fire, at seven the next morning, and Joseph started calling other team members to coordinate plans for the assignment. A little after 5:30 in the afternoon, the radio interrupted Joseph's phone conversation. Three beeps—the signal for a fire call.

"Hold on a minute," he said.

In the next moment, when the dispatcher announced a vegetation fire near Cedar Creek, Joseph knew his plans had changed. He wouldn't be going to San Bernardino with Mortier. Not for a while anyway. Cedar Creek. What a bitch of a place to fight fire. The same roadless ridgelines and yawning canyons that burned in the historic Inaja Fire in 1956, the year before Joseph was born. He'd grown up feeling the weight of that fire, carrying the name of a nineteen-year-old kid swallowed by the flames, his father's best friend, Carlton Lingo.

"Oh shit," Joseph told his colleague over the phone. "This is a really, really bad place."

Following protocol, the Monte Vista Interagency Command Center in El Cajon had dispatched the standard complement for a wildland fire initial attack to Cedar Creek. But Joseph figured standard staffing wouldn't be enough for such a remote spot, especially this late in the day, with air support out of the question until morning. It took him about forty-five minutes to drive to Pine Hills. Along the way, he ordered another strike team of five engines, extra water trucks, a couple of dozers, and more hand crews. That would give him over 300 personnel in all, well beyond the typical force for an initial attack.

A few minutes later, radio transcripts indicate Hal Mortier's voice cut through the radio chatter. "Carlton, I'm not going to San Bernardino until morning, in case you need help. Do you want me to head out to the Country Estates and view this thing from there?"

"That would be helpful, Hal."

"I'm en route right now."

Climbing the hills beyond Ramona, Joseph could see a small column of smoke rising in the dusk ahead. But where exactly was it coming from? Over the radio he could hear a conversation between two engine crews from the Pine Hills station, both led by savvy local guys looking for access to the fire, and neither having any luck.

Damn, Joseph thought, *even those two can't find a way into this thing.*

When he got to Pine Hills, Joseph joined the search. Driving southwest on Eagle Peak Road, a narrow ribbon of dirt and gravel, he got to a point where he could see a glow bleeding into the deepening darkness. *Looks like somewhere near Kessler Flat,* he thought. But still unable to see any flames, he couldn't be sure. At least the firelight didn't seem to be moving or growing, and the smoke column it illuminated was rising straight up. No wind yet.

About that time Mortier came back on the radio with a report from the Country Estates.

"Carlton, I'm up on Thornbush Road, and I can see the entire fire. It's probably about five acres and pretty high up on the slope, difficult to get to. It's just a real rough spot, especially if an east, northeast wind surfaces later this evening."

"Are you available to hang in there for a bit?" Joseph asked. "I'm driving out on Eagle Peak to get a better look at it."

"Yeah, I'll try to stay with you late into the night."

"Thanks, Hal."

Joseph kept driving, looking for any kind of a toehold— somewhere with room to accommodate engines, water tankers, crew buses, bulldozer trailers. When he came to a break in the terrain some five miles down Eagle Peak, Joseph considered getting out of his truck and hiking a little way into the chaparral. Maybe he'd find a vantage point where he could at least see the fire. But then he noticed the smoke beginning to build, and it jolted him a little.

No, no, no, no, he thought. *I don't want to get hung out here too far, have this thing cross the road, and get myself trapped. Time to get out of here.*

At the intersection of Boulder Creek Road and Cedar Creek Spur, Joseph met with a number of other chiefs, all clad in well-worn, flame-resistant jackets and pants. The group included CDF Battalion Chief Ray Chaney and CDF Division Chief Randy Lyle, serving as his agency's official representative and senior officer. Putting their heads together, the chiefs began to plan their attack. They first designated a nearby staging area where the engines and crew buses could park. After that, they turned to their biggest challenge—locating the fire and figuring out how to reach it.

When I first began piecing together the story of the Cedar Fire, I couldn't understand why it took so long for firefighters to pinpoint its exact location. Deputies Dave Weldon and Rocky Laws had reported their latitude and longitude when they rescued Sergio Martinez. But more than one fire chief present along Boulder Creek Road that night told me those coordinates didn't seem to jibe with the location of the glow they could see in the growing darkness a few miles northwest of their position. Why? No one could say for sure.

The official records show a one-digit correction in the coordinates copied by a dispatcher when Weldon read them from his pilot's log, perhaps indicating a transcription error passed on to the chiefs gathered at Pine Hills and explaining why they could only estimate the fire's location. With flashlights and headlamps illuminating topographical maps spread across truck hoods and open tailgates, they tried to nail down what they knew for sure. This ridge in front of us, they agreed, that's Sunshine Mountain. We know Cedar Creek is north of that.

And we know the fire is somewhere north of Cedar Creek. So now they had a rough perimeter, defined by roads that could handle enough vehicles to establish and hold a fire line. It was a sizable chunk of land, probably about 6,000 acres, but with so few roads anywhere near the glow in the distance, it came as close as possible to estimating the fire's location.

For the next several hours, the firefighters kept searching for an access point closer to the fire, somewhere they could mount an initial attack. A few local residents stopped by and tried to help. One had a map that showed a power-line access trail cutting through a private ranch on Eagle Peak Road. Maybe that would work, someone suggested. No, another person countered. You don't want to drive down there; it's not even a road, just an old dozer line. It went on like that, back and forth, with everyone, firefighters and residents alike, contributing bits of knowledge, scraps of memory. One local woman came up and introduced herself to Ray Chaney. She knew where the fire was, she said, and believed she could take him there.

"Excellent," Chaney said. "Let's go."

They took off down a barely passable mountain road, tight with trees and brush. The roadbed was a mess, so rutted and rocky Chaney wished his pickup had four-wheel drive. Even if this neglected old truck trail did lead to the fire, he thought, how were they going to squeeze a fleet of engines and buses in here? For starters, they'd have to strip out branches all the way in. And what about parking and turn-around space?

It was well after dark now, and Chaney was feeling antsy. They were running blind, winding farther and farther into dense chaparral with nothing to show for it. He figured they'd come down to two probable outcomes, and he didn't like either one. They wouldn't find the fire, which seemed more and more likely, or they'd run smack into it and end up trapped. About half an hour into the brush, Chaney's guide gave up.

"This is where I thought it was," she said. "I'm so sorry."

Chaney got on the radio to Joseph. "This is a dead end," he reported. "We're going to start working our way back."

It would be so much easier in daylight, Chaney thought. *Bring in the air tankers and helicopters, hit the fire with retardant, deploy lookouts, and then hike in, cut line, and finish it off. But at night? Without air support, without visibility, without access?*

Carlton Joseph felt stymied, too. As incident commander, he had 350 firefighters ready to go. But he couldn't get them close enough to the fire to fight it.

"You can't just blindly march firefighters over hill and dale into the darkness," Joseph told me later. "You don't hang them out in unburned fuel with no escape route, no safety zone. There's a saying that no bush is worth somebody's life. And it's really not."

Since he couldn't access the fire, Joseph ultimately decided the only sensible thing to do was wait for daylight. Wait and hope like hell the wind didn't surface. If the forecasted Santa Anas failed to materialize, as they had for days now—even if they held off just a few more hours, until sunrise—this fire could be attacked from the air.

Randy Lyle later told me he would've kept searching for a way into the flames. But, he was quick to add, in firefighting situations with so many variables to juggle, it's hard to say any given approach is right or wrong. So Lyle stuck to his role as the CDF liaison supporting the Forest Service commander of a fire on Forest Service land.

"Let's stage this equipment at Pine Hills," Joseph told the group of chiefs. "Get everybody completely organized so we'll be ready for tomorrow, and some of these people can get some rest. If this thing burns to a road and gives us an opportunity to attack it tonight, we can go wake them up."

Chaney, back from his futile search through the chaparral, disagreed. The way he saw it, they were no closer to squelching this fire than when it had first been called in, and most likely Santa Anas were on the way. Forget "mundane." Chaney now believed it was time to gear up for a major incident. He approached Joseph and Lyle and proposed a full command structure—three operational branches and the resources to support them.

"We're not there yet," Joseph replied.

"Then I want to take our guys and go help Kelly," Chaney countered.

Joseph and Lyle agreed.

After rousing the CDF engine crews with orders to follow him, Chaney set out for the Country Estates running Code 3, full speed, lights, and sirens. Even so, they weren't fast enough. Before Chaney and his convoy could travel the thirty-two miles to Ramona, a wicked Santa Ana wind shrieked in from the northeast and blasted the Cedar Fire out of the Cleveland National Forest toward thousands of sleeping people.

Chapter 7

Area Ignition

THE ONCE-PERFECT PLANET MY FATHER taught me to love and respect has suffered under ages of human mismanagement. We've done our best to subdue it to our will, to harness it for our purposes, and in the process we've disrupted much of the way things used to be. Early peoples learned to use fire as a tool, not only for light, warmth, and cooking, but also to clear land, flush game, and encourage fresh growth for grazing animals. Later generations chopped away at virgin forests, making room and hewing lumber to build houses, businesses, towns, and cities. Crowded together in wooden buildings prone to burn at the drop of a candle or hot coal, we learned to fear fire, to see it as a sinister force, wielding terror and tragedy. Everywhere in the nonpolar world, great fires made their way into human history. Many we remember still, not for the cleansing and revitalizing role they played in nearly every ecosystem, but for the damage they caused, the pain inflicted: how much land burned, how many buildings destroyed, how many lives lost.

In the United States, as European settlers populated the East Coast and pushed into the Midwest, timber became a boom industry. By the late 1800s, setting fires to clear the detritus of logging and burn out stubborn stumps had become common practice. Not surprisingly, these "clean-up" fires sometimes wandered off into uncut woodlands or ignited lumberyards and adjacent buildings. Sometimes they burrowed into the forest floor, smoldering for weeks or even months in the remains of yesteryear's dead, fallen leaves, following this underground river of fuel for miles, and then popping up again to start new wildfires in far-flung, unexpected places.

In the West, ranchers moving cattle from one grazing area to another often followed the example of the buffalo-hunting Plains Indians, purposely setting fires to clear brush and woods, ensuring a fresh crop of grass by the time they returned. Whether set intentionally or sparked by lightning, vast seasonal wildfires became so prevalent across the North American continent, especially in the West, that settlers and travelers came to consider smoky summer skies a normal occurrence.

Eventually this wholesale burning of natural resources, punctuated by a number of horrific fires, triggered a shift in philosophy and tactics. By far the deadliest of these decisive incidents began October 8, 1871, near Peshtigo, Wisconsin, a small logging town close to Green Bay. An enormous storm system swirling across much of the Midwest attacked northeastern Wisconsin with tornadic winds. Scattered clean-up fires exploded into monstrous whirls of flames that incinerated 1.5 million acres—ten times the present size of Chicago. Entire towns disappeared in the blaze, and some 1,200 people were killed, 800 of them in Peshtigo alone. In terms of casualties, Peshtigo still ranks as the worst wildfire in US history. Yet we seldom hear of it because the Great Chicago Fire—that legendary blaze mistakenly blamed on a cow kicking over a lantern—happened the same day. The Chicago cataclysm killed 300 people, destroyed much of the city, and dominated the headlines.[11]

Deadly wildfires continued to plague the nation as the century turned. In 1894, a series of fires in Minnesota claimed 600 victims. And in August 1910, an enormous wind-driven wildfire dubbed "The Big Blowup" killed eighty-five people and consumed three million acres of northern Idaho and Montana—an area almost the size of Connecticut. After that, public concern reached Washington, DC, leading to the creation of a new national forest service within the Department of Agriculture and a special firefighting division imbued with military resolve. The US government declared war on wildfire, and the era of fire suppression began. No longer seen as a natural and needed part of ecosystems, fire had become an enemy to attack and conquer.[12]

In California, fire suppression became more important with each passing decade, as millions of snowbelt refugees migrated to the Golden State. Enticed by its temperate climate and promising possibilities, newcomers—Bob and I included— didn't worry about the extreme flammability of California's native vegetation. We should have. Few states are more prone to burn. Southern California, especially, is wildfire country, from its mountain conifers to its mid-elevation chaparral to its coastal sage scrub.

Before 2003, California's largest wildfire could have been the Santiago Canyon Fire, also known as the Great Fire of 1889. Sketchy newspaper reports and one park ranger's impressions implied that a massive blaze charred up to 300,000 acres in San Diego and Orange Counties during a September Santa Ana

---

[11] Denise Gess, and William Lutz. *Firestorm at Peshtigo: A Town, Its People, and the Deadliest Fire in American History.* (New York: Henry Holt and Company, 2002).

[12] Timothy Egan. *The Big Burn: Teddy Roosevelt and the Fire That Saved America.* (Boston: Mariner Books, 2009).

wind event.[13] Some historians, however, believe a complex of smaller fires gave scattered observers the impression of a single enormous blaze.

In 1932, the Matilija Fire burned 220,000 acres and caused eight deaths in Ventura County, establishing an official record as the state's largest wildfire. Almost forty years later, the 1970 Laguna Fire set the record for San Diego County. Sparked by downed power lines during Santa Ana winds, it tore across thirty miles of backcountry in only twenty-four hours, demolishing the rural communities of Crest and Harbison Canyon. Eight people died; 382 houses and over 175,000 acres burned. It would take three more decades, but eventually the Cedar Fire would eclipse both the Laguna and the Matilija fires in size, while killing fifteen people; destroying 2,820 structures, including 2,232 homes; and burning 273,246 acres—427 square miles of charred earth.[14]

At their vantage point looking east from the water tank in the Country Estates, CDF Battalion Chief Kelly Zombro and Forest Service Division Chief Hal Mortier watched the circle of flames in the Cleveland National Forest spread slowly and evenly, taking an hour to double in size from five to ten acres. Neither man felt easy about that. Wildland firefighters always aim to extinguish new fire starts while they're small, and both the Forest Service and the CDF proudly claim 97 percent success in extinguishing California's wildland fires on day one, with limited destruction.[15] The remaining few tend to make the headlines.

---

[13] L.A. Barrett, A record of forest and field fires in California from the days of the early explorers to the creation of the forest reserves, (San Francisco: USDA Forest Service, California Region, 1935).

[14] California Department of Forestry and Fire Protection

[15] CDF, Cal OES, USDA Forest Service, *California Fire Siege 2003, 7.*

On the other hand, the chiefs agreed they still had a good chance of stopping this remote blaze, now officially named the Cedar Fire based on its proximity to Cedar Creek. At such a slow growth rate, even without access or aircraft, Zombro and Mortier, like the incident commander, Forest Service Division Chief Carlton Joseph, figured it would probably keep puttering along until it reached a road where engine crews could mount an attack, and maybe even until dawn, when the air tankers could hit it. But that was only if the wind held off, as it had for the past few days. And no one felt confident enough to make that bet.

"The wind didn't surface right away, but it didn't fool anyone," Mortier told me later. "I mean, it wasn't like, oops, the wind came. From the very beginning we worried about what's going to happen when the wind comes."

As the hours passed and darkness accentuated the bright red and orange flames to the east, a third fire officer joined Mortier and Zombro. CDF Battalion Chief Kevin O'Leary lived in the Country Estates.

"You remember the Mother's Day Fire?" he asked Mortier as they stared together at the distant circle of flames.

"I sure do."

Like the Inaja Fire before it, the 1993 Mother's Day Fire had begun in the same general vicinity as the Cedar Fire. Starting on Sunday, May 9, the last day of a Santa Ana wind event, it traveled down the San Diego River drainage to the Country Estates and then spread south across Barona Mesa, where the flat topography slowed it enough for fire crews to corral.

"You remember how quick it made it from the river to here?" O'Leary asked.

"How quick?" Zombro wanted to know.

"About half an hour, maybe forty minutes."

"You're kidding me!"

"No. We lost two homes here in the Estates, and then it blew around through Barona Mesa."

Zombro took another look at the lazy ring of flames near Cedar Creek. *If we do get an east wind tonight*, he worried, *this thing could just blow up on us.* But without access or air support, what could they do to stop it? O'Leary and Mortier knew of an old road leading from Barona Mesa down into the main river drainage. They had no idea how close it might take them to the fire, but quickly concluded it wouldn't work in any case. If the Santa Anas did surface, anyone headed toward the fire from the west would end up directly in the path of wind-driven flames. Better to forget offense, the chiefs decided, and focus on mounting the best possible defense.

Zombro got to work on a structure protection plan for the Country Estates, considering how best to defend homes and businesses within the community of 9,000 people. Several of Ramona's local engine crews had already deployed along nearby streets. Zombro sent one of them back to the station to make copies of area maps. If this fire exploded, he would need more engines—lots more engines—from wherever he could get them. Out-of-town crews wouldn't have a clue about street layouts, hydrant locations, which areas might be more or less defensible. They'd definitely need maps.

Next, Zombro and Mortier set a trigger point, a way of determining when to put their defense plans into action. They decided on the San Diego River bottom, about halfway between the fire's point of origin and their position at the water tank. When and if the flames hit that point, they'd begin evacuating neighborhoods and assigning engines to structure protection.

Finally, they discussed resources. Zombro wanted five strike teams—twenty-five engines. With over 3,000 houses, plus churches, schools, businesses, and a country club to protect, he could've used a hundred. But so many of the county's resources had been deployed elsewhere, to the huge fires burning north of San Diego, that Zombro knew he had to be reasonable.

"It's a start," Mortier agreed.

When to place the order depended on how long it might take the fire to reach the river. And that depended on its current location—information no one had yet been able to pin down—as well as how many ridges it would have to burn up and over on its way. One, two, ten? Zombro had been working on that question, lining up his topo maps and conferring by radio with the chiefs in Pine Hills—Carlton Joseph and his CDF counterpart, Division Chief Randy Lyle. They tossed projections back and forth, based on what each saw from his opposite view of the fire.

When Zombro noticed an ASTREA helicopter circling overhead—Weldon and Laws back to offer any assistance they could—he radioed them to ask for a fresh latitude and longitude on the fire. Plotting those coordinates on his maps, Zombro came up with a probable site and calculated that flames would take an hour or more to reach the river. Around ten o'clock, he changed his mind. The fire had grown into a huge ellipse, somewhere between 100 and 200 acres in size, still spreading at a moderate rate and still burning without wind. But Zombro had no doubt now that Santa Anas were coming. The smoke column from the fire, as it gained altitude, had begun bending toward the southwest. Soon the wind affecting the top of the column would drop to the ground, and Zombro knew what would happen next. The troops at Pine Hills weren't going to be able to hold this thing in the national forest. The Cedar Fire was taking aim at the Country Estates, and when it hit, it was going to be brutal.

"Hal, I know we agreed the river should be the trigger," Zombro told Mortier, "but we don't have that much time. We need to order now."

Mortier didn't argue. While Zombro contacted Lyle to order five strike teams—twenty-five engines, one hundred firefighters in all—Mortier called Joseph, his fellow Forest Service division chief, to second Zombro's request. But Joseph wasn't yet convinced the fire posed a serious threat to Ramona. He remained optimistic that the firefighters congregated in Pine

Hills would be able to stop it before it escaped the Cleveland National Forest.

"This thing's probably going to find its way to Eagle Peak Road tonight," he told Mortier, indicating that firefighters might soon gain the access they needed.

Randy Lyle wasn't so sure. When he forwarded Zombro's resources request to Rick Henson, the CDF duty chief in charge of resources countywide, Lyle tried to convey the gravity of the situation.

"I know we're low on resources," he said, "but this is going to be a really big fire."

"Give me a minute," Henson said. "Let me make a phone call."

Moments later, at the water tank on Thornbush, Hal Mortier's cell phone rang. He recognized the voice on the other end right away. Although the two men worked for different agencies, Rick Henson was a good friend.

"Hal, you're not going to believe this, but those guys out on the Cedar Fire think they need twenty-five engines in the Country Estates. That's all the engines I got. Can you go out and verify this and see if you can talk them down?"

Mortier laughed. "Those guys would be me, Rick."

"Really? You think you need twenty-five engines?"

"We probably need more than twenty-five, but we're trying to be fair to the system."

"Hal, I can't put the last twenty-five engines in the county in the Country Estates, on a fire that might come there and might not. I've got wind blowing all across North County."

"Then you've got a problem, Rick."

"Will you take ten?"

"Of course we'll take ten."

"OK," Henson said. "I'll do my absolute best to get you ten engines."

Kelly Zombro had never questioned the chain-of-command system, and he understood the difficulty the division chiefs faced.

"I had it easy, to be honest about it," he told me later. "It was a lot easier being me, saying I want resources. It was a lot harder for the incident commanders who had to balance out coverage of this county. They've got the tough choices."

But watching the fire swell against the darkness, feeling the beginning of a breeze in his face, and catching the scent of smoke, Zombro wanted his strike teams, and he wanted them right away. Hearing a CDF colleague turn to a chief from another agency and second-guess the collective judgment of three CDF officers in the field only added to his frustration.

Out in Pine Hills, Joseph and Lyle also noticed the fire swelling in size and began planning a full-fledged command structure for the next day, an organization similar to the one Chaney had suggested earlier. They called in requests for an incident management team and enough hand crews, dozers, engines, water tenders, and helicopters to combat a sizable fire: up to 3,000 acres.

"We ordered knowing we weren't going to get most of this stuff," Joseph told me later, "and that was not considering a fire with wind on it. We knew wind might come; we also knew it had been forecast for the past few days and did not come."

But this night, Mother Nature did not pull her punches. Minutes before midnight, Santa Ana winds slammed into the Cuyamaca Mountains. Still burning downslope toward the San Diego River, the Cedar Fire sucked in that sudden infusion of oxygen and exhaled a shower of embers, each spawning a spot fire where it landed. In the next moment, as Zombro and Mortier watched from Thornbush Road, some sixty acres of chaparral, an area the size of nearly fifty football fields, exploded all at once, a phenomenon firefighters call area ignition. The San Diego River bottom disappeared in an instant, submerged beneath a seething lake of fire that spattered the surrounding shrublands with flaming brands and embers.

Oh my god, Zombro thought, *this is not good.*

CHAPTER 8

FAIR WARNING

Even as Bob and I settled into our blissful new life at Terra Nova, we began to realize that not everyone shared our enthusiasm for the place. When I gushed to my friend Marla Bingham about our wonderful new house in the country, she looked at me for a long moment, her dark eyes level and serious.

"Are you at all concerned about fire?" she asked.

I tried to reassure her.

"Well, of course, we know that's a risk, but we'll take all the recommended precautions."

Marla wasn't buying it. A Native American, a descendant of the ancient Wampanoag tribe that met the Mayflower, she had long ago been identified by tribal leaders as an old soul, someone who understands more than one lifetime's experience can possibly explain. I had come to know Marla well enough to believe it. It was as good a rationale as any for why she sometimes seemed to know things others couldn't perceive. The first time I saw her after the fire, she confirmed it.

"Don't you remember when you told me about your new house, and I asked you if you were worried about fire?" she asked. "Well, I saw it. I saw fire."

Bob was warned, too, in a more pragmatic way, by a group of seasoned firefighters he met while photographing a search-and-rescue workshop. He liked the guys right away, finding them affable and bighearted. During a break, conversation somehow turned to our new house in the chaparral. One of the men cut straight to the heart of the matter, at least from a firefighter's perspective.

"What zone are you in?" he asked, referring to a universal one-to-ten scale for ranking wildfire risk.

"Nine."

"Oh man, you're toast."

Bob and I had moved to California in 1976, the year after we married, so we'd experienced our share of earthquakes and seen a few wildfires—from a safe distance. We'd driven past flames climbing a hillside on their way to burning dozens of homes not far from downtown San Diego. We'd sat in front-yard lawn chairs well into the night, watching a fire front stretch across a distant peak like a glittering orange necklace. In all that time, only one incident—the 1985 Cowles Mountain Fire—occurred anywhere close to our home.

A rare chunk of urban wilderness, Cowles makes a majestic statement. Rising to nearly 1,600 feet over San Diego's eastern suburbs, it's the highest point within the city limits. At any given time, dozens of hikers crowd the hairpin trail to the summit. Those who make it all the way enjoy a 360-degree view of the county—braided mountains giving way to glinting ocean. The day Cowles Mountain burned, sirens wailed, helicopters circled, and smoke hung heavy over our neighborhood, about a mile from the fire. But we weren't evacuated, and no structures burned. In fact, only the first couple of streets closest to the mountain ever seemed to be in any real danger. In the end, the

Cowles Mountain Fire amounted to no more than an exciting diversion from our normal routine.

Taken together, all these experiences led Bob and me to think we knew something about wildfires, when of course we didn't at all. Rather, we'd come to think of fire watching as a kind of spectator sport, thrilling, sometimes even a little frightening, but, from a decent distance, not really all that dangerous. In the process of buying Terra Nova, we waded through stacks of papers full of fine print and signed our names over and over again. We even signed papers confirming we'd signed other papers. Some of those documents verified that we'd been informed, either verbally or by receipt of brochures or booklets, about certain risks inherent in our new property.

We were officially notified, for example, of our parcel's vulnerability to floods (slim to none), earthquakes (high, but no more so than anywhere else in California), and wildfires. This legal confirmation that we'd be living in zone nine of ten in terms of wildfire hazard should have alarmed us, or at least given us pause. But to be honest, it only made us worry about whether our insurance company would follow us from the suburbs to the backcountry. If not, we knew we'd have to resort to the state's Fair Access to Insurance Requirements (FAIR) Plan, a government-mandated safety net for Californians living in wildland areas considered too dangerous to qualify for regular insurance coverage.[16]

The FAIR Plan offers less coverage for much more money than standard policies, but it's better than nothing. Even if our regular carrier had turned us down flat, we probably would've taken a FAIR Plan policy rather than give up our paradise found. So we signed the notice of zone nine fire risk along with

---

[16] To help protect more consumers, the California Fair Access to Insurance Requirements (FAIR) Plan requires all insurance companies that sell homeowners policies in the state to assume a share of the highest fire risks.

all the other escrow paperwork, officially documenting that we understood full well we were moving into wildfire country.

No question, then, Bob and I knew more than enough about the threat of wildfire to be concerned about the safety of our new home. The problem was, we thought we also knew enough to protect ourselves. The best information we could find—and we did do our homework—indicated that minimizing wildfire risk depended primarily on two things: careful construction and vegetation management.

Randy and Sue Fritz had taken care of the first point, designing and building the house with fire protection in mind. In contrast to many backcountry homes—rustic log cabins and clapboard farmhouses, which somehow managed to survive for decades—Terra Nova seemed a fortress. Its thick stucco exterior and concrete tile roof complied with optimal "firewise" recommendations. Its eaves and soffits were sealed and stuccoed, its vents screened, leaving no exposed wooden beams, no openings where sparks might blow into the attic, no architectural details where embers might lodge and ignite. An interior sprinkler system, connected to a 10,000-gallon water tank on the hill behind the house, was rigged to turn on automatically when temperatures inside rose too high. The sprinklers, in turn, would set off a big red fire bell attached to the outside wall of the family room, alerting neighbors and summoning help. Finally, a spigot in the driveway was fitted to accommodate a fire hose.

All these precautions, plus the fact that the nearest fire station was no more than ten minutes away, convinced our insurer to cover Terra Nova despite its fire-prone location. But it was going to cost us. We'd be paying five times more for our homeowners' policy. Still, we felt heartened knowing that insurance underwriters, reputed for hedging their bets, had judged our new home safe enough to be insurable.

Another good sign: The local fire departments and the community itself had responded admirably to past threats.

Once, when fireplace ashes dumped outside started a small brush fire in the neighborhood, two fire trucks responded—one from Lakeside, three miles south, and one from the Barona Indian Reservation, two miles north. Even before the firefighters' prompt arrival, a small army of neighbors showed up and doused the fire, short-stopping any real damage. A bigger blaze had occurred in the area just the summer before. On our first visit to Terra Nova together, Bob and I noticed the evidence—two lines of red-stained rocks running from Wildcat Canyon Road to the top of the ridge across from our new house. The blaze had started when a car backfired, sending sparks into dry grass on Sue and Randy's side of the road. Sue and several other neighbors noticed the smoke and called 911. Even as they watched, breezes blowing in off the ocean pushed the flames across the asphalt to the east. The spreading line of fire skirted two houses nearest the road, but devoured a wide piece of the mountain above them before air tankers arrived and bracketed the blaze with red retardant, allowing firefighters to snuff it out.

Beyond firewise construction and savvy firefighting, we knew we had to remain vigilant about protecting our new home, especially when it came to managing the native chaparral that surrounded us on all sides. We'd have to create and maintain what firefighters call "defensible space," enough cleared ground, devoid of fuel, to stop, redirect, or at least slow an approaching fire. Randy and Sue had cleared a buffer zone immediately around the house. We decided to be extra cautious and extend it.

Exactly how much land to clear was a subject of debate. Varying requirements called for anywhere from thirty feet to one hundred feet or more. But in a confusing twist of bureaucracy, fire codes sometimes conflicted with environmental laws and even with each other. Not until after the Cedar Fire, for example, did the San Diego City Council set a single citywide standard of one hundred feet for vegetation management.

Ecologists, meanwhile, worried about protecting California's native habitat from overzealous homeowners, especially in San Diego County, a biodiversity hotspot, home to dozens of threatened and endangered species. The environmentally responsible approach, experts claimed, would be thinning and cutting back native plants rather than pulling them out by the roots. They labeled this approach "vegetation management," as opposed to "clearing brush." Environmental statutes also limited the extent of defensible space homeowners could create. In one celebrated case, a Ramona couple who cleared the area they said a CDF representative recommended were later ordered to replant half of it or face stiff fines for destroying too much sensitive native habitat.[17]

Trying to make sense of this confusion, we asked our local firefighters for advice. But Bob's conversation with one Lakeside chief only further muddied the issue in our minds.

"I've seen a fire jump across 500 feet of bare dirt," he said.

That bothered us. Our five-acre parcel measured 330 by 660 feet. Were we supposed to completely denude it, destroying the natural environment that had drawn us to the backcountry in the first place? There had to be a better option. So we called Mike Pratko, a no-nonsense, plain-talking, God-fearing arborist with thirty years of experience beating back California chaparral. Mike had done a lot of work for the county in the past, maintaining parks and clearing suburban canyons. More recently, as owner of his own tree service, he'd taken care of our trees in the city, before we moved to Terra Nova. While most yardmen tending suburban San Diego lopped and chopped, leaving landscapes looking scalped, Mike and his men cut with care and precision, turning tangled messes into living lace. If anyone knew how to manage vegetation, it was Mike Pratko.

---

[17] Kathryn Balint, "Thicket of regulations can keep county homeowners guessing," *San Diego Union-Tribune*, February 10, 2004.

When he arrived, dressed in green work pants and long-sleeved shirt, Mike pumped Bob's hand and took an appreciative look around at the blue sky and green mountains stretching away to the horizon. Hands on hips, he drew in a big breath of canyon air and turned toward us. A smile softened his weathered face.

"I can see why you moved here," he said.

We explained that we wanted to cut enough vegetation to be safe from fires without spoiling the natural beauty of the place, and then we walked around the house together, giving Mike a chance to appraise the situation. His heavy work boots seemed to cover the territory in only a few strides, and he talked as he walked, gesturing broadly to illustrate his plan.

"We'll cut everything back to those rocks," he said, pointing toward various clumps of boulders that thrust up from the ground a hundred feet or so from the house. All that granite would help stop a fire, too, he said. "And we'll take that big, cleared area all the way around. Then, for extra protection, we'll cut a second firebreak beyond that, about twenty or thirty feet farther down the hill."

He sounded confident, matter-of-fact, as if cutting firebreaks to protect life and property was something he did all the time, which, of course, it was. We asked him to go ahead and get started on the job. Mike's crew worked for two weeks—half of September—cutting back and hauling away truckloads of chaparral. When they finished, Bob and I both felt relieved and a lot safer facing our first fire season in the backcountry.

By now, after investing so much time, thought, effort, and money in fire protection, we'd begun to adjust to living with the risk of wildfire.

"You know," Bob said one day. "We just ought to assume that it's going to happen at some point."

We were sitting atop one of the broad boulders out front, looking up the hill at our new home. Behind us, the canyon stretched away to Mexico. It was all so beautiful.

"What's going to happen?" I asked.

"It's going to burn. We ought to just accept the fact that if we live here for the next twenty-five or thirty years, at some point during that time, Terra Nova is going to burn. So we plan for that. And then when it happens, we'll be sad, but we won't be devastated."

How can you say that? I wondered. *How can you even think it? It's one thing knowing it could happen and taking every precaution to minimize the risk. It's quite another to flat-out assume it will.*

But I said nothing as the awful possibility trickled through my brain like ice water. Could Bob be right? Planning for the worst. Wasn't that the reason I'd rented an oversize safe deposit box at the bank, where I kept critical documents and a few special treasures—old coins, high school medals, negatives of our wedding photos and the girls' baby pictures—with plenty of room left for Bob's best transparencies and family snapshot negatives? I'd long intended to assemble them in a notebook of sleeved vinyl pages. I only had to order the supplies from one of Bob's photography companies and then make time to sort through all my boxes of photos, the accumulation of a predigital lifetime.

"So we put all the negatives in the safe deposit box," I said finally, "and we copy special papers and scan the photos we don't have negs for, like my mother's wedding picture."

"Right."

"It's a good idea. That's what we'll do."

I still think it was a good idea. And no doubt, if either of us really believed Terra Nova was doomed to burn, especially so soon, we would have acted on it right away.

CHAPTER 9

CHAOS IN THE COUNTRY ESTATES

LIKE ANY GOOD HORROR MOVIE, our last night at Terra Nova began with an opening scene so benign no one would ever guess it could deteriorate into mayhem and terror. As Sergio Martinez lit his signal fire in the chaparral, Bob and I dressed up in Hawaiian shirts and kukui nut leis and drove off for an early Halloween party, accompanied by our two Newfoundlands, Terra and Charter.

Here is where I must admit that Bob and I belong to a dog club, a regional chapter of the Newfoundland Club of America. Every recognized dog breed is championed by a similar group, whose members tend to vary in every way except one: They love their dogs with a passion that approaches insanity. What else could explain a group of grown-up men and women, plus a herd of huge, slobbering beasts—all in Halloween costumes—gathered on the patio of a fancy Italian restaurant? Terra and Charter, collared in garlands of fake flowers, looked underdressed alongside fairy Newfs with pink gossamer wings, Newfs in sunglasses and goofy hats, and one big guy white-striped down the back to impersonate a giant skunk. Two women came as condiments—one, ketchup; the other, mustard—with their Newfs each encased in giant fabric hotdog buns. And one couple, along with their dog and infant granddaughter, arrived wearing home-sewn bunny suits, complete with ears, noses, whiskers, and tails.

Big, shaggy Onslow, always the class clown, served as our host, since it was his folks, Nancy and Eric Wolf, who'd arranged our evening. Onslow had turned heads the Halloween before in a shiny black cape and red horns—typecasting, considering his devilish resistance to all attempts at obedience training. This year his mischievous eyes peeked out from under a bright green dragon hood. Even Nancy Wolf, always a style-setter with her long blonde hair, longer legs, and classic wardrobe, looked silly in a fabric shark's head. Reprising an old *Saturday Night Live* skit, she sidled up to each new arrival and muttered the land shark's punch line: "Candygram." Eric Wolf, sporting a splendid court jester's hat, helped get the party going by handing out glasses of wine. Except for his colorful headgear, he had come as himself, the impeccably dressed uptown attorney, right down to his perfectly polished wingtips. We could not have known that night, as we laughed together over wine and pasta, that we would spend the next three days with the Wolfs, huddled together in a downtown San Diego hotel—four people and three Newfoundlands, all wildfire refugees wondering when, if ever, we could go home.

The air still felt warm when we left the restaurant around ten o'clock. All week the weather had been beastly hot, and dry enough to make your skin sting. Elsewhere in Southern California, the arrival of Santa Ana winds had turned high temperatures and low humidity into prime fire weather. A rash of wildfires had broken out in the mountains surrounding Los Angeles. Two massive blazes near San Bernardino, both set by arsonists, had caused six deaths and destroyed hundreds of homes.[18] To be honest, Bob and I didn't pay much attention to any of this until our daughter Lauren called from Seattle to check on us. She'd seen Southern California's killer fires in the national headlines.

"Don't worry," I told her. "We're fine. San Bernardino is a hundred miles away, and the Santa Anas aren't blowing in San Diego."

We still didn't notice on Friday, the twenty-fourth, when the National Weather Service issued a red-flag warning for San Diego County, citing "very low humidities" and a high likelihood of Santa Ana winds. A front-page story in Saturday's morning paper advised readers of extreme fire risk in the backcountry. The CDF had canceled days off, the article said, staffed its stations around the clock, and recalled five of ten air tankers scheduled for routine maintenance. But we missed all that, too.

Looking back, it's astonishing to me how clueless and apathetic Bob and I were during those dangerous days leading up to the Cedar Fire. Much of Southern California was burning, and many of San Diego's firefighters had traveled north to fight the biggest blazes, depleting resources at home despite an escalating fire risk in our own region. But the only incident on our personal radar was the Roblar 2 Fire at Camp Pendleton. Even that was a good forty miles from us, and firefighters had kept it confined to undeveloped land. Hardly worth worrying about.

---

[18] Burning in the mountains above the city of San Bernardino, the Old Fire destroyed 91,281 acres, 993 homes and caused six deaths, five of those attributed to heart attacks. The adjacent Grand Prix Fire stretched nearly to Los Angeles County, where it joined a smaller blaze, the Padua Fire. Together, these two fires destroyed 80,340 acres and 194 homes, and threatened the densely populated communities of Rancho Cucamonga and Alta Loma. Source: CDF, Cal OES, USDA Forest Service, *California Fire Siege 2003, 68, 71.*

It was still hot enough when we got home from our Halloween celebration to close up the house and turn on the air conditioner. Bob went up to bed soon after, around eleven. I stayed downstairs and stretched out on the family room sofa to read for a while. The dogs had settled down for the night, too. Within a few minutes, I fell asleep to the sound of sweet Terra snoring softly from her favorite corner. In the meantime, Sergio Martinez's signal fire was about to blast out of the mountains and tear our lives apart.

In Ramona, on Thornbush Road, CDF Battalion Chief Kelly Zombro watched the Cedar Fire's midnight explosion and knew he had just inherited responsibility for protecting San Diego Country Estates from an onslaught of flames. He turned to a sheriff's lieutenant who'd joined the group of chiefs gathered at the water tank.

"Get your sergeant on the phone," Zombro said. "I want this evacuation started."

The sergeant was already on it.

"I didn't mean to circumvent you," he told Zombro over a cell connection, "but I was here ten years ago for the Mother's Day Fire, and I know what I'm looking at. I've already ordered evacuations."

Zombro turned and saw the red and blue lights of sheriff's cruisers sprinkled along the darkened streets of San Diego Country Estates. He let out a tense breath. At least the people were going to be all right. But no resources had arrived yet to join the local Ramona engines patrolling the Estates. Where were those strike teams he'd ordered? It had been a couple of hours since he'd called in his request. Forest Service Division Chief Hal Mortier, still standing by, radioed his colleague, Forest Service Division Chief Carlton Joseph, at the command post in Pine Hills, near Julian.

"Carlton, could you confirm ordering those two strike teams we talked about? Wind's picking up, and we're seeing quite a bit of fire activity."

"I have not ordered the two strike teams," Joseph said. "We're just kicking around the idea of possibly sending one of the CDF strike teams we've got over that way."

Zombro's eyes widened. A few moments later, when a CDF battalion chief called from the dispatch center at Monte Vista for an update, Zombro let loose.

"I'll tell you the truth. I'm not trying to tell the duty chiefs what to do, but I'm watching area ignition like you can't believe on this thing, and I still have nothing responding here."

"You're getting area ignition?" the battalion chief asked. "How big do you think the fire is now?"

"I'm going to say 300 acres, but I think it's way over that. I want strike team orders, and they aren't doing it, and I've got ashes landing here."

"All you're going to get is like two strike teams."

"I know, but it's something. The last time this thing burned apparently was at the tail end of a Santa Ana, and that's what saved most of the homes. This is the beginning of the Santa Ana, so I've got real concerns about it. I want to get this now."

But, like the chiefs at Pine Hills, the chief at Monte Vista couldn't see the alarming view from Thornbush or grasp the immediacy of the threat.

"I'm just trying to figure out what's going on," he said, "because we don't have a very clear idea."

"Well, let me tell you." Zombro worked to keep his voice under control. "We had a sixty- or eighty-acre area ignition going about five minutes ago, and I'm watching probably well over one-hundred-foot flames right now just rolling."

"Do you have an east wind?"

"Oh yeah. It started about five, ten minutes ago. And now the smoke's starting to dip down over the ridge and right into the Country Estates."

"Then we're going to be getting 911 calls, too."

"Oh yeah, you are."

In the meantime, Mortier had called Joseph with an update. Fire activity had picked up considerably, he said, with long-range spotting and wind speeds of eight to ten miles per hour. Evacuations were under way in the Country Estates and beginning on Barona Mesa.

Joseph replied that he was on the phone to dispatch, ordering two strike teams.

"Are you going to want to increase that?" he asked Mortier.

"Well, we've wanted five all along, if we can get them."

"OK," Joseph said. "I think from what you're telling me, I'll see about ordering the whole gamut, five strike teams."

Firefighters call it "alignment," when everything comes together to create ideal conditions for catastrophic fires. The day's red-flag environmental conditions set the stage. Add to that an inaccessible location. Drop in a lost hunter, desperate enough to set a signal fire, late enough in the day to preclude air attack. Now trigger a Santa Ana event, ensuring two days of sustained winds blowing thirty to forty-five miles an hour, with gusts up to seventy-five. Devil winds. The deciding factor leading to cataclysm.

That's perfect alignment.

With so many high-risk factors in play, the Cedar Fire would help rewrite modern wildfire history, becoming known as one of the planet's first "megafires," born of a changing climate and ever more dangerous fire conditions.[19] During the fire's weeklong siege, a succession of highly trained and

---

[19] Jerry Williams, et al., *Findings and Implications from a Coarse-Scale Global Assessment of Recent Selected Mega-Fires*, Food and Agriculture Organization of the United Nations, May 2011.

experienced men would lead the fight against it as incident commanders. None had ever encountered any fire remotely like this one. Even their combined know-how, pooled through the military-efficient structure of unified command and elite incident management teams, proved inadequate to the task. Each admitted to consistently underestimating the speed and reach of the flames—the unforeseeable behavior of a fire without precedent. Each felt the bone-deep frustration of not being able to end the fire's mad gallop, of needing a thousand times the available manpower and resources to wage a war they'd spent their lives preparing to fight.

"Nobody had ever experienced a Cedar Fire," commented Hal Mortier, a national incident commander with thirty-three years of experience. "You can have all the fire history in your head and all the events that took place in your own career, but you can't predict something nobody has experienced."

That first night in the Country Estates, Mortier initially estimated the flames would take hours to reach the community, if they ever did. And Zombro, who shortly after midnight predicted the fire's arrival within one hour, quickly radioed an update: "I've got a spot fire now less than a half-mile away, so speed to these structures is increasing."

Before either Zombro or Mortier could post another report, the Cedar Fire gathered itself and blasted into the Country Estates, torching trees, seizing houses, and catapulting the community into chaos. Although the evacuation had begun at least an hour earlier, families were still spilling out of their homes, stuffing their vehicles with possessions, and heading west out of the area. Sirens wailed in the smoky darkness, and traffic stacked up along the community's main thoroughfare, as ashes and embers rained against windshields. Many other residents refused to evacuate, choosing instead to stay and try to save their homes. Silhouetted against rising orange firelight, dozens of dark figures teetered on rooftops, garden hoses in hand.

The fire hit the easternmost streets of the Country Estates first, and then quickly broke into two fronts, a phenomenon firefighters call "splitting the head." Flames leapfrogged up Mount Gower on the community's northern boundary, climbing so high that Zombro's command post on Thornbush lit up like daylight as the fire shot west toward the ocean. At the same time, on the opposite side of the development, flames raced south toward Barona Mesa. Soon, all across the Country Estates, burning houses lit the night, like a scattering of bonfires along a darkened shore.

Hal Mortier knew then that the Cedar Fire would not be easily corralled. "When you have two heads, and you weren't handling one to begin with," he said to me later, "it tells you this is a completely whole new story."

Even as the Cedar Fire took aim at Ramona, Monte Vista got word of another new incident, this one at Santa Ysabel, near the Inaja Fire Memorial outside of Julian. CDF Battalion Chief Kevin O'Leary, who had kept watch with Zombro and Mortier at the water tank for a few hours before the wind came up, left to lead the initial attack. Unlike Carlton Joseph in Pine Hills, O'Leary found himself blessed with easy access via California Highway 79. Local fire crews, not yet called to duty on the Cedar Fire, pitched in and helped the CDF troops snuff out the small blaze, dubbed the Schoolhouse Fire, just in time, before the wind came up.

"We got real lucky there," O'Leary told me later.

If only that luck could have spread to Pine Hills. Returning to Ramona shortly after midnight, O'Leary found the Cedar Fire rolling upslope toward the Country Estates in a high-rise wave. He immediately checked in with Zombro and then linked up with a sheriff's deputy to help evacuate Barona Mesa.

As they reached Four Corners, the center of the community, the southbound fire front blew right past them. O'Leary shook his head. There would be no catching this monster as they'd caught the Mother's Day Fire ten years before.

At least crews were finally en route. Kelly Zombro knew that now. Yet it was half an hour after houses began to burn before the first ten engines began to arrive from various points around the county. As each reported to the designated staging area, Mortier met them with a copy of the map Zombro had known they would need. Around 1:00 a.m., the troops from Pine Hills arrived to join the fight.

Zombro had upped his order to eight strike teams, drawing the last reserve engines from the San Diego area, and from Orange County, too. To the west, at Camp Pendleton, the incident commander of the waning Roblar 2 Fire contributed significant reinforcements by releasing a few of his crews from mop-up duty. More than one chief would look back at the Roblar 2 incident as a blessing; without it, even more of San Diego's firefighting resources probably would have been assigned to fires elsewhere and not available to battle the Cedar and Paradise fires closer to home. Dozens of engines would pour into the Country Estates over the next few hours, the first of hundreds to respond to the Cedar Fire over the coming days, bringing a total force of more than 5,800 firefighters to San Diego from all over the western United States.[20]

In the meantime, Kelly Zombro had never felt so frustrated. Surrounded by fire, breathing smoke, he could only watch helplessly as flames claimed house after house. With so few engine crews, all in defense mode from the moment they arrived, the best any of them could do was bump and run— steer the fire around a house and then rush to the next one. Over and over and over. Zombro purposely kept his command

---

[20] CDF, Cal OES, USDA Forest Service, *California Fire Siege 2003*, 45.

structure loose. He wanted each strike team free to respond as rapidly shifting conditions demanded, without having to report to him first. And he wanted them to stay safe.

"Never extend yourselves to the point where you need help," he told each crew as they checked in for duty, "because I can't guarantee you any help at all. If you leave this community, I want to know about it. Otherwise, just keep moving."

On the move now himself, Zombro followed the progress of the firefight from his truck. Around nearly every corner, houses were burning. It galled him, knowing most had ignited not from direct flames but because of embers blown under a deck, into an attic vent, between roof tiles. Normally, fire officers send a fresh batch of engine crews in behind the first wave to check for ember fires. But Zombro had no one else to deploy, nor could he order any engines to backtrack without losing houses on the leading edge of the fire. All he could do wasn't going to be enough this time. He found himself pounding his fist on the dashboard, spouting expletives, even stopping occasionally to stamp out embers.

Make this stop, he prayed. *Just make this stop!*

Worst of all, Zombro knew now that the Cedar Fire was going to take more than structures.

"I knew people were going to die," he told me later. "There was just no way we could get to everyone. I had to keep putting it out of my mind, but it was always in there, gnawing at me. We just did not have the resources. And the sheriff's department was as bad off as we were. Nobody has that kind of staffing."

I was asleep on the family room couch, still dressed for a luau, when Bob came clomping back downstairs around 1 a.m.

"Sandra, wake up." His voice was loud and edged with alarm. "I smell smoke. I've never smelled it this strong before."

I pushed up from the sofa and tried to clear my head. The wine from dinner had carried me into a pleasant slumber, and I didn't want to wake up. Smoke? I couldn't smell anything. I opened the door to the deck and stepped outside into an otherworld. Hot, murky wind, acrid as vinegar, blasted me in the face. Ashes streaked past like sleet. From beyond, in the darkness, came the sounds of tree limbs writhing and creaking. Spooky, that's how it felt, as if the night itself were screaming.

I couldn't see any signs of fire anywhere, no flames, no glow. No reason for hysteria. We just needed to find out what was going on. There'd be nothing on TV or radio so late at night, so I sat down at the kitchen table with my laptop and searched online for news of fires near San Diego. All I found was a brief mention of a tiny fire in the Cleveland National Forest near Cedar Creek, wherever that might be, and it had reportedly been contained. Not a likely cause of so much ash and smoke.

"Maybe it's the Pendleton Fire," I suggested. "It's been burning for days."

"Maybe," Bob said.

It didn't occur to either of us that the northeast wind pummeling our house would drive any lingering smoke from Pendleton west, out over the ocean, rather than east toward us.

"I'm going to call someone who can tell us something," I said.

"Don't call 911," Bob cautioned. "We don't want to tie up emergency lines."

I agreed. I only needed information. First I tried the Lakeside Fire Department's main office but got a recording. So I called the station at Barona. To my relief, a firefighter answered the phone.

"We're about two miles south of you on Wildcat Canyon, and we're smelling smoke here," I told him. "Is it just the Pendleton Fire or what?"

"There is a new fire in Ramona," he said, "but it's burning west, so if you're south of us, you're safe."

I liked the sound of that. His next words, though, something about "you might smell smoke; you might even see flames," sounded a little garbled. Had he said to leave if you smell smoke or see flames? I didn't think so. I'd just told him we already smelled smoke. So I took him to mean: Don't panic, even if you see distant flames. Later I wished I'd asked him to clarify. But he sounded so calm, so nonchalant, and he was telling me what I wanted to hear.

"He knows all about it," I relayed to Bob. "He says it's in Ramona, headed west, so we're safe. Those were his exact words, 'You're safe.'"

Ramona was a good twelve miles away, maybe fifteen. A 20-minute drive up the canyon. I thought back to the day Cowles Mountain burned just a mile from our house in the suburbs, yet we were never evacuated, never in danger. Of course, that was city stuff. Now we lived in fire country.

"I don't know," Bob said. "I think maybe we ought to stay up and get a few things together, just in case."

"I'm not even sure where all our pictures are," I said. "There are still boxes of them stacked in the garage I haven't touched since the move."

I was back on the computer by now, searching for anything about a fire in Ramona. Bob disappeared for a few minutes, came back with a big, bulging packing box, and set it on the floor beside me. I pried open the top flaps to reveal stacks of family photos and envelopes full of negatives.

"This is one of them," I said. "We've got a couple more like this, plus all the albums. And your negatives. You know, we've got to get them into the safe deposit box."

"I'm working on it."

We sat at the kitchen table a while longer. I thought about the red-stained rocks just across the canyon, a permanent reminder of how close the last fire in Wildcat Canyon had come. I thought about all those neighbors standing around watching the air tankers put out the flames, like front-row spectators at an aerial sideshow. This was our first season in fire country, our first time smelling smoke in the wind, and we didn't feel anywhere near that sanguine about it. But we knew now where the fire was—miles away and not even burning in our direction. A firefighter had said we were safe. Besides, we'd done everything we could to protect ourselves. Obviously, we were going to have to learn to live with nights like this, to adopt the old-timers' attitude and not worry so much.

My computer clock read 2:23 a.m. It didn't occur to me that daylight savings time had ended at two, making the actual time 1:23.

"I'm exhausted," I said finally. "I've got to get a couple more hours of sleep at least. Then we can reevaluate."

"OK," Bob said. "But tomorrow let's spend some time getting our stuff together, figuring out a plan."

Randy Fritz had designed the big windows in our bedroom to make the most of the canyon view. We loved leaving the shades open and waking to muted mountains against peach sky. Sometimes a pale ocean of fog filled the canyon where it dropped away to the south, broken only by a chain of mountaintop islands. Now we peered out the other direction, north toward Ramona. I had to search a second or two, but then I saw it, and there was no question what I was looking at. A red glow hugged the horizon, throwing the farthest ridgelines into silhouette. A prickle of alarm spread through my body.

"My gosh, there it is."

"Look at that." Bob's voice sounded hushed, almost reverent.

The red light swayed and rippled along the black line of mountains, a reflection of swelling flames beneath.

"Those poor people in Ramona," I said. "God help them."

Bob took a last look and went to bed, but I sat up a while longer, perched on the edge of our old plaid armchair, hugging my knees and watching the distant red light play along the ridges. Across the canyon, high on the mountain, a pair of headlights came alive and traced a slow, twisting path through the darkness toward Wildcat Canyon Road. We hadn't yet met our neighbors at Blue Sky Ranch, a complex of houses on the other side of the canyon. We didn't have their phone numbers, didn't even know their names. But we'd seen them come and go, just as they no doubt could see us from their vantage point a close mile away. Now I wondered what kind of people they were. Savvy backcountry veterans who knew something we didn't? Or over-reactors who worried every time a neighbor lit a barbecue? Probably, the truth lay somewhere in between. Probably, they just didn't have as much information as we did and decided to play it safe. I couldn't blame them. With so much smoke, ashes flying in the wind, and now a red sky on the horizon, if I didn't know the fire was so far away and moving in another direction, I'd be packing up my valuables and leaving, too. Instead I turned away from the windows and crawled into bed beside Bob. He reached out and pulled me close.

"I don't know about this," I said. "I don't know about going to sleep with a red glow in the sky. I mean, we can see the thing."

Bob gave me a squeeze. His body felt warm and strong.

"What should we do?" I whispered.

"Trust," he said. "Trust and learn."

I have no idea why he said that, nor does he, but at the time it sounded reassuring enough to ease me into sleep. Looking back, no words could have proved more naive. Or more prophetic.

CHAPTER 10

WILDCAT CANYON

Ray Chaney rushed west in his chief's truck through the darkness from Pine Hills to Ramona, siren screaming and lights pulsing. The wind slashed at his windshield as he drove into San Diego Country Estates over streets littered with ashes, leaves, and broken branches. Coming across an evacuation checkpoint manned by two sheriff's deputies, Chaney drove up and drafted one of them to ride with him as a departmental liaison. It was a tactic fire officers used often, designed to speed up authorization when needed.

Shortly after Sheriff's Lieutenant Randy Siegel climbed aboard, Chaney pulled up to an intersection where at least fifty cars waited in line to turn left out of the Country Estates. Minivans full of families. Sedans stuffed with possessions. Oversize pickup trucks pulling loaded horse trailers. But cross traffic made it impossible for any of them to move. Another line of frantic drivers was attempting to enter the area, some looking for friends or family members, some with empty trailers, intent on saving their animals.

"Get on your radio and have a deputy sent over here to expedite that left turn," Chaney told Siegel. "If somebody doesn't get here before the fire does, everybody in that line is going to die."

With the flames clearly out of control now, Chaney's primary mission had shifted from fighting fire to saving lives. He knew that hundreds of people lay sleeping in some 300 houses scattered throughout Wildcat Canyon, the next community in the fire's path. Hundreds more—guests and staff—no doubt filled the Barona Resort & Casino halfway down the canyon. And there would likely still be a crowd gathered at the nearby Barona Speedway, closest to the approaching flames, where fans camped overnight on the grounds after Saturday night races.

Leaving the Country Estates, Chaney turned south onto Wildcat Canyon Road and found a spot with a view to the east where he could pull off on the shoulder for a quick check on the fire's progress. Clearly visible through a saddle between two hills, a solid line of flames pushed hard and fast across Barona Mesa to the east, flooding the land like water. Chaney turned to Siegel.

"We've got less than five minutes before this thing overruns where we're sitting right here. We've got to get the racetrack evacuated fast. Call your people on the radio."

"We can do it faster ourselves," Siegel suggested, and Chaney turned back onto the road and hit the gas.

As he'd imagined, an assortment of camping rigs cluttered the speedway grounds. Clots of two and three people stood outside, puzzling over the strange red and orange glow in the eastern sky. Chaney asked for the track manager.

"You've got to get everybody out of here!" Chaney told him. "Everybody needs to evacuate north, toward Ramona. Not—I repeat, not—south down Wildcat Canyon, because that's where the fire is headed."

He broadcast the same message to the crowd over his truck's loudspeaker as he drove out, hitting his siren a couple of times for emphasis. People scurried to their vehicles. As

Chaney and Siegel rushed on toward Barona, the radio blurted out an emergency report: A group of residents and two sheriff's deputies were trapped by fire about four miles into Featherstone Canyon, off Wildcat Canyon Road. The turn lay just ahead of Chaney's headlights.

"Let's go," he said, and Siegel nodded.

It was a dirt road, tight with trees and shrubs. Chaney made it about half a mile before a curtain of heat and flames cut him off. He shook his head, looked at Siegel, and broke the bad news.

"Your guys are on their own."

San Diego sheriff's deputies Mark Johnston and Mariano Tano, each in his own cruiser, had ventured a long way into the chaparral from the two-lane blacktop of Wildcat Canyon Road to evacuate the remote ranching neighborhood of Featherstone Canyon. Starting at the far eastern end of the tiny community, where the fire would hit first, they rushed from door to door, banging and shouting, doing their best to wake up each household. Tano's K9 partner, a German shepherd named Uoschi, waited in the car. About a dozen residents, along with several horses, fell in behind the deputies' vehicles as they started back out through heavy smoke at around 2 a.m. But they were all too late. Fire jumped across the road ahead of the convoy, cutting off their only exit route.

Everyone scattered to find whatever shelter they could. Johnston radioed the sheriff's command center and reported that at least twelve people, including two deputies, were trapped in Featherstone Canyon.

"Get a fire crew over here!" he shouted into the radio.

Within minutes, a dispatcher called back to say no one would be able to reach them until the fire blew through. The words "nothing we can do" stuck in Johnston's head. Then the dispatcher asked for an exact headcount and the deputies' I.D. numbers.

Tano listened from his own car. *Oh god,* he thought. *I'm about to become a statistic.*

The deputies could catch only sporadic radio traffic after that, mostly frantic requests for help from others trapped by fire. None of the dispatchers broke out of their usual dispassionate tone, but both Tano and Johnston found the solemnity in their voices unnerving. At one point the command center advised the deputies to take shelter in a building. While Tano stayed in his patrol car with Uoschi, Johnston pulled his vehicle as close as he could through nearly opaque smoke to the nearest structure, a handsome, fairly new stone house. Inside, he found two men intent on riding out the firestorm. But the place was filling with smoke. Better to return to his car and retreat to a clearing he'd noticed nearby, Johnston decided. He tried to convince the two men to come with him, but they insisted on staying to defend the house.

Johnston sprinted back outside through darkness, heat, and smoke to his vehicle, and both deputies moved their cars into the center of the clearing. They parked side by side, facing opposite directions. Within moments, the fire was everywhere, howling (a loud and strangely mechanical sound) and spewing little tornadoes of fire and embers. A frenzy of flames surged to within forty, maybe thirty yards, and frenetic winds spun by the fire itself rocked the cars, creating a weird sensation of speed.

All either man could do now was keep his vehicle's motor and air conditioner running, recycling the air in the car to keep the smoke out, and pray for the fire to pass. The heat was terrific. Tano's uniform darkened with sweat, and behind him in the backseat, Uoschi panted heavily. *God,* Tano thought, *this fire is going to eat us.* He tried not to think about what that might feel like.

Just a few feet away, his cruiser at times invisible in the smoke, Johnston already knew how it would go. It wouldn't be the fire itself that got them; both cars sat well out of the flames' reach. The real danger was in the air—superheated, full of smoke and poisonous gases. He fingered his cell phone, thought about calling his wife, but decided against it. Why torture her with the knowledge he was about to die? Johnston couldn't come up with a good answer to that. He waited for some sort of symptom to tell him his lungs were shutting down—a cough, a gasp, a constriction. But nothing happened. Time passed; the fire raged; the toxic wind churned. And still Johnston and Tano and the dog kept breathing.

Hours later, the air finally began to cool and clear. Smoke gave way to stars and, bit by bit, a gray, gauzy semblance of daylight. Tano and Johnston climbed out of their patrol cars and celebrated with a high five. The clearing still reeked of smoke, and as far as they could see in the gloom, small fires flickered red against blackened ground. *As if resting up for another go at us*, Tano thought. But he couldn't dwell on that now, couldn't stop to consider how close the three of them had come to death. First, they had to find the people they'd come to rescue. It didn't take long. Somehow, despite the devastation, despite the smoldering mounds of ash and mangled metal where their houses had stood, the residents of Featherstone Canyon, humans and horses alike, had all survived, huddled together in a low spot in the middle of a horse corral.

Johnston and Tano got back into their cruisers, negotiated the four miles of dirt road through a blackened moonscape out to Wildcat Canyon, and turned south. If they'd made it, surely others had, too. They had to find them. The deputies searched through endless ruins for survivors but saw no one. And then, on Strange Way, another dirt road winding eastward into the hills, Tano and Johnston came upon the colorless hulks of two cars corroded by fire and, near them, the charred remains of three human victims.

Just south of Featherstone Canyon, bisected by Wildcat Canyon Road, lies the heart of the Barona Indian Reservation—a cluster of eighty homes anchored by a school and cultural center at one end, and a tiny Catholic church at the other. In between sits the high-rise hotel and casino complex, which since 1984, when the impoverished tribe first got into gaming with a bingo hall, had mushroomed into a megabucks enterprise that sustained the entire Barona community.

Perhaps more than anyone in the path of the fire, the Native people living at Barona understood it. Descendants of the ancient Kumeyaay, a people who once populated all of modern-day San Diego County and parts of northern Mexico, they could remember, if only in their genes, a time when humans lived in symbiosis with the land. A time when wildfire seemed not so much an evil invader, but rather a part of all that is and must be, a natural power worthy of respect.

As long as twelve thousand years ago, the Kumeyaay, like other indigenous groups, learned that fire could be domesticated, even cajoled, into service. A small flame could cook food, warm huts, light moonless nights. A bigger fire could drive game into the open or eliminate venomous snakes. Even untamed, fire played an essential role in the Kumeyaay world, cleansing the land of excess vegetation, pests, and disease; triggering renewal. Wildfire did not come often, usually no more than once a generation, but when it did, it came on its own terms—roaring, raging, all-consuming. There was no negotiating, no cajoling then. Nothing to do but run. Hundreds of generations of Kumeyaay had seen wildfires come and go. This generation would be no different.

The Barona tribal members may have understood the fire and why it came, but their understanding did not lessen their terror. The Cedar Fire swept in by night, whipped by devil winds into a frenzy of enormous flames and red froth, moving so fast that most people had no more than twenty minutes' warning. Twenty minutes to spread the word, grab children and animals and a few belongings, and flee their homes.

The phone calls began sometime after midnight. Anxious voices shouted staccato warnings: "A fire is coming. Hurry up and get out." Some did, leaving right away, heading down Wildcat Canyon Road through smoke and blowing ash. Others lingered to help family and neighbors evacuate or try to protect their property. Soon the Barona residents could see the fire, a solid wall to the east, rushing toward them over the mountains. It came in fast, and it came in loud, tribal members said, turning the world orange and black.

"The fire was up; it was down," one person recalled. "It was east; it was west; it was north; it was south. It was everywhere."

Even so, some people stood their ground for as long as they could, trying to fight the flames. The priest at the Barona Mission was one of these brave souls. Armed only with his faith and a garden hose, he managed to save the historic structure. But most tribal members were forced to run for their lives. Just too much fire, they said, and, in the words of one young witness, "It was grabbing houses." Thirty-nine reservation houses burned before the night was over. Nearly half the community.

Two neighbors who stayed, working together in an attempt to save both their homes, soon found themselves pelted by a rain of fire. Chunks of burning wood and debris fell all around them. When a huge fireball hit the ground nearby and shattered, throwing embers everywhere, they knew it was time to leave. One of the men ran to his all-terrain vehicle and revved it up.

"Get on," he yelled. "We've only got one chance, and if we blow it, we're dead."

The second man took a final look back, just in time to see another neighbor's house going up. *It's over for the houses,* he realized. *Now we've just got to save our lives. If we can.* He straddled the ATV, and the two men careened off over a bank and down a trail. Their eyes stinging from the smoke, both strained to find a landmark in the darkness, some clue pointing the way to safety. And then they caught sight of red emergency lights flashing through the murk.

"What are you doing here?" a firefighter shouted when the ATV materialized out of the smoke.

"We just came through hell," one of the men said.

After leaving Featherstone Canyon, CDF Battalion Chief Ray Chaney and San Diego County Sheriff's Lieutenant Randy Siegel kept pushing south down Wildcat Canyon Road, the fire chasing them in the rearview mirror. Passing a neighborhood of tribal residences, they could see the blue and red lights of emergency vehicles flashing among the houses. Good, they agreed, evacuation is underway there.

Just north of the casino, Chaney pulled off at the Barona fire station and met briefly with the chief, letting him know he was on his way to lock down the hotel and casino. Even so late at night, Chaney knew the place would be full of people—upward of 2,500 staff and guests, either working, asleep, or engrossed in their gambling, and all oblivious to approaching danger. They'd never be able to make it out ahead of the fire. People would overreact and crash their vehicles, creating an instant logjam across Wildcat Canyon Road, their only escape route. Hundreds of people would be trapped in their cars, and then the fire would sweep through. An image flashed into Chaney's mind, a news photo from the first Gulf War. It depicted a stretch of road dubbed the "Highway of Death," littered with burned-out cars and the skeletal remains of people trapped in traffic and bombed as they tried to escape.

"We're going to shelter everybody in place," Chaney told Siegel.

The resort buildings themselves were newly constructed and surrounded by acres of open areas—lawns, ponds, parking lots, and a golf course. Defensible space that could take a lot of heat. Chaney knew vehicle fires posed the biggest danger. If one or more cars caught, it could easily set off a whole line of fire and lead straight to the buildings. He'd have to warn the security guards about that. On the way into the complex, he stopped for a moment to brief a California Highway Patrol (CHP) officer paused at the main entrance.

"Send all vehicles you see south on Wildcat Canyon," Chaney told him. "The road north is blocked by fire."

He drove on to the hotel's main entrance and rushed inside with Siegel.

"Who's in charge?" Chaney asked.

"I am."

The night manager stepped up, casting a speculative eye at his two unexpected callers—Siegel in his sheriff's uniform, Chaney in full turnout gear—yellow flame-resistant jacket and pants, white chief's helmet, red radio vest, and heavy black boots.

"Listen, I need to talk to you right now somewhere private," Chaney said.

With a few guests standing nearby, the last thing he wanted to do was start a panic in the hotel lobby. The manager led the way to a back room, and Chaney spelled out the situation.

"You've got about ten, fifteen minutes, and a 200- to 300-foot wall of flame is going to hit this casino."

The manager took a step back.

"We're going to do this thing called shelter in place," Chaney continued. "Shut down the HVAC system and post a roving patrol on each floor of your hotel to keep the guests calm. Make sure all of the windows and drapes are closed in every room. And nobody leaves. You've got a lot of cleared space out there; the fire should burn around the buildings. But I have to make this perfectly clear to you. If anybody leaves this complex, they will die. Do you understand?"

The manager nodded. The resort's head security guard had now joined the meeting.

"Your guys are going to be watching the parking lots as well," Chaney told him. "Report any vehicle fires."

Both men stared back at him, wordless. Chaney tried to bring them back to life.

"Hey! As long as everybody stays inside, you'll be OK."

Leaving the resort complex, Chaney blocked the exit with his vehicle and warned the CHP officer to take cover inside. His timing couldn't have been closer. Moments later, a wave of flames rolled up and broke over the casino grounds. Fire ran over and under Chaney's truck, short flames rendered powerless by the expanse of asphalt, followed by a torrent of embers. Chaney got on the radio to Zombro.

"We're leaving the casino, and I'm basically being overrun by fire right now."

"Ray, you all right?"

"We're fine. I'm in a good spot. It's a little hot and smoky, but I'm not worried."

"OK, well, be careful."

For the next hour or so, Chaney and Siegel crisscrossed the reservation's back roads, dodging fire and searching for people in trouble. Whenever they came across a house not already burning, one or the other ran to the door and pounded to make sure no one was left inside. In places, the smoke hung so thick they could hardly see the road ahead. At one point, Chaney nearly hit two horses running loose. They'd both been burned; he could see the terror in their eyes. Siegel started to open the door of the truck to try to help them, but Chaney stopped him.

"If you get out," he said, "you won't make it back."

John and Patti Cipro had checked into the hotel at Barona on Saturday afternoon. They'd come for that night's US Marine Corps birthday ball, a tradition revered by leathernecks everywhere. As a retired master gunnery sergeant—the Marines' highest enlisted rank—John Cipro wouldn't have missed the occasion. Like him and Patti, most of the partygoers took rooms rather than attempt to drive home down Wildcat Canyon Road after a festive evening of dining, dancing, and toasts to the Corps.

At around 3:30 a.m., John woke to a heavy smell of smoke and an orange glow seeping in around the window curtains. He got up and hit the lights, but nothing happened. So he walked over to the window and pulled open the draperies. As far as he could see, up and down the canyon and all the way to the most distant ridgelines, the world was on fire. Even in Vietnam he had never seen anything like this. In another moment, Patti was standing beside him. At first, neither spoke.

Oh my god, she thought, *we're going to die here at Barona.*

As if he had heard her, John laid a hand on her shoulder.

"We're going to be OK," he said. "The building is new; it's fire resistant, and even if it did catch fire, the golf course isn't going to burn. We could run out there."

Well, that's much better than what I'm thinking, Patti decided. *I'm going with that.*

They could tell the fire had already taken an unsuccessful run at the buildings. White vinyl fencing all around the parking lots had melted to the ground, and the edges of the lawns looked charred. Outside those perimeters, they could see huge flames swirling, houses burning, and every tree on fire. Noise filtered in from the hallway outside the room. Someone was shouting for guests to evacuate. John and Patti turned from the window, dressed quickly in the orange light, and left. Caught in a press of people shuffling through the dark corridor, they felt relieved to hear a voice they knew, another Marine from their group. He had a flashlight and led them to the stairwell. At each landing on the way down, a hotel employee with a light guided them on.

When they reached ground level, the crowd pushed along the corridor leading to the casino. Entering that vast space, still alight and noisy with the clang and clatter of electronic gambling games, took them instantly back to normality, or at least a reasonable facsimile of it. No one was leaving; the doors were locked and guarded. Otherwise, nothing seemed amiss. The usual overnight crowd of Barona patrons sat fixated at slot machines and blackjack tables, the smoke from their cigarettes masking any awareness of the fire outside.

John and Patti made their way to the backside of the casino area, where wide windows normally framed a placid view of ponds and golf greens. But there, too, fire had overtaken the horizon; flames danced across the hills to the west. The Cipros were surrounded by fire, surrounded and trapped inside a locked building. It was too dangerous to leave, the guards told them, too hot and smoky outside. They'd have to stay until the fire passed.

With nothing else to do, the couple headed to the buffet line, hoping to grab a cold sandwich while they had the chance. Who knew how long they'd be stuck here or when the food would run out? They noticed a steady stream of fire refugees trickling into the building. Medics treated the injured; the others blended into the crowd. One of them, a tiny elderly woman, came up to Patti. She seemed a bit dazed.

"Do you mind if I cut in line?" she asked. "I need a glass of water."

"Sure," Patti said. "Get in front of me."

The older woman looked up with vacant eyes.

"My house just burned down," she said. "Everything is gone."

CHAPTER 11

STRANGE WAY

As if Kelly Zombro didn't have enough problems in the Country Estates and Barona Mesa, Ray Chaney had called back after his close encounter with the fire front at Barona to report grim news from Wildcat Canyon.

"We've got people trapped down here," he said. "As soon as you can give me some resources, I need to start doing search-and-rescue operations on these 911 calls we're getting."

Zombro promised Chaney one strike team and a hand crew. It wasn't much, but then he didn't have much to give. "Take this and I'll see what I can get you as we go along," he said, "but I'm telling you I've got structures burning all over the Estates right now. So bear with me."

It's the toughest thing about being a fire manager, the chiefs say: when the need outweighs the resources. "We were consistently getting reports of structures threatened here and there," Zombro told me later. "That's when it's my job to say, 'OK, I've got five companies, and they're all committed to other homes. I can't help.'"

Chaney and Siegel didn't wait for reinforcements, but continued south down Wildcat Canyon on their own, rousting as many people as they could. Every time they got out of the truck to knock on doors or talk to residents, they could hear the continual karump, karump of propane tanks blowing in the distance. Sometimes it happened closer by—a huge concussion, a towering torch of flames. More than once, Chaney found himself ducking behind his truck, and then standing up again to find everything around him ablaze, or already incinerated. Sometimes houses exploded into flames, setting even the ground around them on fire. Chaney asked Siegel to count the number of burning structures they saw, but he quickly lost track. The fire was everywhere now, exhaling great clouds of smoke, broken only by swirling cyclones of red embers or sudden glimpses of houses afire. At one point, a power line came out of nowhere and bounced off the hood of Chaney's truck, scaring them both.

By the time strike teams began arriving in Wildcat Canyon from the north, some from as far away as Orange County, several massive oak trees had burned and fallen across the road near the casino, blocking the engines' way south. Chaney called in a CDF crew to cut the road open, and then directed each team of engines into place, first to addresses where people had been reported trapped, and then to specific roads, one after another.

"Essentially, you're engaged in search and rescue," he told the newcomers. "If you can suppress a structure fire quickly, do so, but we're not here to put the fire out now; we're here to save lives."

Every engine crew rallied to the task. "They were just driving through fire," Chaney told me later, "burning paint off fire engines to get into these houses to search for people who might've been trapped."

Transcripts of the 911 calls streaming into emergency centers as the Cedar Fire chewed through Wildcat Canyon magnify the chaos, zooming in on just a few of the thousands of individual dramas played out that night. On one end of the line, frantic residents begged for help. On the other end, frazzled dispatchers tried to offer reassurance, although they had no help to send. Every available firefighting unit in the county was already run ragged, jumping from house to house, business to business.

Those of us caught in the fire didn't know any of this. Surrounded by flames, we couldn't think past the immediate danger to imagine the magnitude of the crisis—the reach, the speed, the intensity of the flames. We didn't realize how few engines there were to cover miles and miles of fire front, or what those fire crews faced, that they might as well have been trying to stop a tsunami or a hurricane, a tornado or a blizzard. It's probably fair to say that few of us believed any fire could be unstoppable. Rather we believed, as children believe, that if ever there were a fire, if ever we needed help, firefighters would come in their big red trucks, pull out their ladders and hoses and axes, and help us.

"I need the fire department here at my house," one desperate caller told a dispatcher. "My house is about to catch fire."

"OK, sir, you need to take some deep breaths. Slow down, because you need to get through this," the dispatcher counseled. "We'll try to get you some fire engines down there as quickly as we can, OK?"

Another caller seemed stuck on procedure. "So what's the process?" he asked. "What's going to happen?"

"We don't know," the dispatcher replied. "I mean, it's Mother Nature. We're trying to do the best we can."

In places, where fire or fallen trees blocked roads, residents couldn't get out, and rescuers couldn't get in. One dispatcher fielded a wrenching call from a woman trapped on Old Barona Road, just a mile north of Terra Nova.

"We're totally engulfed in flames," she said. "We have a well and a Jacuzzi. What's the safest place?"

"Whatever is going to be farthest away from the brush," the dispatcher advised.

"Nothing's far away from the brush."

"OK, we'll try to have somebody come in there. What's your address?"

"We need a helicopter. . . . Please, send someone fast. You don't understand. I'm not exaggerating."

"We're trying to get something over there."

"So we just cover with wet blankets?"

"I, I can't give you any advice. I don't know what your situation is, all right? We're trying to get somebody over there."

"Please. Please."

Beyond honest effort, there were blunders, of course: "Human beings making the decisions human beings make," as Kelly Zombro put it later. Like us, some citizens said they talked to 911 operators who told them not to worry; the fire was nowhere close; go back to sleep. Minutes later, their homes caught fire. Firefighters, too, had to cope with misinformation, and sometimes downright lies. Six or seven times during the night, Zombro sent crews to rescue people who had falsely reported being trapped, hoping to draw fire crews to save their homes.

"People were lying because they wanted their house to be number one," Zombro explained. "It really pissed me off, because I was telling my guys, 'OK, I have people trapped. I can't send you any backup but go get them.' And then the people weren't there. Maybe they did have something they felt was imperative, but bottom line, they caused me to send these crews into situations with that piece of knowledge to take undue risk because that is what we do if there's a life involved."

Despite the chaos and close calls, everyone on the Barona Reservation and everyone on Old Barona Road survived the fire. But just outside the reservation borders, eight of their neighbors did not.

I wish I had known Galen Blacklidge. I think we would have become good friends. At fifty, she was exactly my age when the Cedar Fire snatched her away from the tranquil, backcountry life she and her poet husband, Jim Milner, had crafted for themselves high on a mountainside overlooking Wildcat Canyon. They'd met through an old-fashioned personal ad that a friend had convinced Jim to place in a local newspaper. He first balked at the idea but then realized he could make it work for him by tailoring an ad only someone he'd truly want to meet would bother to answer. It went something like this: "Writer, 35, poor and a student, looking for a woman of refined sensibilities." Only one woman answered that ad. And just as Jim had naively imagined, she turned out to be exactly the woman he was hoping to meet.

Galen Blacklidge was beautiful, artistic, deeply spiritual, and destined to find Jim Milner. After a year of commuting back and forth between Wildcat Canyon and her home in Fallbrook an hour north, she moved to the retrofitted chicken coop where Jim lived on a dirt road called Strange Way, about two miles, as the hawks fly, from Terra Nova. Gradually, Galen transformed Jim's humble cabin into a stunning, two-story aerie accented with her own paintings. Friends loved gathering there to talk about art and literature, or to enjoy Galen's elaborate themed parties.

Greek night, for instance. Everything worked together: the invitations, the cuisine, the drinks, the table colors, even the after-dinner entertainment—a video of Zorba the Greek. Above, beneath, and through it all, Jim recalled Galen's joyful laugh and her generous, welcoming spirit. She had a daughter,

Jennifer, when they met, and eventually a granddaughter. Not having fathered a child with Galen himself, Jim loved to watch her care for little Madison. So tender and present, he recalls. So selfless.

"She really knew how to love," he told me.

Jim and Galen's neighbor, Molly Sloan, and her family had lived on Strange Way for thirty of Molly's eighty-four years, occupying a cluster of homes nestled at the base of immense granite boulders. The Sloans' compound perched so high on the mountain that on clear days they could spy San Jacinto Peak rising above Palm Springs, more than sixty miles away. From that vantage point, Molly had seen plenty of wildfires come and go. But they never seemed to do much damage. Firefighters always jumped right on them. The Sloans never even considered evacuating. For them, fire watching became almost fun, an exciting event peculiar to backcountry life, like occasionally glimpsing a golden eagle or a mountain lion.

Molly Sloan's best friend on Strange Way was Ralph Westly, a seventy-seven-year-old retired retailer who lived in a rustic rental cabin just down the road. After Molly's husband died, she and Ralph sometimes took hikes or day trips together. She admired his spirited approach to life. He was always engaged in some kind of adventure—backpacking, exploring Mexico, growing organic vegetables, even reading Chaucer in its original Middle English. As a lover of words, Ralph found two more kindred spirits in Jim Milner and Galen Blacklidge. The three of them often got together to talk about literature.

Late that Saturday night, October 25, Molly woke to the ring of the telephone. Her daughter Mary, who lived next door, smelled smoke. It was so typical of Mary to call in the night warning of possible dangers. A nurse like Molly, she impressed everyone as the ultimate nurturer, always concerned about others. Mary next called her seventeen-year-old niece, Jennifer, who lived with her mother, Robin, in the third house on the Sloans' property. Jennifer was alone. Robin wouldn't be home from working the late shift at the El Cajon Walmart until around midnight. Finally, Mary called Jennifer's father, Charlie, who lived in a trailer about a mile away; he and Robin had separated several months earlier. Charlie didn't answer, so Mary drove to his place to be sure he wasn't home, and then returned to Robin and Jennifer's house, the best viewpoint for fire watching. Molly joined them there.

For the next hour and a half, the women studied the horizon to the northeast, where they now saw a glow. Hoping for news about the fire, they turned on a radio and television, but found only the usual late-night reruns and infomercials. Robin joined them shortly after midnight. Less than an hour later, way off in the direction of San Diego Country Estates, they saw flames.

Mary called the area fire departments, Lakeside and Barona, but the firefighters she talked with didn't sound too concerned. Don't worry, they said. Still, the Sloans couldn't help but worry, enough to stay awake and keep watching. Around 2 a.m., they suddenly saw flames again, much closer this time, and ripping across the chaparral so fast they couldn't believe it. This wasn't like any fire they'd seen before.

The four women scattered, each running home to gather a few belongings before jumping into their cars. Molly grabbed an armful of clothes and stuffed them in a bag. She found her good silver, a box of important papers, and a couple of photo albums. And then the lights went out. Within moments, someone was banging on her front door.

"There's a fire coming," a man was yelling. "Get out. Get out now!"

It was a neighbor's son, visiting from Los Angeles for the weekend. Molly opened the door, her arms full of albums. Forget all that, the man said. Just get out.

"I've got to get the dogs," Molly shouted back.

She had three. The visitor helped her put them all into her car. Then he ran off to his own car, and Molly started her engine. As she pulled away from her house, she heard a horn honking behind her. Mary.

"Mom, have you got the dogs?" she yelled.

"Yes," Molly shouted back and then took off, relieved to know Mary was right behind her.

Jim Milner had smelled smoke fairly early that evening. After dark he hiked out to a view point and scanned the horizon in every direction, but saw nothing. So he and Galen went to bed. Sometime after midnight, they woke to thick smoke and a glow outside the bedroom window. Jim phoned the fire station at Barona. A fire was coming, a firefighter told him; they were beginning to evacuate the reservation. Jim next tried to call his neighbors to warn them, but could only reach two people; one of them was Ralph Westly. Jim and Galen rushed to pack a few essentials, but already they were out of time. Jim saw flames jump into view about a mile away. In just the few seconds he stood watching, he could see more fire blowing in from the north, crowning the hilltops.

Oh shit, Jim thought.

He turned to Galen.

"This is bad," he said. "We need to leave now."

"It'll be OK," she answered.

That was all there was to their last conversation.

They each grabbed one of their two dogs and rushed to their cars. Galen pulled out first. Not far down Strange Way, past an oak grove where the road straightens out, they ran up against a screen of fire completely blocking their way a hundred or so yards ahead. Galen hesitated. Jim was about to get out and talk with her about what to do when her car lurched forward and disappeared into the flames. Instinctively, Jim punched his accelerator to follow, but almost immediately had to slow down to avoid losing control of the car. He couldn't see in the smoke and swirling embers. And the heat through the windshield was terrific, like standing next to an open oven.

Jim knew the road turned sharply right just ahead; he was watching for it, but with so little visibility, he missed it anyway and almost careened down an embankment into the worst of the fire. Instead, his wheels hit a ditch and the car jolted to a standstill. There was nothing to do now but get out and run for it. He called his dog, Sarah, to follow him, but she spooked and ran the other way.

Sprinting down Strange Way under the familiar canopy of oak trees, now a searing ceiling of fire, Jim felt certain he was going to die. But even through his fear, random questions ran through his head. How would it happen? What would it be like? Would the asphalt burn his feet? Would he breathe in superheated air? What happens to consciousness after it leaves human form? Suddenly a pair of headlights broke out of the smoke behind him. Galen! But no. Someone else's car.

Molly Sloan still doesn't know how she made it down the mountain. By the time she'd traversed the steepest portion of the road and hit the flat, the smoke was so bad she couldn't see at all. For the next mile, she figures, she was feeling her way, hugging the berm running along the left shoulder. Maybe all the sparks and embers flying overhead lit her way just a little. Then, somewhere in the smoke, she came upon a man running down the road and realized it was Jim Milner. Molly pulled up to him.

"Jim! Get in!"

"Let me drive," he insisted. "I've got to find Galen." Molly slipped across the seat.

When they hit Wildcat Canyon Road, Jim first searched for Galen among the gaggle of residents gathered there. She'd been ahead of him. *She should be here by now.* But she wasn't. He knew then that she hadn't made it out. Still, he called his sister and Galen's daughter, hoping one of them had heard from her. They hadn't.

"I'm afraid we've lost her," Jim told his sister, and his voice betrayed his anguish. "If only we'd gone together."

Meanwhile, the fire kept coming, racing down Wildcat Canyon. It was almost on top of them again. They had to keep moving. Jim kept Molly's car, and a woman Molly didn't know at all offered her a ride out of the canyon. Someone else, driving an SUV big enough to hold Molly's dogs, volunteered to take them. It would be a week before she saw them again.

At the bottom of Wildcat Canyon, Molly Sloan asked her driver to stop and wait for a bit while she watched the cars coming down the hill, looking for Mary and Robin and Jennifer.

"Why aren't they coming?" she wondered aloud. "Why aren't they coming?"

Finally, at around 3 a.m., Molly told herself they must have taken shelter at the casino. She could look for them there, but first she had to reach safety. Grabbing a ride with yet another stranger, Molly made her way to her daughter Peggy's house in El Cajon. She beat on the door and yelled as loud as she could, but her voice caught and quavered.

"Peggy! Peggy! I can't find Robin and Mary and Jen. And everything is burning."

On Strange Way, the fire front had blown through, making the road passable, though the chaparral all around still blazed.

Through the smoke, Jim Milner looked for any sign of his wife, Galen, even tire tracks headed over the dirt berm along the road's edge. For three hours he searched, getting out of the car when he could, holding a wet cloth over his face to cut the smoke and protect his face from swirling embers. Eventually, he found his dog, Sarah, dead.

Soon after that, he saw Galen's car, the driver's door open. And then, about fifty feet away, he found Galen. She was lying on her back, her knees drawn up. It took him a long time to reach her. Every few steps he dropped to the ground, screaming and crying. For a long while, Jim sat with Galen's body, touching her forehead, telling her he loved her, that he would miss her, telling her goodbye. He did not know how much time passed, how much wailing and jamming his hands into the blackened, still-warm earth it took before he was able to stand again and, finally, to walk away. He knew only that dawn had broken.

It would be much longer before the Sloans found out what had befallen Mary, Robin, and Jennifer. As early as Sunday afternoon, family members broke through the police barricades blocking Wildcat Canyon Road, checked the casino to no avail, and pushed back up Strange Way. They found all three cars—Mary's and Robin's both sitting beside the smoking heap of ashes that was Mary's house, Jennifer's headed down the hill—and all three were empty.

With no help from the authorities, the Sloans searched the rubble on their own, each manning a different sifting station. Hours later, Peggy's sister-in-law found Mary's bathtub and started pulling out hunks of debris. Pieces of metal, scraps of wallboard, shards of pottery. At the bottom of it all, she came across a gold ring. Mary's ring. And then, close to the tub, she found another ring. Jennifer's ring. Eventually, a search-and-rescue team showed up and took over. They managed to uncover tiny pieces of human bone, definitive proof that the women had taken refuge in the house and died there when the fire arrived. The Sloans can only try to piece together what happened. They have to guess why Mary got out of her car and took refuge in her bathtub, taking her little Chihuahua with her. They don't know how Robin and Jennifer ended up nearby. So many unanswerable questions.

In the ruins of a concrete block outbuilding behind Molly's house, the Sloans found another body, the remains of Ralph Westly. Most likely, he died from smoke inhalation, a lack of oxygen, or even a single breath of superheated air. Why Ralph had detoured to the Sloans', with the fire bearing down on them all, will remain another mystery. He'd started to evacuate—they found his fire safe sitting outside his house. Was he trying to warn his good friend Molly? Seeking protection from the fire among the enormous rock outcroppings near her house? Eventually, county officials showed up at the Sloans' to retrieve Ralph's body. Molly remembers that the coroner wore a white, long-sleeved shirt, such a contrast to the blackened ruins of her home, of her life.

Three other people died on Strange Way. Gary Downs had bought his home and forty acres of property in Wildcat Canyon just a couple of years before. An optimist with a generous heart and a ready sense of humor, he owned a company that provided motorcycle escorts for funerals and parades. Gary was fifty and divorced, living alone and constantly immersed in remodeling projects. He seemed to be on a mission to rework his house into a perfect country retreat, a place to savor the long views of canyon and mountains for years to come. Authorities found his body, and those of his two cats, near his packed car. They concluded that Gary had driven off the road in his attempt to escape the fire.

John Leonard Pack and his wife, Quynh Yen Chau Pack, both twenty-eight, met in a San Francisco restaurant where Quynh worked. John was a San Diego native; Quynh was born in Vietnam. After moving to San Diego with her new husband, she enrolled at California State University San Marcos and had nearly completed a degree in accounting. Family and friends say the couple loved their life in the country, their little cabin, and their two dogs. Fire officials found what was left of the Packs' car on Strange Way where the fire had stopped it. It was pointed toward their cabin, leading sheriff's deputies to conjecture that the fire had blocked the couple's escape and forced them back toward home. Quynh and the dogs died inside the vehicle. John's body lay nearby in the roadway.

It is difficult to think about burning to death, difficult to imagine a more horrifying, painful way to leave this world. In wildfires, it often happens in an instant, and from the inside out. A single breath of the superheated gases that roll like a wave just ahead of a big fire is more than enough to sear the lungs, shut down the brain, and pinch out a life, leaving only a corpse for the flames to conquer. It doesn't always happen this way, this quickly. And even when it does, there's little if any comfort for those left behind. But in remembering the victims of wildfire, in facing the awful reality of their final moments, and in thinking about what well could have been my own final moments, it's all I have found to hang on to.

CHAPTER 12

A FUNNY FEELING

LAKESIDE FIRE PROTECTION DISTRICT DIVISION Chief Andy Parr was out east of town on business late Saturday afternoon when the initial dispatch came through on his truck radio for a fire in the Cleveland National Forest near Cedar Creek. It didn't strike him as unusual. After more than twenty years as a firefighter—he'd started at nineteen—Parr expected frequent wildland fires during the dry season, as often as once a week. Usually, the one-two punch of air attack and ground pounders caught a nascent fire small, snuffed it out, and few people even heard about it. Still, Parr never took a backcountry fire for granted. Too many of the homes he was responsible for in the Lakeside district lay on the outskirts of town, where civilization intruded into undeveloped chaparral—a dangerous boundary called the wildland-urban interface. Especially on days like today, with a red-flag warning in effect and Santa Anas in the forecast, Andy Parr never let his guard down.

After hearing the dispatch to Cedar Creek, he made his way to a high point and scanned the horizon. Sure enough, off to the north, a wispy plume of smoke floated straight up, proof of a small blaze unaffected by wind. Nothing really alarming. Nothing for Lakeside to do but stand by. After work, Parr continued to monitor the talk on his home scanner. It sounded routine at first, typical of a wildland initial attack. But as the hours passed and multiple attempts to access the fire met dead ends, he noticed a change in tempo, vocal cadences picking up. These were people he knew—seasoned, respected fire chiefs who'd seen it all and handled it all.

If they're talking fast, Parr thought, *I'd better be listening.*

At 11 p.m., he checked the television news, hoping for an update, but no one reported anything about a fire in eastern San Diego County, known locally as East County. Parr didn't find that reassuring. He pulled a blue duty uniform over his brawny frame, smoothed his mustache, ran a hand over his blonde buzz cut, and kissed his wife good bye.

"I've got a funny feeling about this fire," he said. "I'm going back to work."

Fifteen minutes later, as Parr walked into his station, the phone rang. It was CDF Battalion Chief Kelly Zombro, calling from Ramona, asking for help in San Diego Country Estates. Lakeside had already sent one of its four engine crews north to the Old Fire in San Bernardino, but Parr didn't think twice about sending a second engine to Ramona. Like every other fire agency in California, Lakeside depended on mutual aid. Nobody could afford to keep enough resources standing by 24/7 to tackle a big incident on their own.

Besides, he had a reserve engine and an extra duty crew to help cover the home front, and based on past incidents Parr figured it would take a couple of days for a fire in Ramona to burn as far as the Barona Reservation, where Lakeside normally would pitch in with further resources. In the meantime, the best thing Andy Parr could do for Lakeside was help stop the fire in Ramona. He arranged with Zombro to meet him in the Country Estates, climbed into his official chief's vehicle (a Ford

Expedition stuffed with gear), and started north on Wildcat Canyon Road. Beyond Barona, just past the racetrack, Parr met another chief's truck running south at Code 3, lights and siren. Both drivers braked to a stop in the middle of the road. Parr recognized CDF Battalion Chief Ray Chaney, got out of his truck, and walked over to talk with him.

"Where are you headed, Ray?"

"To the casino. Thinking about starting evacuations."

"How's it look in Ramona?"

"I don't really know. Kelly just asked me to get down here and take care of things."

"OK. If you need help, let me know. I'll send some crews from down below."

"Thanks. I'll do that."

The whole exchange took no more than thirty seconds. Chaney continued south, and Parr drove the remaining three miles to the Country Estates. Pulling into the parking lot where he and Zombro had agreed to meet, Parr found a sheriff's rep and two Forest Service division chiefs—Hal Mortier, who'd stood watch with Zombro all evening, and Carlton Joseph, the Cedar Fire incident commander, who'd just arrived from Pine Hills, near the fire's point of origin. Zombro never made it. He was busy fighting fire. The wind had come up, strong and searing, bringing the fire with it, and houses at the far end of the Country Estates were engulfed in flames. Within another five minutes, a shower of embers forced the men back to their vehicles.

This is ugly, Parr thought. *We don't have any control here whatsoever. This fire is in charge, and we're just playing defense.*

His instinct told him to hurry back to Lakeside, call in his people, and support Chaney. By dawn, he figured, they'd probably need to evacuate the hotel and casino at Barona. But Parr had barely started down Wildcat Canyon when fire sheeted across the road in front of him and blocked his way. Later he would look back on that unexpected encounter and his momentary meeting with Chaney as fortuitous, alerting him to the Cedar Fire's unprecedented pace and the immediate need to deploy Lakeside's engine crews, plus reinforcements from other districts. This fire wouldn't wait half an hour for him to drive the detour route back to Lakeside. Parr jumped on the radio and ordered an immediate full wildland dispatch—seven engine crews—into Wildcat Canyon from the south. As word of the advancing flames spread, an eighth crew responded independently from the San Diego Rural Fire District, giving Parr a tiny contingent to lead into battle.

Still, the fire beat them all to Barona. After speeding south to Lakeside down California Highway 67, the alternate route, Parr cut back over to Wildcat Canyon Road and headed to the casino ahead of the engines from the south. He skidded to a stop a good mile from his destination when a wave of flames rolled right over his truck, scattering pea-size embers in its wake. By the time he could make a U-turn and beat a retreat, a sea of smoke had swallowed him whole. His stomach went sour.

This sucks, he thought. *I don't have any way to put out this fire; it's just blowing over my head. I can't get to the casino from either direction. I have no idea if anybody north of here got out, and I can't do anything to help them.*

Driving south again as fast as he dared through the murk, it was all Parr could do to stay on the road and hope he didn't run into anyone. After about a mile, he met the first of the engines he'd requested. He sent two or three of them down Old Barona Road, the closest cross street, and others into the isolated neighborhood of Muth Valley.

Terra Nova lay halfway in between.

"There's no way we're going to put this fire out," Parr told the crews. "So there's no firefighting. Don't even take the hoses off the truck. Just wake up as many people as you can and get them out. I don't care if you have to put them in the fire engines. And then get out yourself because we've got a hundred more houses to go."

For the next two or three hours, Parr stationed himself in the center of Wildcat Canyon Road, barring access to the north and moving methodically south as crews emerged from one road and headed for the next. In places, firefighters kept working as the fire closed in and even after it had blown past, with some crews doubling back into still-burning areas to find and rescue survivors.

All this, and they were only catching the flank of the fire. The front had slammed through farther north up the canyon, where Parr first encountered it crossing the road. Spurred by terrific winds and feasting on dense, dry chaparral, the Cedar Fire galloped across the land with extraordinary speed. The smoke was dense and choking, the air alive with embers. Parr stayed on the radio, monitoring each crew's location, warning them repeatedly not to extend too far or stay too long.

Each time he sent an engine in, he worried. He knew what they were up against. Feeling your way half a mile down some sketchy dirt road, choked with brush on both sides. Not knowing where it goes or how far, whether there's anywhere to turn around at the end of it, whether a panicked driver might come careening out of the smoke and nail you head-on. Or if, at any moment, fire might explode all around you. Or if anyone even lives on the road or not. And when you do finally arrive at a house, what if no one answers the door? How do you know the residents have really left? Maybe they're just sound sleepers. Or deaf. And what if you kick in the door and find a dog or cat left behind? Do you try to take it with you? Do you grab a family portrait you see on your way out, to give people about to lose their home a memento to help them start over? What about people who flat out refuse to leave? How much time do you spend trying to convince them, when hundreds of their neighbors may still be asleep and unaware? So many decisions, each one agonizing. And only a few seconds to make them. Parr's worst nightmares had never approached this kind of hell. When another Lakeside chief arrived and asked how he could help, Parr immediately sent him back down the canyon.

"What I really need you to do is go back to the dispatch center and talk to them face to face," he said, "because over the radio I can't make them understand how bad this is. Tell them the truth. Be as serious as I am to you right now. Tell them to get all the chiefs in on this. Tell them to order big-time resources."

Soon after that, dispatch called and assured Parr that more engines were coming. From San Francisco. He got on the radio and made an announcement to all eight of his engine crews.

"You know what, guys? We're it."

I do remember half-waking once or twice that night to the sound of a siren passing on Wildcat Canyon Road, but it didn't alarm me. I knew there was a fire north of us in Ramona, so it only made sense that emergency vehicles would be headed that way. Still, why no one on our road heard the evacuation warnings, why none of us woke until the light of the fire itself brightened our windows, I can't say. Perhaps an engine crew peering through dense smoke just couldn't see the steep, skinny road leading to Terra Nova. Maybe they saw it and judged it too risky to try with a vehicle as big as a fire engine. Or maybe they never even made it that far into our neighborhood. But what about our neighbors closer to Wildcat Canyon Road? The Pontes family, who lived in a distinctive wooden dome house visible to passing traffic, didn't wake up until after Bob and I left.

"Everybody knows the dome house," Andy Parr told me after the fire. "There was a lot of activity right there for a long time, maybe fifteen or twenty minutes. I'm telling you, these guys were running their sirens and air horns; they were trying to make as much noise as they could. How anyone slept through that I will never know."

Neither will I. What I do know now that I didn't know then is this: Dozens of fire and law enforcement officers risked their lives that night in a frantic attempt to warn the sleeping residents of Wildcat Canyon and nearby Muth Valley. Sheriff's deputies Dave Weldon and Rocky Laws, the helicopter crew that rescued Sergio Martinez, skimmed ahead of the spreading flames in ASTREA3, shouting warnings to residents over the loudspeaker. They came so close to the fire so many times that they took to calling their chopper "The Moth."

Because ASTREA pilots typically fly at higher altitudes than firefighting aircraft, mitigating the dangers of power lines and uneven topography, Weldon wasn't limited by a cutoff rule prohibiting night flying. But on this night, heavy smoke obscured everything downwind of the flames, including the homes most in jeopardy, those directly in the path of the fire front. At times, with almost no visibility, he had difficulty judging his altitude and finding houses below. Adding to the challenge, the wind had arrived in full force, blowing at a steady thirty-five miles per hour and gusting at times as high as seventy. The danger zone for aircraft starts at thirty. Knowing lives were on the line, Weldon and Laws kept flying through the smoke and turbulence. Only when it got so bad that their helmets crashed together did they concede it was time to land before the winds took them down. Even then, they traded the chopper for a squad car and rejoined the desperate efforts to find and evacuate people on the ground.

The two deputies had an advantage. They knew the territory. Most of the first responders converging on Wildcat Canyon to join the evacuation effort—firefighters, deputies, highway patrol, and police officers—came from other parts of the county and beyond. None had any reason to know their way around the tangles of narrow asphalt and dirt roads carved into San Diego's backcountry. At one point during the night, Ray Chaney heard a CHP officer he knew come up on the radio.

"Be careful," Chaney warned him. "This thing's moving so fast. Don't go down some winding road you can't get out of."

But the patrolman took crazy risks anyway, trying to save as many people as he could. Before the night was over, the taillights on his police cruiser had melted. Weeks later over beers, he and Chaney compared their fire experiences.

"You know," the patrolman said, "I got a decoration for what I did in the Gulf War. And that pales in comparison to what we were doing out there during that fire."

CHAPTER 13

THE BOBCAT

I HAD BEEN WRONG ABOUT OUR neighbors across the canyon. Seeing headlights creep down the mountain as Bob and I headed back to bed, I'd told myself that someone was probably overreacting to the smoke, not knowing, as we did, that the red glow on the horizon came from a faraway fire headed in another direction. Actually, all twelve residents of Blue Sky Ranch knew much more than we.

Artist and astrologer Ingrid Coffin had founded the Blue Sky community some fifteen years before. She'd since seen a number of fires come and go in Wildcat Canyon, enough to underscore the risk and justify a neighborhood evacuation plan. During fire season, everyone at Blue Sky kept keys in vehicles, cat carriers and dog leashes in plain sight, and a box of vital papers and favorite possessions by the front door. Ingrid tested their readiness with occasional fire drills. On the night of the Cedar Fire, her foresight paid off.

Around 1:30 a.m., one of the Blue Sky residents, a county park ranger, got a call from her boss saying scanner chatter warned of a big fire headed toward Wildcat Canyon. Immediately she spread the word, and people started packing to leave. Another Blue Sky neighbor came tearing in from his night job to load the community's truck. First the dogs and then as much stuff as he could fit in—those pre-packed boxes of valuables, plus computers, cameras, and the like.

With everyone else rushing to pack and leave, Ingrid began phoning her canyon neighbors. Since we hadn't met yet, she didn't have our number, but she did call Sue and Randy Fritz, who lived next door to us. Sean, their twenty-three-year-old son, answered the phone.

"Sean, there's a big fire coming down the canyon!" Ingrid said. "You need to grab whatever you want to save and get out now."

Sean seemed hard to convince.

"I don't see any fire," he said.

"Can I talk to your mom?"

"She's not here. She and Dad are visiting my uncle in Missouri."

"Sean, you've got to leave."

"I don't see any fire."

"Well, by the time you see it, it's going to be too late, so go now or your mother's really going to be mad at you."

Forty minutes after the residents of Blue Sky Ranch learned about the approaching fire, they drove out of Wildcat Canyon in a caravan, headed for a prearranged meeting place in Lakeside. Once there, Ingrid counted heads and came up one short. Her husband, Bob, hadn't shown up.

"Where's Bob?" she asked.

"He wouldn't leave," someone said. "He was trying to turn the sprinklers on."

"He's a Sagittarius," Ingrid explained to me later. "Heroic."

Ingrid's anxiety lasted only about twenty minutes, until Bob called to say he'd made it out of the canyon, barely. The fire had come so fast, he said, that just in the time it took him to open the sprinkler control box and turn on the water, the horizon changed from smoke to flame.

Sean Fritz had invited a few friends over for the evening to watch a movie. When they left around 1 a.m., he walked them out. They all noticed that something seemed off. *Must be just a really dark night,* Sean thought at first, *maybe a new moon.*

"Whoa, it's really smoky," somebody said. "Like there's a crazy fire or something."

Then they noticed the ash falling.

Better check, Sean decided. He got in his car and followed his friends out as far as the crest of the neighborhood road, just past our driveway. From there he could see miles to the north and even farther from east to west. Except for the usual twinkle of house lights, the entire horizon lay dark. No flames anywhere in sight.

Sean had been twelve when his family moved to Wildcat Canyon, a place where the smell of smoke struck him as pretty normal. The Fritzes had seen wildfires flare up nearby at least three times. Each time, a firefighter or deputy came to the house and alerted them, but they never had to evacuate. Air tankers and helicopters always arrived promptly and extinguished the flames. So where was this fire? Sean drove back home, turned on a radio, and started flipping channels, checking for news. After what seemed a long time, he found something.

"A small fire up around San Diego Country Estates," Sean heard the newscaster say, and then something about firefighters hoping to contain it soon. The news also included a reminder of the switch from daylight savings to standard time, so Sean set the clock back and went to bed. Not long afterward, Ingrid Coffin's phone call woke him. The news that Blue Sky Ranch was evacuating ahead of a big fire took Sean by surprise.

Wow, he thought, *I guess it's a little bigger than I figured, and it's not really being contained.*

He drove to the crest of the road again and studied the canyon to the north. This time, far in the distance, he could see a glow. Not much of a threat, but it wouldn't hurt to start packing a car. He called his parents to find out what they'd like him to take, but they didn't answer. So Sean made his own choices—photo albums, computers, some of his personal stuff. Still he couldn't make up his mind about leaving. There'd been no official warnings, after all. He checked the radio for a news update but couldn't find one.

What he really wanted to do was go back to bed. It was almost three now, standard time, much too early for the sun to come up, although it already seemed to be growing light outside. Sean went to a window, looked out at an orange sky, and felt a jolt of alarm. He threw a few last things into the car, grabbed the cat, and took off. When he came to our driveway, he stopped and blew a long blast on his car horn, keeping it going even as he drove away. Taking a last look back at our house, Sean saw a light come on.

It had been only forty-five minutes since he'd last checked the horizon to the north and seen a distant glow, but this time when Sean crested the hill of our neighborhood road, all he saw was fire, fire stretching across the entire horizon. On the other side of the canyon, huge flames and billowing smoke obscured Blue Sky Ranch. By the time Sean drove down the steep asphalt grade and bumped over the rutted dirt and gravel leading to Wildcat Canyon Road, flames were blasting through Oakoasis Open Space Preserve next door. Meanwhile, across the canyon, high up on the mountain, fire had leaped south from Blue Sky Ranch to a point directly across from our bedroom windows.

All around us in the canyon, from Old Barona Road to Muth Valley, household after household woke to its own nightmare. Some heard the sirens or megaphones; some were warned by phone calls or frantic pounding on the door. Some knew nothing until jarred from sleep by the crash of breaking glass or a roar outside their windows—a sound, they reported, like a jet taking off. And some, like us, had already sensed the change in the wind, already smelled the smoke, called 911, and been sent back to bed. Nothing to worry about, they'd been told. The fire was far away, to the north, to the east, over the ridge. Now, much too late, we all realized the authorities had been wrong. Just in our little neighborhood, nine other households scrambled for safety. Sean Fritz was no doubt the first to leave, making it out just ahead of the flames. For the rest of us, it was a haphazard exodus, complicated by smoke, fire, and fear.

Frank and Sandra Cozza had moved to Wildcat Canyon only a few weeks before the fire, desperate for a fresh start after losing both a baby and a business the year before. By the night of the fire, they'd converted a rustic clapboard cabin into a comfortable home, hung a bassinet from the upstairs bedroom rafters, and welcomed a new son, two-week-old Franco. It felt like things were finally beginning to turn around.

Sometime before midnight Saturday, the Cozzas smelled smoke, and Frank called 911.

"Don't worry about it," the dispatcher said. "It's a fire so far away it's never even going to reach your area."

Frank wasn't so sure. Before turning in at around 10 p.m., he walked outside and checked the horizon, a stunning 270-degree view stretching at least two miles up the canyon. But there was nothing to see. A few hours later, when little Franco woke up hungry, it took a moment for the groggy new parents to separate their baby's cries from the wild shrieking of a fierce Santa Ana wind. And then, peering out into the night, they saw trees bent double, a luminous orange sky, and a long line of tall flames closing in from a distance of only 200 or 300 yards. Already a soaring eucalyptus tree close to the house stood ablaze from ground to crown.

There wasn't time to find clothes. Sandra grabbed the baby and one of the dogs, and sprinted outside in her nightgown toward the car. It was parked under a huge tarp set up at the base of a hill behind the house. Running barefoot close behind her, dressed only in his underwear, Frank slipped on the stairs, tumbled all the way down, and found himself smacked against a wall, with the couple's other pup licking his face. He scrambled to his feet, scooped up the dog, and kept going—until he got to the open door.

"I looked out and saw a silhouette of Sandra and the baby against an orange background; flames were coming over the hill toward them," Frank told me later. "And the car was locked; she couldn't get in."

He stepped back inside the house and plucked the car keys off their hook by the door. As he stepped out again—two seconds, maybe three?—the fire snatched the canvas suspended above his wife's head and swirled it upward into instant ashes. With her face tucked protectively toward her child, Sandra didn't even notice. Frank screamed, taking in a gulp of smoke that knocked him to his knees, and crawled the rest of the way to the car, gravel biting into his bare legs.

When he finally got the car door open, he pushed Sandra inside, along with the baby and both dogs, scrambled in himself, and hit the ignition. As they shot around the house toward the road, the fire kept pace, igniting the chaparral outside the car windows. Angels. Frank believes it's the only explanation for how they made it out of Wildcat Canyon, careening through an orange tunnel of flames, with Sandra praying aloud all the way. The Cozzas' wooden home never stood a chance. In their last glimpse of it, Frank said, "It looked like the sun had set where the house was."

Upslope from the Cozzas, Leslie Nunez woke up wondering why the house felt so hot. In the next instant, she saw flames outside the windows. When she ran to the living room for a closer look, she noticed the double-paned glass in the room's sliding doors bulging inward. Leslie's screams woke her husband, Dave, who rushed downstairs to the garage to start their big red sedan. But as he opened the garage door, fire and embers swept inside.

"It's too late," he yelled upstairs. "We're going to die!"

"Like hell we are," Leslie shouted back.

She still doesn't understand why, but she felt calm, confident.

"Get that damn car started. We're leaving."

Somehow the couple found a path through the smoke, down the sloping curve of their driveway and past flaming telephone poles, to Wildcat Canyon Road. Rather than try to outrun the line of flames pushing south, Dave Nunez turned north into the black, where the fire had already passed, and the couple took refuge at Barona. As they walked into the casino, a man complained about the lockdown, saying he wanted to leave.

"No, you don't," Dave told him. "I just drove through that stuff. Believe me, you don't want to be out there in it."

If anyone in our neighborhood was prepared for wildfire, it was Lisza Pontes, whose wooden geodesic dome house sat on the flat land near Wildcat Canyon Road. After researching wildfire risks and recommendations, she'd completely retrofitted the property, replacing wooden decks, adding a second water tank and fire hose connection, clearing almost every twig of vegetation, and coating the entire house with elastomeric paint—high-tech, high-dollar, and highly fire-resistant stuff. She'd written out three separate evacuation plans based on how much time she, her husband, Ross, and their twenty-five-year-old daughter, Sharid, might have to pack up and leave—one hour, thirty minutes, fifteen minutes. Then she ran family fire drills to rehearse each scenario.

Reading the newspaper that particular Saturday morning, Lisza saw the front-page red-flag warning Bob and I had missed and scuttled her usual Saturday errands. Instead, she spent hours watching the horizon and soaking her landscaping. Just before midnight, Lisza smelled smoke and called around until she connected with one of the area fire stations.

"It's the Pendleton fire," the guy who answered told her. "It's way up north."

Feeling relieved, Lisza and her family went to bed and slept until Sharid woke up to an orange room and flames striking at her windows.

"Mom," she screamed, "the fire's here!"

Lisza clicked into crisis mode. "OK," she yelled. "We're on the fifteen-minute plan. The fire department should be here any second; in the meantime, everybody knows what to do."

They didn't know every other house in the neighborhood was already burning, or that everyone else had already left. But they quickly realized they didn't have fifteen minutes. Grabbing only wallets and dogs, the Pontes family jumped into Ross's truck. Halfway down their driveway, a neighbor's propane tank blew, knocking the pickup into an adjacent ditch. Ross ran to get another vehicle. Lisza and Sharid waited in the truck as long as they could, until it caught fire, and then they hurried out into a shower of embers just as Ross pulled up in Lisza's car.

Smoke obscured the road all the way down Wildcat Canyon, and everything around them was ablaze. Lisza slapped at sparks eating holes in her shirt, her dogs' fur, the car upholstery. Sharid had been burned while racing from the truck to the car; her elastic pajama waist melted in the heat, searing her lower back and reeking of burned rubber. Now she was talking to her boyfriend on her cell phone, telling him how much she loved him, telling him good bye.

Oh my god, Lisza thought. *I've tried so hard, but I can't protect my daughter.*

And then suddenly the smoke cleared. They'd made it.

At first, I thought our escape might actually be easy. Pulling away from Terra Nova, Bob and I drove into a pocket of clear night that put the swirling embers and brilliant flames behind us. It seemed my fears about reaching the main road, half a mile down the mountain on the canyon floor, had been overblown. All I had to do was drive out. But just past the edge of our property, where the chaparral closes in tight, we hit the smoke. Dense, dark, impenetrable. Like looking out the window of a plane into a thunderhead. Something inside me, something more knowing than thinking, shouted: *The brush here is ready to explode. Go! Move! Get out of here! Now!*

I wanted to hit the accelerator, but I couldn't see the pavement. I couldn't see anything, and the shoulder of the road, cut into the hillside, fell off sharply to the right.

"I can't see," I yelled.

"Don't wreck the car!" Bob shouted back.

He reached toward the dashboard and hit the recirculate button, a brilliant move that kept the car from filling with smoke. "Just don't wreck the car!"

What he meant was, don't drive off the edge. We'd rounded the big boulder that forced the road into a sudden swerve. That much danger at least lay behind us. But just ahead I knew the asphalt narrowed into that steep, skinny grade, and I couldn't begin to find it.

"I can't see the road!"

"You'll just have to remember where it is!"

Bob was barely in his seat, clutching the grab bar above the door with his right hand like a commuter on a lurching subway train. He wanted to be driving his truck instead of riding shotgun in my sports coupe. He wanted to feel more protected, more in control. His voice sounded odd—forced, almost cracking—and I realized I was having trouble talking, too. My mouth was so dry my tongue barely worked.

"I can't see," I kept saying. "I can't see the road!"

It was all gray, all pea soup. I tried my high beams. Even worse.

"I can't see anything!"

At that moment, some kind of animal, something fairly big, jumped out of the chaparral and landed directly in front of my right headlight, maybe even glanced off the bumper. My foot found the brake pedal.

Did I hit it? Oh, I hope I didn't hit it.

I felt relieved when the animal immediately righted itself and dashed off. What was it? A coyote? No, not a coyote. Something different.

Animals run just ahead of fire. That knowing voice again.

And then I realized: *Oh god, this fire is right on top of us.*

Bob and I both had seen the creature. A blur, hardly more than a phantom, it charged straight ahead, visible in the headlights for only an instant before disappearing into the murk, its feet seeming never to have touched ground. Except I knew they had. Just as before, early one morning on my way to work, here in this same place—and right in the middle of the road.

It's the bobcat. It's on the road. Follow it.

I gunned the engine, aiming for the spot in the smoke where the animal had disappeared. When we got there, I could make out two rows, no, two fields of fuzzy red lights spreading right and left, and a dark path between them.

"Oh my god!" I heard myself shouting. "Oh my god!"

Everything below us was on fire.

It never occurred to me to turn back; it never occurred to me that we might die. We had to keep moving; we had to get through. That was all. I gripped the steering wheel with both hands, aimed the Acura toward the darkness that was the road, and we crept down the steepest part of the mountain, finding asphalt all the way. At the bottom, where the pavement gave way to dirt and gravel, we burst into an alien dimension, a dark world veiled in smoke, lit only by throbbing red and orange smears of lights. I could see a little farther now, but not far enough. A drainage ditch at the road's edge loomed just ahead.

"Watch it!" Bob's voice cracked the darkness.

I swerved back toward the center and tried to hold a steady course, negotiating as best I could between the lines of fire. Bob talked me through it. Right, left, straight. It took both of us to find the way. The fire front must have already passed through, leaving everything simmering in its wake. In places, currents of embers snaked across the road. And more than once, I had to punch through a low, red fence of flames, driving as fast as I could in the smoke, thinking all the time of the gasoline tank suspended underneath us. *Maybe it's like running a finger through a candle flame,* I thought. *If I move fast enough, it won't burn me.*

Somehow we made the final turn that pointed us toward Wildcat Canyon Road. Soon, any second now, we'd be there and on our way out of the canyon. But we were still enveloped in smoke, guided only by the fire on either side of us. In the next moment, we slammed into something, a glancing blow. Not enough, thank God, to trigger the airbags. A dirt bank to our right crystallized for an instant in the headlights. I jerked the wheel the other way, and the car bounced back toward center, but the surprise impact rattled me. I had no idea where we were now, except for knowing we should be close to the main road. Where was it? Why weren't we there yet? I tightened my hold on the steering wheel and started praying out loud.

"Lord, help us out of this fire. Be with us and help us find our way out."

"Yes!" Bob agreed. He was still barely seated, still hanging on to the handle over the door.

The smoke thickened, darkened. I felt my tires skid over a patch of gravel and grab hold of solid pavement. In the next instant, my headlights picked up the yellow and white center lines of Wildcat Canyon Road materializing through the murk. We'd made it. And I'd lurched blindly into an intersection almost always full of traffic. For a moment, my mind tried to juggle competing feelings of relief and horror. But I didn't have time to sort it out now. We were still inside the fire.

Orange flames swayed in the smoke, taller, closer than before, and on both sides of the road. I put the car on top of the center lines and stayed there, keeping as far away as possible from the gauntlet of fire. I could still see only a few feet before the smoke blotted everything out. *Just keep driving*, I thought. *Faster, as fast as you can.* How fast? I have no idea. I didn't check the speedometer, only kept my eyes on those painted lines and my foot on the accelerator. I didn't think, as Bob confided later that he did, about the possibility of running into anything. Oncoming traffic. A stalled car. An animal. A fallen tree or downed power line. And somehow, we didn't.

We'd come about a mile from Terra Nova when the flames lining the road yellowed and flared, reaching up and across as if to meet in the middle like overhanging branches. For a moment, I thought they might completely block our path.

"Oh my god!" I sounded louder this time, and then I flattened the gas pedal. The Acura shot through the flames and burst out the other side, newborn into an ordinary night, dark, clear, and clean. Just like that we'd put the fire behind us. Like waking up from a nightmare.

"Nice job, Cutes!" Bob said. "Now find a place to pull over, so I can drive."

His demand caught me by surprise.

"I think I'm doing a pretty good job, actually."

"Well, pull over anyway so I can tie my boots."

We were coming up on a wide spot along the shoulder of the road, just big enough for one car. I slipped into it. Bob opened his door, the dome light came on, and I watched him swing his feet out onto the pavement. While he cinched his shoelaces, I scrounged through my purse, searching for my cell phone to call our veterinarian, Peter Slusser, in Muth Valley, obviously the next community in the fire's path. We'd gotten to know him and his family as neighbors and friends by now; I had his number in my phone. But I couldn't get through; the line was busy. Probably a good sign, I told myself. At least he's awake. He'll be OK.

"Sandra!" Bob was looking back toward Terra Nova.

"What?"

"The whole mountaintop just exploded."

I looked back too, scanning desperately for a landmark amid the brilliant orange mass consuming Terra Nova and everything around it, including the road we'd just traveled. For an instant, near the ridgeline where our house should be, I thought I could pick out squares of orange framed within a black rectangle. Walls and windows silhouetted against flames? I couldn't decide. It was only a glimpse, a puzzle in my mind even then, and later I wondered if I'd really seen even that much. There wasn't time to be sure. We'd barely cleared the fire. It had to be right behind us.

"Bob, we've got to go. It's coming."

He pivoted back inside the car and yanked the door shut, and I steered back onto the pavement. Ahead on our right, the headlights of three cars lit the long grade of Muth Valley Road descending to its intersection with Wildcat Canyon. How many other people had already left? How many were still asleep?

"Do you think our neighbors made it out?" I asked Bob.

"I don't know."

At the intersection, we came up behind a yellow fire engine parked in the middle of the road. A firefighter standing beside it gestured me to stop, and I rolled the window down.

"Lady," he said, "we're not going to stop this fire."

"No shit, my house is burning right now."

"I know."

"There may still be people up there," Bob yelled across me.

"I know."

The firefighter motioned us past, and we drove on through the darkness, the only car on the only road out of Wildcat Canyon.

From Ruin to Renewal
The Cedar Fire Story in Pictures

(Please enjoy full-color versions of these images at sandrayounger.com.)

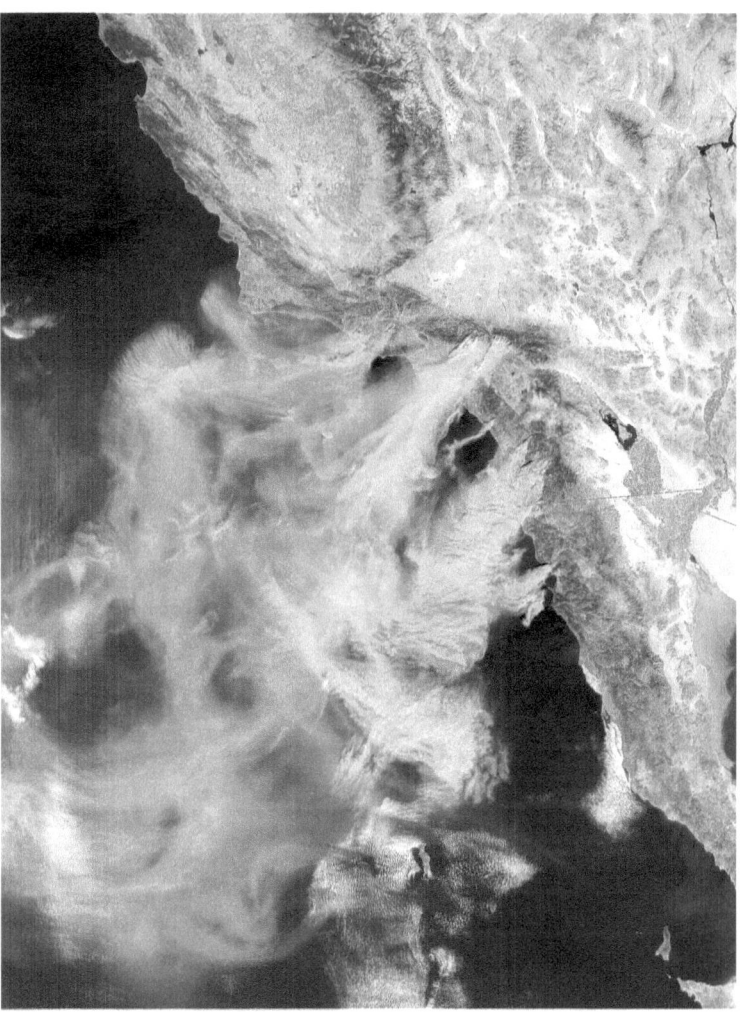

Seen from Space: Smoke from fourteen separate fires streaks the skies during Southern California's 2003 Fire Siege. Most are clearly visible in this satellite view taken at the height of the Cedar Fire, October 26, 2003. From north to south: the Piru, Verdale, and Simi fires north of Los Angeles; the Grand Prix and Old fires near San Bernardino; the much smaller Roblar 2 Fire near USMC Camp Pendleton; the Paradise Fire in Valley Center; the Cedar Fire stretching across central San Diego County, and the Otay Fire along the international border. A fire can also be seen in Mexico. JACQUES DESCLOITRES, MODIS RAPID RESPONSE TEAM, NASA GSFC

Wildcat Canyon: The view from Terra Nova. © 2003 Robert E. Younger

Terra Nova Before: The original house shortly after the Youngers moved to Wildcat Canyon in the spring of 2003. © 2003 Robert E. Younger

Terra Nova After: Reduced to rubble. © 2003 ROBERT E. YOUNGER

Terra Nova After: So little left. © 2003 ROBERT E. YOUNGER

Overwhelmed: Despite firefighters' desperate efforts in the San Diego Country Estates, the Cedar Fire claims the first of 2,232 homes destroyed throughout San Diego County. © 2003 DAVE GATLEY

Sinister Brilliance: A tsunami of fire surges toward a backcountry home near Wildcat Canyon. © 2003 JOHN GASTALDO/ U-T SAN DIEGO/ZUMAPRESS.COM

Lives Lost: An abandoned car found in Wildcat Canyon bears mute witness to the tragic final moments of canyon neighbors lost in the fire. © 2003 DAVE GATLEY

Unstoppable: The fire line dwarfs an engine (upper left) as flames approach the San Diego suburban community of Scripps Ranch.
© 2003 JOHN GIBBONS/U-T SAN DIEGO/ZUMAPRESS.COM

Bird's-Eye View: San Diego Sheriff's deputy and ASTREA helicopter pilot Gene Palos looks toward the Cuyamaca Mountains where smoke defines the "backdoor," or trailing edge, of the Cedar Fire, early Sunday morning, October 26, 2003. DAN MEGNA

Apocalyptic Skies: Smoke boils across the sky, obscuring the sun, as the southern front of the Cedar Fire jumps Interstate 8 and spreads into the communities of Harbison Canyon and Crest, Sunday afternoon, October 26, 2003. DAN MEGNA

Air Attack: A water-dropping helicopter appears lilliputian against towering flames as it joins the battle to protect homes near the mountain village of Descanso.
© K.C. Alfred/U-T San Diego/Zumapress.com

Lunarscape: Weary firefighters descend a ridge blackened by the Paradise Fire.
© 2003 Dan Trevan/U-T San Diego/Zumapress.com

Coming Home: Scripps Ranch residents return to their neighborhoods, braced for the worst. © 2003 Howard Lipin/U-T San Diego/Zumapress.com

A New Season: Sandra and Bob Younger enjoy another spring in Wildcat Canyon after rebuilding Terra Nova. © 2006 Ericmillettephotography.com

CHAPTER 14

MUTH VALLEY

THE BLAZING CHAPARRAL WE'D DRIVEN through in our flight to Wildcat Canyon Road marked only the wake of the Cedar Fire's wild gallop toward the ocean. Leaping through unbroken shrublands, flames quickly topped the ridgelines forming the canyon's west wall and roared down the other side into Muth Valley. Following the sinking contours of the land like water, fire tumbled toward the region's nadir, a thousand-acre body of water known as San Vicente Reservoir. Undeterred even by that wide, watery buffer, embers and burning debris blasted across on the wind and ignited an island at the lake's center.

The fire hit Peter Slusser's house at almost the same time it got to us. By the time I tried to call him, he had already left, his pickup loaded with dogs, cats, and birds. Other than that, he'd had time only to grab his laptop, his pilot's logbook, and a camcorder filled with family videos. The busy signal I'd taken as a good sign really meant Peter's home was already burning. Nearby, Randy Fritz's brother, Jeff, cut it even closer. Driving out as the flames arrived, he took extra moments to stop and open a corral gate in the futile hope the family's two horses might escape and outrun the fire.

At the same time, firefighters and law enforcement officers worked deep into the web of dead-end roads that defined the tiny community. Flashing lights, piercing sirens, staccato commands over loudspeakers—they tried it all in a desperate attempt to wake up every sleeping resident and send them down Wildcat Canyon Road.

Closest to the reservoir—and farthest from Wildcat Canyon—lay the gated neighborhood of Lake View Hills Estates. With the fire already tearing into the north end of Muth Valley, an engine crew pulled up to the black iron gate leading into the community of ten households. The steep narrow roads beyond twisted precipitously toward the reservoir below—a challenge for a cumbersome vehicle like a fire truck to negotiate even in the best of conditions. With the flames closing in at warp speed and their own chances of escape dwindling by the second, the firefighters realized they could go no farther. Reluctantly, the crew turned around and headed out of Muth Valley.

As in so many other neighborhoods targeted by the fire, the residents of Lake View Hills Estates woke to the sounds of a furious wind, phone calls, car horns, and doorbells. As with all the rest, they burst into action and scrambled to their vehicles. It was around 3:15 a.m., the same time we left Terra Nova, when the first of them fled through the iron gate and started toward Wildcat Canyon Road. Falling into a line of vehicles, they felt their way through the smoke, braving intense heat and a noisy hail of debris carried by the wind, threading between walls of flames that stretched higher than they could see. Everyone in this initial group made it out.

Living in the house closest to the gate, Cheryl Jennie and her partner, Stephen Shacklett Sr., had spent twenty-three years watching the sun set over the lake. He was fifty-five; she was fifty-nine. They'd worked together to remodel the place and loved sharing the ambiance with friends and family, often hosting get-togethers of sixty or more people.

The couple's dogs—a shih tzu named Muffie and two enormous Irish wolfhounds—commanded the center of attention, begging for treats and attention from each guest. Cheryl and Stephen both enjoyed showing the Wolfies, and often spent vacations in their motorhome traveling to dog shows. Cheryl loved watching Steve trot the dogs around the ring. A bear of a man at six feet four inches and 300 pounds, yet light on his feet, he and his giant canine partners made perfectly proportioned teams.

The night of the fire, Cheryl woke around midnight and smelled smoke. She walked outside and circled the house, checking in every direction, but saw nothing. So she called the Barona Casino and asked if anyone there could see a fire. "The fire you smell is way out near Julian," she was told. "Don't worry."

It's still hard for me to understand why so many of us in the fire's path got such ill-informed advice that windy, smoky night. No one, especially firefighters and 911 operators, should have tried to dismiss our concerns. Granted, no one could have imagined how fast the Cedar Fire would run, consuming 100,000 acres overnight. A "normal" wildfire might have taken two or three days to advance as far. But the truth is, wildfire is just that—wild and unpredictable, scornful of assumptions.

About three hours later, Cheryl woke again, this time to the sound of wild winds buffeting her patio umbrellas. Going out to close them, she found herself facing a line of flames headed straight toward her kitchen.

"Steve!" she screamed. "Get up, get up, get up! Oh my god! Oh my god!"

Stephen hobbled out of the bedroom. He'd broken his left leg just a week before, and the cast slowed him down.

"You're panicking," he said. "Now stop. Go start the motorhome."

Cheryl ran outside and tried but couldn't coax the engine to turn over. When Stephen arrived, she helped him with the cast as he climbed into the driver's seat, and then dashed back to the house for the wolfhounds. She could tell by their jumpiness that they sensed the danger now, too. Each dog far outweighed her, yet taking one at a time, Cheryl somehow managed to wrestle them into the RV.

"I'll take my car and meet you at the gate," she told Stephen.

After a final trip inside for Muffie, Cheryl dumped the little dog into the passenger seat and left the driveway at 3:30 a.m. A little past the gate, she stopped and waited for Stephen as promised. He quickly pulled up behind her, and she started out of Muth Valley. But around the first bend in the road, Cheryl ran dead into the fire. The flames were huge; heat and smoke filled the car, making it hard to breathe.

I'll never make it through, she thought. *I'd be engulfed in an instant. I've got to turn back.*

She threw the transmission into reverse and lurched backward. For a heartbeat or two, her tires caught in a ditch, and then broke free. Driving back past the motorhome, Cheryl looked up, trying to find Stephen behind the wheel, but the smoke was too thick.

Goodbye, Steve, she thought. *I love you.*

She believed she was going to die.

By now other vehicles behind Cheryl were turning around, too, but in her rearview mirror it looked as if the motorhome and an SUV directly behind it were going on through the flames. With so much smoke, it was impossible to know for sure, but she hoped so. Bigger vehicles probably had a better chance of breaching the fire and reaching safety, she reasoned.

Cheryl had no idea now where she was going, only that she had to get away from the fire. Looking ahead, she could barely see the road, but soon made out a fork in the pavement. Which way should she turn?

"Oh God!" she prayed out loud. "Oh God, help me!"

For no conscious reason, Cheryl cut right. In the murk ahead, she caught sight of faint red taillights and followed them, all the way to the driveway of a house belonging to neighbors she'd never met—Larry Redden and his wife, Laureen. As the Reddens pulled into their garage, Laureen's parents, who lived with them, arrived in a second car. Cheryl grabbed Muffie and scrambled out into a barrage of wind and smoke, beneath an orange sky raining fire. She sprinted into the garage, and the big doors rolled down behind her, barely muting the roar of wind and flames outside.

"Let's go to the lake!" Cheryl screamed.

"That's the last place we want to go," Larry Redden shouted back.

He had retired just the year before as a captain with the San Diego Fire Department. Even with his family's only escape route blocked by flames, Larry didn't flinch. His thirty-five years of experience told him they'd be fine as long as they stayed inside the house. No need to stress. Just take shelter until the main fire blows past, and then go outside and extinguish anything that's burning. That's what firefighters do, what he'd wanted to do when he first got the call from a neighbor and looked out his windows to see every ridgetop from one end of the horizon to the other alive with flames blasting straight into Muth Valley.

But his wife had been desperate to leave, so he went along. Reaching the gate, Larry found a gaggle of cars just sitting there, as if waiting for a cue. He pulled around them and headed to the front of the line, shouting at each driver as he passed.

"C'mon, let's go if we're going!"

But like Cheryl, Larry didn't make it too far beyond the gate before confronting the fire. Sky-high flames. Heat prickling his skin through the windshield. *This is no good*, he thought. *We've got to go back.* He made a quick U-turn and again drove down the line of cars, again shouting at the drivers.

"Go back to your homes," he told them. "Get inside and stay there until the fire passes."

Back in his own garage, he led the way upstairs to the living room and repeated the same instructions to his family and Cheryl.

"Stay here. Don't go outside! I'm going to be checking all around the house."

As the firestorm swirled and crashed overhead, Larry kept moving from room to room, methodically canvassing the structure from top to bottom. Smoke thickened the air, and every smoke detector in the house was blaring. In the attic, Larry grabbed his old turnout gear and suited up. In the basement, he stuffed wet towels under an outside door to staunch a flurry of embers shooting through and flying around the room. Meanwhile, Laureen found a broom and punched each smoke detector into silence. Terrific gusts of wind battered the house with embers, burning brands, and random debris. Huge branches littered the driveway.

As soon as the worst of the firestorm blew past, Larry tied a bandana over his face, went outside, and started putting out spot fires, the worst burning a corner of the wooden deck. Despite his warning, Laureen went out, too, and turned the garden hose on another part of the deck that had caught fire. When the pressure gave out, she and Larry both scooped water out of the swimming pool to throw at the flames.

Inside, Cheryl paced through the smoke from one end of the house to the other, patrolling for new flare-ups. When a spot on the deck came back to life, she went out herself and dumped a pan of water on it. All the while, through the big windows at the back of the house overlooking the lake, she could see surrounding homes ablaze. It seemed to last forever—the smoke, the flames, Cheryl's pacing and praying.

"Oh my God, help us. Oh my God, help us. Oh my God, help us."

Finally, the light began to change. Firelight gave way to dim daylight. *Did we really make it?* Cheryl wondered. *Did we really live through this?*

As the sun rose, Larry Redden and his father-in-law drove out to inspect the ruins of Lake View Hills Estates. When they returned, Cheryl could read bad news in their faces. Her house was gone. But all she cared about now was finding Stephen. She'd already called and asked her daughter to check the Lakeside grocery store parking lot where the couple had agreed to meet. But Stephen wasn't there.

So Larry Redden ventured out again to look for the motorhome. Just beyond the gate, he ran into an engine crew of firefighters. They'd found two RVs, they reported, one intact, sitting in the middle of the road; the other charred, caught in a ditch. Larry went with them to search the burned vehicle. It didn't take him long to discover the bodies of a man and two huge dogs. Larry Redden pulled out his cell phone and called home.

Oh god, Cheryl thought when Laureen relayed the news. *In just a few hours, I've lost my whole life.*

Retirees Bob and Barbara Daly had also been forced back by the flames. Awakened by the sound of the wind rearranging their patio furniture, Bob Daly had immediately roused his wife, who began packing the couple's valuables. He then drove up the steep, winding grade to the automatic gate that guarded the entrance to the neighborhood and opened it. He didn't want anyone to be trapped in case the electricity failed. By the time he returned home and picked up Barbara, the fire had cut off their escape. Bob Daly thought about running for the reservoir down a narrow dirt access road adjacent to their property, but quickly rejected the idea as too risky. It was a long way to the water, at least a third of a mile, through heavy brush all the way, and the road itself was in terrible shape, so they'd have to walk. *We'd never make it,* Bob decided.

Another neighborhood family did start down that narrow roadbed. The Shoharas—James, Solange, and their thirty-two-year-old son, Randy—drove to the trailhead in two vehicles. Solange led the way in a pickup loaded with a filing cabinet; the two men followed in a Toyota compact.

Bob Daly saw them starting down the access road on foot against terrific winds, even as flames descended the next hill, only a few hundred yards away.

"Don't go down there," he shouted. "It's too rough."

Pelted by embers and out of time, the Dalys took refuge in their swimming pool, on the leeward side of their house. No one used it anymore. In fact, for a couple of years now, they'd talked about having it filled in. Now they huddled in the cool water alongside rabbits, rats, and snakes, all of them seeking shelter from the firestorm, all of them functioning purely on survival instincts.

When the Santa Anas drove the flames into the Dalys' house, a patio wall catapulted the worst of the killing heat up and over their heads, likely saving their lives. Within fifteen or twenty minutes, their home and everything in it had collapsed into ashes. As it burned, chunks of lumber and other debris rained down into the pool. To escape the barrage, the couple climbed out and clambered down a set of burning wooden steps to a paved turnaround circle in the road. Barbara took refuge on a rock in the center of the clearing and stayed there. When the worst of the fire had passed, Bob followed a bend in the asphalt road and found the couple's detached RV garage untouched by the flames. He extinguished a few hotspots that threatened the building and pulled their motorhome out in front. For the next few weeks, it would be the Dalys' only home.

The Shoharas had moved to Lake View Hills Estates from Ramona only a year before, after completing the house Solange had dreamed of for years and planned to the last detail. Eight-foot-tall family portraits lined the walls surrounding a spiral staircase just off the marble entry. Chandeliers, a wine cellar, even a koi pond—Solange had conceived it all, with James's support.

They grew up on opposite sides of the world—James in Hawaii and Solange in France—and met at a swimming pool in her hometown while James was stationed nearby with the US Air Force. He was twenty-one; she, only seventeen when they married. Within two years, James was transferred to California, where Solange learned English by watching television soap operas. After all three of her children had graduated from high school, she took an unorthodox turn, enrolling in a peace officers academy to become a prison guard. James retired from a second career as a civil service employee and followed his wife's lead. Both worked at the Richard J. Donovan Correctional Facility, a state prison near the Mexican border. They put in long hours, banking the overtime pay to build their retirement home.

Randy was the youngest of the Shohara children. A natural athlete, he'd competed as a professional bodyboarder, even earning one of eighty-six invitations to a world championship tournament. Boarding was Randy Shohara's life. As he grew older and the sponsors began to drift away, he still drove to the beach every morning to practice.

The older Shohara son, Andy, lived in Ramona with his wife, Claudia, and their two preschoolers. Hearing reports Sunday morning that the Cedar Fire had spread down Wildcat Canyon, Andy Shohara called his parents to check on them, but he couldn't get through. It didn't concern him at first. Phone lines were down all over, and neither his mom nor dad was allowed to carry a cell phone at work.

The next morning, Monday, Andy got a call from his sister, Kathy.

"Have you heard from our parents?" she asked.

"No," Andy said, "but we're not too worried."

"I don't know. It's not like Mom not to call. We're going to drive over there."

"You can't get in. The roads are closed."

"We're going to try."

When Kathy arrived in Muth Valley later that day, it fell to Bob Daly to tell her what had happened. Sunday at dawn, he'd set out on foot to check on his neighbors, hoping that everyone had survived the night. But barely beyond the end of his own driveway he had come upon the charred hulk of Solange Shohara's pickup. The burned Toyota sat nearby, and inside it, two bodies, the remains of James and Randy. Bob Daly got out his cell phone and called 911.

"We have victims in Muth Valley," he told the dispatcher.

"OK. I'll send an ambulance."

"Send the coroner," Bob said.

When the authorities arrived, they found a third body—Solange Shohara—about fifty feet down the road leading to the reservoir.

The Shohara family had planned to take a cruise together that December. Everyone was going, even Solange's relatives from France. Instead, they all gathered two months early for a triple funeral. James, Solange, and Randy Shohara were laid to rest in a single grave at Fort Rosecrans military cemetery, overlooking the Pacific Ocean.

Despite their tragedy, the Shohara family found consolation in one fortunate coincidence. Or perhaps it was providence. On Saturday, while Sergio Martinez wandered lost in the Cleveland National Forest, Kathy, her husband, and twin toddler sons were having fun at Disneyland, a two-hour drive from San Diego. At the last minute they decided on a change of plans—staying over in Anaheim, rather than driving back to San Diego and spending the night with Kathy's parents in Muth Valley.

By 3:30 a.m. on Sunday, Lakeside Division Chief Andy Parr knew it was time to head south toward the bottom of Wildcat Canyon. He hated like hell to pull out, but after two mad hours working to evacuate the area, fearing all the while for those beyond his reach, he could do no more. Fire had swallowed everything to the north and now everything in Muth Valley, too. Sitting side by side in their trucks at the intersection of Muth Valley and Wildcat Canyon Roads, Parr and Mike Rottenberg, a fire chief in the nearby city of Santee, looked out at walls of flames closing in, leaping down both sides of the canyon and drawing a curtain across Muth Valley Road just behind them. In only a minute or two more, fire would overrun their position. Already, Parr had sent the eight engines under his command to safety, leaving only himself and Rottenberg to hold on as long as possible, just in case. Of what they weren't sure. But no matter now. They were headed out.

Just then a burning car burst out of the fire obscuring Muth Valley Road and skidded to a stop near the chiefs' trucks. Parr and Rottenberg rushed to pull the driver out and help her into Rottenberg's vehicle. Moments later a convertible with shattered windows emerged from the flames. Two women and a big dog clambered out onto the road. One of the women was burned; the other seemed dazed. Parr shoveled gear off the seats and into the rear of his Expedition to make room for two passengers, one in front and one in back. They had a bird, too; he wedged its cage alongside his gear. The dog squeezed into the only spot left in the vehicle, the footwell of the front passenger seat, and settled down, laying its head on top of the center console and fixing its eyes on Parr as he drove. The women, never speaking, reached out to one another across the seatback and clasped hands. For the first time that night, Andy Parr felt something had gone right.

CHAPTER 15
PARADISE LOST

You'd think San Diego County had enough to contend with as Saturday slipped into Sunday. Shortly before midnight, when Santa Ana winds slammed into the Cleveland National Forest, the Cedar Fire broke free and galloped wild through Ramona. Its rampaging flames sent more than 9,000 residents scrambling out of warm beds into a nightmare of blinding smoke, flying embers, and desperate decisions.[21] CDF Battalion Chief Kelly Zombro led the frantic attempt to defend San Diego Country Estates against the stampede, deploying every last engine, bulldozer, and water tender available. Meanwhile his colleague, CDF Battalion Chief Ray Chaney, sped south down Wildcat Canyon, a backcountry Paul Revere hoping to warn sleeping residents of a coming apocalypse.

Yet in the midst of this chaos, another fire sparked to life on the Rincon Indian Reservation, nearly twenty-five miles to the northwest. Frenzied by the wind, it jumped quickly

---

[21] 2000 US Census, US Census Bureau.

into Valley Center, a rambling rural community tucked into the inland mountains. Paradoxically, considering the hell this new incident would create, firefighters dubbed it the Paradise Fire, after nearby Paradise Creek. The night air was still warm, 78 degrees, when it began; humidity had plunged below 10 percent. Add to that Santa Ana winds screaming in from the northeast at a steady 35 miles per hour with gusts to 45, and you had an arsonist's dream.[22]

Rarely does one individual cause as much tragedy and devastation as the person who lights a fire destined to burn out of control. There is no older or purer means of terrorism. It happens all the time, and most perpetrators get away with it. Because it's rarely witnessed and leaves little evidence, arson is notoriously hard to prove. In 2003, the year of Southern California's great fire siege, US law enforcement agencies reported more than 71,000 arson incidents, but only 16,163 arrests. Those same 2003 statistics tell us that most suspected arsonists—nearly 85 percent—were male. Half were under eighteen; almost a third, under fifteen.[23]

I have always been able to accept the fact that Sergio Martinez was a desperate man who did a desperate thing when he lit the signal fire that devoured my home and killed twelve of my neighbors. However horrific the outcome of his actions, he meant no harm. But I cannot fathom how anyone could light a fire with malicious intent to destroy, even to kill. The reasons confessed vary from pragmatic to psychotic to petty. Sometimes, it's simply a matter of money; most people who start structure fires hope to collect an insurance payout. Ironically, some firefighters become firebugs, whether because of a psychological quirk, to create work for themselves,

---

[22] California Department of Forestry and Fire Protection and USDA Forest Service, The 2003 San Diego Fire Siege Fire Safety Review, 2004, 21.
[23] Federal Bureau of Investigation

to appear heroic in responding to their own fires, or simply because they're bored.

Investigators suspected arson caused at least three of the fourteen major blazes burning across Southern California in October and November 2003. Two of those, the Old Fire and the Grand Prix Fire near San Bernardino, which pulled so many firefighting resources out of San Diego County in the days before our own week of fire, merged into a terrifying and deadly forty-mile front that destroyed 1,134 homes and caused six deaths. Five of those fatalities were men who suffered fatal heart attacks while evacuating or watching their homes burn.[24]

Law enforcement agencies launched an all-out effort to identify and apprehend the perpetrators. They established a telephone hotline to collect anonymous tips. They published police sketches based on multiple reports of two twenty-something males in a white van near the Old Fire's point of origin; witnesses said one threw a lit flare from the passenger's window into heavy brush. San Bernardino and Los Angeles Counties each offered a $50,000 reward for information leading to the arrest and conviction of the arsonists.

Yet for six years, the investigation went nowhere. Finally, in October 2009, officials indicted Rickie Lee Fowler, by then twenty-eight and a convicted felon, on five counts of murder, one count of aggravated arson, and one count of arson of an inhabited structure. Fowler, they alleged, was the passenger in the white van who had thrown the burning flare. The driver had since died. In late 2012, a jury in San Bernardino decided that Fowler should die too, in a state execution chamber.[25]

In San Diego County, after a $200,000, fifty-interview investigation, officials concluded that the Paradise Fire was

---

[24] CDF, Cal OES, USDA Forest Service, *California Fire Siege 2003*, 68, 71.
[25] As of 2023, capital punishment remains a legal penalty in California. But there have been no executions in the state since 2006 because of litigation that led to a federal court order, and a 2019 gubernatorial moratorium.

deliberately set, but they couldn't nail down a suspect. Several Rincon tribal members told reporters they knew who did it, but no one was willing to name names. Despite ongoing efforts, including a $25,000 reward posted by the Rincon tribe and another $10,000 by the CDF,[26] investigators could never amass enough evidence to arrest, let alone convict, anyone for starting a wildfire that charred 56,700 acres, destroyed 221 homes, and killed two people.[27]

The grim task of leading the fight against the Paradise Fire—with paltry resources pitted against perfect fire conditions—fell to Ray Chaney's godfather, CDF Division Chief Bill Clayton. A trim, grizzled veteran with forty years of firefighting behind him, Clayton had for most of the week been assigned to the Roblar 2 Fire at Camp Pendleton. By late Saturday, with the blaze finally corralled at approximately 8,600 acres,[28] he'd been able to cut loose a few engines and send them inland to Ramona in response to Kelly Zombro's desperate midnight pleas for resources. After that Clayton went to bed, hoping to grab a few hours of sleep. But by 3 a.m., he was driving into Valley Center to take command of the new incident there. He arrived to find fifty or sixty houses already burning, close to 2,000 acres consumed, and flames tearing across fresh territory.

Few, if any, firefighters working the lines that memorable week had more experience than Bill Clayton. The son of a fire chief, he'd dabbled in the old man's profession as a seasonal

---

[26] Jo Moreland, "Paradise Fire Still Stumping Investigators," *North County Times*, October 26, 2005.

[27] California Department of Forestry and Fire Protection, *Paradise Fire—Final Update*, November 6, 2003.

[28] CDF, Cal OES, USDA Forest Service, *California Fire Siege 2003, 67.*

firefighter while working his way through two business degrees and a teacher's certificate at San Diego State University. But after hanging his diplomas on the wall and trying an office job for a couple of years, Bill Clayton realized his real love was firefighting. Even after he hit retirement age, he came back on a part-time basis, working as much as regulations allowed.

Arriving at the Paradise Fire staging area, Clayton joined a group of firefighters hurrying to marshal available resources and defend as many homes as possible. Among them was CDF Battalion Chief Kevin O'Leary, who served as chief of the Valley Center Fire Protection District. O'Leary had already been working for hours—first volunteering to help monitor the Cedar Fire from the water tank near his home in the Country Estates, then squelching the Schoolhouse Fire at Santa Ysabel, and after that returning to Ramona to help evacuate Barona Mesa. When the Paradise Fire flared up, he hurried to Valley Center and stepped into the role of operations chief under Clayton. O'Leary's knowledge of the surrounding terrain enabled him to predict the fire's path in time to warn hundreds of people in its way, no doubt saving lives.

In the meantime, with the Cedar Fire sucking up every engine left in the county, plus reinforcements en route from outside the region, Bill Clayton's urgent order for reinforcement troops and equipment fell flat. Headquarters had nothing left to send him. So he got back into his chief's truck, along with Larry Natwick, a volunteer aide, and drove out to assess the situation on the ground. They'd just left the staging area when the first fatality report came in—a woman caught in the fire while trying to escape her home on Yellow Brick Road.

Her name was Nancy Morphew. She was fifty-one, tall and strong, a devoted equestrienne whose life revolved around her family and her Arabians. When the fire came, she rushed toward the barn with a truck and trailer, determined to save her beloved horses, and likely lost her way in dense smoke. The Arabians would survive. But Nancy's truck veered off the road into a deep ditch. The trailer overturned. Her body was found nearby. Clayton did what he could to comfort the woman's distraught husband, who'd been defending the couple's log home, while Natwick doused a still-burning corner of the house with a garden hose.

And then another alarming report came over the radio: people trapped in a vehicle near Fire Station 73 on Lake Wohlford Road. Clayton and Natwick arrived to find an ambulance crew loading a severely burned young woman. People standing nearby shouted to them about a car still stranded on a road next to the station, behind a curtain of fire. Clayton waited until the flames ebbed just enough, and then drove into the heat. Amid the red and black of fire and charred earth, he and Natwick found a burning vehicle smashed into a tree. In the backseat was the body of sixteen-year-old Ashleigh Roach.

The Roach family, plus a few friends staying over after a Halloween party, had sat up most of the night worrying about the fire burning to the northwest on the Rincon Indian Reservation. For a while, Lori and John Roach watched the glow of the flames with a group of neighbors gathered at Station 73, just a quarter of a mile from the Roach property. About 3 a.m., they went home to rest for a bit while their twenty-two-year-old son, Jason, took over the task of monitoring the fire. By dawn, it looked like the danger had passed them by. Finally, they could all relax and get some sleep. But at eight o'clock, John and Lori woke to the strong smell of smoke. On their feet in an instant, they checked outside and saw nothing but blue skies. Yet within the next couple of minutes, two sheriff's deputies drove up to the Roaches' gate with the news that the fire had changed directions and was now headed toward them.

"It's coming," they said. "Get out. You've got twenty minutes."

They didn't have ten. Just after the deputies left, the Paradise Fire surged through the canyon below the Roach property, flared up, and enveloped their house.

"Everybody out!" John Roach screamed. "Run! Run!"

He opened the front door to a swirl of fire and embers. Sparks flew inside and landed on the living room carpet. Already, the porch was burning. John grabbed a garden hose and sprayed it down, hoping to create an escape corridor for his family and friends, who all came tumbling out of the house and scattered toward various cars.

John and Lori had to leave first. His truck blocked everyone else in. Their older daughter, twenty-year-old Allyson, and a friend who'd joined her for the party got into his car and fell in behind them. Ashleigh and her brother Jason came last in his brand-new Mustang. To the right, the driveway fell away down a slope. Trying to maneuver through smoke and embers, Allyson's friend lost his way, and his car slid down the bank. He and Allyson tumbled out and found themselves in tall, flaming grass.

Heat. All Allyson can remember is the heat, unbearable and inescapable. Like sitting too close to a roaring fireplace, she told me, and not being able to move away. The intensity of it drove her to the ground, but she kept clawing her way back up toward the driveway on hands and knees. Her eyes felt as if they were drying out, so she squeezed them shut, a reflex doctors later said saved her vision.

At the top of the slope, Allyson stood up. She looked down at her hands. Acrylic nails hung off her fingertips; her skin reminded her of melted candle wax. She couldn't find her friend in the smoke; somehow he'd found his way out of the fire on his own. Suddenly, Jason's car materialized in the haze. Seeing his sister at the edge of the driveway, he stopped. Ashleigh jumped into the backseat to make room in front, and as soon as Allyson climbed in, Jason took off again. But only a little farther down the drive, he hit another vehicle in the smoke, and the Mustang canted off the road into a flaming pepper tree. Burning branches grasped the car in a white-hot embrace. Jason scrambled out and turned toward Ashleigh in the backseat. He shouted at her to come with him. But Ashleigh wouldn't move.

Jason waited as long as he could; he was gulping smoke, and he could feel his skin burning. Knowing they must be almost to the fire station, he decided to go for help. Allyson, meanwhile, had dragged herself across the center console and followed Jason out the driver's side door. She, too, begged Ashleigh to come with her, but Ashleigh wasn't coming. At last, Allyson turned and stumbled toward the fire station. The smoke was so thick she had to watch her feet one step at a time to make sure they stayed on the asphalt. But she knew if she just kept going, the road would lead her to safety.

Waiting in the fire station's parking lot, just beyond the reach of the flames, John and Lori couldn't understand why the other two cars hadn't yet joined them. A few minutes later, they saw Jason, walking barefoot, emerge from the smoke and collapse, and then Allyson appeared, her face white with ash.

"Where is Ashleigh?" John asked them.

"Back there," Jason said.

John Roach went mad. Screaming Ashleigh's name, he started toward the flames. A sheriff's deputy grabbed his arm and tried to hold him back, but John broke away and ran to rescue his daughter. A few steps into the smoke, he collapsed, unable to breathe. The sheriff's deputies, who'd followed him, helped him back to safety.

Lori still stood, as if hypnotized, where he'd left her. At last she became aware of a paramedic shaking her, pleading with her. "Lori, I need your help," he was saying. She was an emergency room nurse, by protocol the senior medical person at the scene. The paramedics needed her help to treat her own son and daughter. Amazingly, Jason got away with relatively minor burns. Allyson suffered second- and third-degree burns over 86 percent of her body. Doctors estimated her chance of survival at less than 15 percent. She would spend four months in the hospital, fighting through surgery after surgery, infection after infection, to beat those odds.

A few years after the fire, I sat with Allyson and her parents, John and Lori, in the living room of their beautifully rebuilt home, and watched haunting home videos of Ashleigh Roach. Such a young girl, so full of dreams, dressed in a short green embroidered skirt, hands at her hips, blonde hair bouncing, feet flying through an Irish step dance. It was her way of celebrating the family's heritage, her parents told me.

Like them, I wished she were back. If only she'd followed her brother and sister to safety. She belonged here with her family, still smiling, still dancing. Why hadn't she tried to escape her brother's burning car? It's a question that will always haunt the Roach family, a question they've each tried to answer.

"She was just like me," Lori said. "When I'm terrified, I freeze."

John Roach speculated that Ashleigh felt safe in the car. It wouldn't have made sense to her to get out into the fire, he said. Allyson worried that the awful sight of her burned and melting face and hands may have stunned her sister past action.

After the fire, miracles kept the Roach family from succumbing to trauma and grief. Lori Roach told me sheriff's officers who first reached the burning car reported seeing two figures inside. Grasping for explanations short of supernatural, Lori came up empty. She is convinced an angel made sure her daughter didn't die alone.

At Fire Station 73, CDF Division Chief Bill Clayton's radio brought news of a new crisis. The fire now threatened a nearby casino, with people trapped inside. Dodging flames on their way south on Lake Wohlford Road, Clayton and Natwick came across a man in shorts and a T-shirt, running full tilt down the asphalt and losing ground against an oncoming wave of flames. Clayton pulled up beside him, and Natwick jumped out into the heat. Embers blew into the car through the open door. Clayton got out, too, just long enough to help Natwick push the terrified man into the backseat.

At the front entrance to the Valley View Casino, Clayton turned his injured passenger over to the care of security guards, and then he and Natwick hurried inside. In the dim, smoky glow of emergency lighting, they found a hundred, maybe two hundred nervous people, plus an injured horse, scared and running loose among the card tables and video games. Some well-intentioned animal lover had brought it inside to escape the fire. When the horse kicked a man sitting at a slot machine, Clayton jumped in front of the animal, waved his arms, and hollered to back it off. Security guards took the opportunity to grab a rope dangling from the horse's halter and throw a T-shirt over its eyes to calm it. Across the room, a man dropped to the floor, and Natwick rushed over to offer first aid. Just then a fire crew burst in the front door, dragging a hose line. They pushed through the crowd to the back of the room to attack flames that had breached the exterior rear wall of the building.

That's all we need, Clayton thought. *If fire burns inside the wall to the attic, the roof will catch, and we'll have a bunch of people trapped inside a burning building and a major fire burning outside, too.*

The air reeked of smoke, and the noise level rose as people edged closer to panic. Any minute now, someone was bound to try bolting through an exit. Clayton knew he had to keep them inside. He climbed up on a chair.

"Let me have your attention," he yelled over the din. "Everybody calm down. I know you're worried, but you'll all be OK. The fire department is here, protecting the building."

He thought of the bodies he'd just seen, the curtains of flames cutting off the roads.

"This building is the safest place to be. Stay right here. If you do, you'll live. If you leave and try to drive out of this fire, your chance of survival will be slim."

Clayton must have been convincing. The crowd stayed put while the flames rolled by outside and the engine crew saved the building. The fire next threatened to trap residents and firefighters in multiple neighborhoods south of the casino. Clayton and O'Leary somehow recruited a few air tankers and helicopters to attack the flame front, and the Paradise Fire veered east, creating a critical window of escape.

It was good of Bill Clayton to tell me his fire story. He didn't want to. He seldom talks about the devastation he's seen over forty years of fighting fire. Why consciously revisit the piles of rubble, the blackened bodies, the stench of death through the smoke? It's bad enough that it all comes back sometimes, unbidden in his dreams.

CHAPTER 16

WEST OF WILDCAT

Bob and I needed water. Our mouths were so dry we could barely talk. Fear can do that to you. Usually, when we reached the four-way stop at the bottom of Wildcat Canyon, we drove straight ahead to access the freeway. This time I turned right toward a convenience store and gas station at Willow Road and California Highway 67. Already an assortment of vehicles—cars, pickups, and a horse trailer or two—crowded the sprawling asphalt lot. People rushed back and forth in the predawn darkness, backlit by the store lights. Others stood in clumps, looking up at the mountaintop that defined the western edge of Wildcat Canyon.

I stayed in the car with Terra and Charter, who came to attention and scanned the scene from their backseat windows, while Bob ran in to buy two bottles of water. Despite the hour, the place was so busy he had to wait in line to pay. On the way back to the car, he took a moment to follow the crowd's gaze and saw the entire ridgeline fringed in flames, red and yellow fingers reaching toward a luminous orange sky. Wildcat Canyon brimmed with fire.

I wish now that I'd gotten out to look, too, but at that moment the car felt safer than the rest of the world, and I wasn't done running. We took a few seconds to gulp down the water, a wet, cold miracle in our mouths. No question, we had to keep moving; the fire was still chasing us. But where do you go when you can't go home? We felt unmoored. We had no relatives in San Diego, so we ticked through a short list of friends we felt comfortable calling in the middle of the night. Jeri Deneen and Jon Powell came to mind first. They lived in the city, not far from our old neighborhood. I punched their number into my cell phone but got only a voice-mail greeting. So I left a quick message Jeri kept for years: "Hi, it's Sandra. There's a huge fire in Wildcat Canyon. We're OK, but the house is probably gone. We thought about crashing with you for a while if you're home. Call me."

We couldn't yet think of another plan, but wherever we went, I knew it had to be west, away from the flames. I steered the Acura to Interstate 8, wide open as far as my headlights could reach, and started toward the ocean. We were safe now, the fire finally far behind us. *Thank you, God!* My thoughts tumbled over one another as I drove.

But the house, our beautiful house. There's no way it could've survived. All those embers, like red rain, flying all around us. So much fire everywhere. And what about our neighbors? Did they make it? There was no time to warn anybody, no time at all. The fire was right there. We didn't see anyone on the road, not a single car. Were we the last ones out? Where was everybody? Where was Peter? I couldn't call anyone else; I didn't have anyone else's number. God, let them be all right. Was there any way the house might have survived? We did have the brush cleared at least. Defensible space. And we had the right roof. Concrete tiles. Sealed soffits. We'd done everything we were supposed to, hadn't we? So maybe. Maybe.

"Sandra, you've got to speed up. You're on the freeway."

Bob's voice interrupted my mental chaos. Switching out of autopilot, I checked the speedometer and noticed also that we needed fuel. By now we'd reached familiar territory, our old neighborhood at the foot of Cowles Mountain. I took the next exit and drove to the closest gas station. While Bob manned the pump and the dogs jostled around the backseat, I found the restroom and took stock of myself in the mirror. Frayed jeans, faded college T-shirt, white gym socks, and black flats. No make-up, unbrushed hair and teeth. What a mess. But who cared? I was alive. Alive! For the first time, I noticed Bob's glasses perched atop my head. Now I remembered; I'd grabbed a pair off the kitchen counter on my way out of the house, thinking they were mine.

"I've got some good news for you," I called to Bob on my way back to the car.

"What's that?"

"I found your glasses."

Sometime during this pit stop, Bob popped the trunk to see how the cockatiel had fared on our way down the mountain. He'd had to turn her cage on its side to make it fit next to the laundry basket, and still it crunched a bit when he slammed the trunk lid. Yet there was Chelsea, hopping around as lively and alert as ever. Except something about her didn't seem right. She looked short and stumpy, like a gray Easter chick. Suddenly I realized why; she'd lost her tail and all her long wing feathers. She must have flapped so hard against the cage that they fell out. Looking closer, we noticed tiny spatters of blood all around. Why? We couldn't tell. All we knew was that Chelsea had suddenly become more important than ever to us, and we didn't want to lose her.

"Let's take care of the bird," I said. "She's probably about all we have left."

We weren't far from a twenty-four-hour emergency vet clinic, where the young staff working the overnight shift took us all in without hesitation—Bob and me, Chelsea in her dented cage, and both Newfoundlands. There's a huge fire, we told them. Houses burning. Until then, they'd had no idea; we were the first evacuees to seek their help. For the next hour or so they wrapped us in concern, bringing coffee in Styrofoam cups for Bob and me, and shiny stainless-steel bowls full of fresh water for Terra and Charter, who slurped it up with enthusiasm and then settled down to nap. As long as we were all together, their world felt snug and complete.

While Bob carried Chelsea back to an exam room to meet with a vet, I waited with the dogs in the darkened lobby, sinking into one of two long, hard, wooden benches that faced each other across the narrow space like chancel pews. Slanted beams of fluorescent light spilled out from behind the reception counter as if in benediction, illuminating a makeshift desk wedged into a front corner. A curtain of plastic sheeting hung across an opening on the opposite side of the room; gaps in the floor tile showed where a wall had stood.

"We're remodeling," the woman behind the desk explained. "Such a disaster. Sorry for the inconvenience."

"It's OK," I must have said, because I distinctly remember feeling grateful for that improbable sanctuary, its subdued light, the cool air flowing in and out of my lungs, the quiet hum of conversation from the back rooms, the solidity of the wooden bench beneath me, the normality of it all.

After a bit, Bob came out with good news: Chelsea was fine. The vet inspected her tiny body for injuries and listened to her breathing to check for smoke inhalation. The blood came only from broken feathers. Thinking it might be difficult in our uncertain circumstances to accommodate a bird, the office staff offered to keep our little friend for a day or two, until we could come back for her, and we gratefully accepted.

As we were leaving, another clinic employee arrived. A young woman with long black hair and wild eyes, she burst through the front door with two more canine evacuees, her own.

"Lakeside's on fire," she announced to her colleagues. "Get ready."

After the Cedar Fire's wild stampede through Muth Valley, Lakeside Division Chief Andy Parr expected it to spill over the western ridgelines of Wildcat Canyon. But he'd hoped it wouldn't jump California Highway 67 into the sprawling Lakeside community of Eucalyptus Hills. If fire did take hold among the eponymous trees that lined the neighborhood's winding, up-and-down roads, it would be nearly impossible to stop. Eucalyptus grow thick and tall, and they're so full of oily sap it tends to ooze out of the bark. You could hardly plant a more flammable tree.

Close to dawn, during a lull in the wind, flames topped the ridge near the dam at the base of San Vicente Reservoir and cascaded out of Wildcat Canyon like a waterfall, spraying walnut-size embers everywhere. Parr watched from his truck near the intersection of Highway 67 and Willow Road, where Bob and I had stopped for water. Within moments, a scattering of smoke columns rose where the embers had landed—lots of small smokes and one bigger one. *A bunch of little field fires,* Parr thought, *and only one house ablaze. Not so bad after all.* He'd braced himself for much worse. He kept working by radio, coordinating the firefight with engine crews he'd positioned in Eucalyptus Hills. Soon their reports turned grim.

"We're losing houses right and left."

"What do you mean?" Parr asked. "How can that be?"

Suddenly he realized what he'd been looking at. Each little plume of smoke signaled a house on fire; the big one was a water-bottling plant just up the highway.

Oh great, Parr thought, *now we're not just losing houses, we're losing jobs, too.*

Worse turned to worst when the wind came back. As if taunting the fire crews, flames skipped over the highway and sprang all the way up to the ridgeline on the other side. Leaping tree to tree, the Cedar Fire spread through Eucalyptus Hills with terrifying speed.

After leaving Chelsea in good hands, we loaded the Newfoundlands back into the Acura and continued west, stopping en route at an all-night grocery store to buy toothbrushes, toothpaste, and dog food, and then moving on to search for a hotel room. We started with a place we'd heard accepted pets, but Bob returned from the front desk without a room key.

"They said they don't take dogs."

"What? I'm pretty sure they do or at least they used to."

"I even explained this wasn't a normal situation," Bob said, "that we'd been driven out of our home by a fire, but they said they didn't have any rooms."

"So now what?"

"We're going downtown." He frowned and fingered a slip of paper with a name and address written on it. "They suggested a sister property they've got there, some place called The Bristol Hotel."

"Oh great, a downtown hotel that takes big dogs? I can hardly wait."

"It's probably going be an adventure," he agreed, "but let's go see."

Despite our fears, The Bristol was no flophouse, but a contemporary boutique establishment in the gentrified central city. It was still dark as we pulled into the front drive, but when we climbed out of the car, the hotel's outside lights revealed how narrowly we'd escaped tragedy in our mad rush through the fire. The front bumper of the Acura had detached on the right side, popped out by our collision with the bank just before we reached Wildcat Canyon Road. Even more ominous, at the back end of the car, brown scorch marks streaked the white paint. Later I learned that firefighters consider scorched paint evidence of a brush with death.

The bellboy who met us at the curb was kind enough not to comment on our luggage, a beat-up laundry basket crammed full of photographs and negatives, which I refused to leave in the car. He loaded it onto his cart as he would an ordinary bag and walked it into the lobby. I followed, feeling conspicuously out of place in my grubby clothes, accompanied by two enormous, shaggy, black dogs, both grinning with excitement. The polite young woman behind the counter never raised an eyebrow as she proceeded to tick through the usual check-in questions— number of beds, smoking or nonsmoking, make and model of car, debit or credit. I responded with the usual answers, until we hit an impasse.

"How long will you be staying with us?" she asked.

"I don't know," I said, and for the first time my voice faltered. "I think our house just burned down."

She stared at me for a wordless moment before turning back to her keyboard. Then she finished typing and pushed the paperwork toward me to sign.

"I've left your departure date open," she said.

As dawn drew near, the rising light gave CDF Battalion Chief Ray Chaney his first glimpse of the devastation in Wildcat Canyon. He'd never seen anything like it, such complete and endless destruction, such a naked world. Wherever he looked, the vegetation was gone; the animals, gone; the buildings, gone. An acrid brown haze hung from sky to ground like a dirty gauze curtain. Red, yellow, and orange remnants of fire licked at the blackened stumps of trees, the only color amid the dull grays of burned vehicles and the white mounds of ashes where houses had stood. Wildcat Canyon looked like a scene from an old black-and-white sci-fi movie—a moonscape, an alien planet, a post-apocalyptic Earth. Shaken, Chaney called his wife and tried to describe it, tried to express the bleakness threatening to swallow him whole, but it was too much to capture in words.

At around 6:30 or 7 a.m., with the sun well up, he got a call from a Lakeside battalion chief.

"Ray, I need your help. I'm in Eucalyptus Hills, and I'm getting the crap kicked out of me. Do you have anything you could send me?"

"I wish, but everything I've got is engaged up here in Wildcat Canyon."

"Well, as soon as you can, send me something or come down and help me."

Chaney rethought his situation. The fire had done its worst in Wildcat Canyon. There was no one left to warn, nothing left to save. Why not go somewhere his team's efforts could be better spent? He got on the radio.

"We're done here," he told his crews. "Everybody regroup at the bottom of Wildcat. We're going over to Eucalyptus Hills."

Watching the wind shoot embers far ahead of the fire front and flames torch trees and houses from one end of Eucalyptus Hills to the other, Andy Parr feared the Cedar Fire would gallop into the adjacent city of Santee. He even imagined fire leaping from there to nearby Rattlesnake Mountain. And if it made it that far, there would be nothing to stop it from rolling downhill, straight through the neighborhoods and business districts of El Cajon, a major municipality with 95,000 residents.[29]

---

[29] 2000 US Census. US Census Bureau.

But Parr and his crews finally caught a break. The Santa Anas let up for a bit, and the fire hesitated, prancing for a while at right angles to the wind, a behavior firefighters call flanking. Meanwhile, the reinforcements Parr had waited on all night finally showed up. Ten engines grabbed the chance to get out ahead of the fire and intercepted its westward advance toward Santee. Andy Parr's worst fears hadn't materialized after all.

After contributing his engine crews to Parr's growing forces in Eucalyptus Hills, Ray Chaney drove north up California Highway 67 to meet Kelly Zombro at an intersection about halfway to Ramona. The chiefs quickly compared notes and penciled out their next phase of operations before heading back to work. It was almost 8 a.m. now, and the fire front had just jumped to the west side of the highway. They could see it running flat out across open chaparral, heading simultaneously north toward Poway, a city of 48,000 surrounded by lavish estates and horse ranches, and south toward Scripps Ranch, an upper-middle-class community within the San Diego city limits, where nearly 30,000 people lived in clusters of master-planned suburban neighborhoods.[30] Chaney shook his head. Somewhere up the line, well beyond his purview as a battalion chief, county emergency operations managers should be sharing information with those city fire departments.

"I hope they know they've got some major fire headed their way," he said.

---

30 City-Data.com

A bit farther toward Ramona, the fire had devoured the ravines and rises immediately west of Wildcat Canyon and now threatened a narrow corridor of some 300 homes stretched along Mussey Grade Road. It's no wonder folks living there love the place so fiercely. It would be hard to find a more picturesque drive anywhere in Southern California. Century-old coast live oaks bend over the two-lane blacktop, joining branches to create a leafy green passage into an almost mythical world far from urban workaday distractions.

Mussey Grade Road is a historic thoroughfare, opened in 1888 to provide access southwest to San Diego from Julian's mining camps and Ramona's farms and ranches. For more than fifty years, until the completion of California Highway 67, it was the only town-and-country route in the area. It must've been quite a sight to see stagecoaches, six-horse freight wagons, and eventually tin lizzies winding through oaks and chaparral to and from the big city. That all came to an end in 1943 with the construction of San Vicente Reservoir, which filled the lowlands at the bottom of Mussey Grade's gentle descent with drinking water for San Diego's growing population.[31] Even today you can see where the old pavement melts away into the water, leaving the community's residents with only one way out of a box canyon filled with lush vegetation, a deceptively lovely invitation to disaster.

Diane Conklin had seen the fire coming hours before it hit. Awakened by the gusting Santa Anas, she looked across the vast expanse of open land to the east of her ridgetop home just off Mussey Grade and saw a line of flames spilling into Muth Valley. From her vantage point, she could see nearly

---

[31] MusseyGradeRoad.org

every house hugging the hills on the far edges of San Vicente Reservoir, including the home of a good friend. Diane ran to the phone and called the woman, but no one answered. Without any other contact numbers for Muth Valley, Diane could only watch helplessly as flames hopscotched through the neighborhood. So she turned her attention to her own neighbors, calling everyone she could reach. By daylight she and her husband had joined a long line of evacuees creeping northward out of Mussey Grade, just ahead of flames blown horizontal in a furious wind. By the time they returned, 129 of the canyon's homes would be leveled.

One of those houses belonged to Art Bale, a retired CDF fire captain, and his longtime companion, Pearl Ellis, herself a former volunteer fire chief. The couple awoke in darkness early Sunday morning to the barking of their two big Bouvier des Flandres dogs. Looking northeast, Bale saw the red radiance of a major wildfire on the move. In the thirty years they'd lived on Mussey Grade, enough time to grow mature trees and bury nine Bouviers, Art and Pearl had seen the glow of numerous fires. And of course they knew the drill. Art got out the hoses and wet everything down. Pearl filled her car with artwork and other irreplaceable possessions, loaded the dogs, and left. Art stayed behind, protecting their home with a garden hose until around 11 in the morning, when the water ran out and he saw flames surging along the closest ridgeline. He knew then it was time to leave. He knew also what he'd be coming back to—a black, barren hilltop, stripped of everything familiar except the rows of rocks marking the graves of his departed pets.

CHAPTER 17

AIR ATTACK

CDF Captain Ron Serabia, AIR tactical group supervisor at the Ramona Air Attack Base, had gone to bed Saturday night certain the tiny column of smoke he'd reported that afternoon would grow into a real problem overnight. How big a problem depended on the wind. Around 2 or 3 a.m., Serabia woke to the sound of wild gusts ripping through the big sycamore next to his house. He stepped outside to assess the weather, and his heart jumped. All the way across the horizon to the south, a line of flames split the darkness.

That's eighteen, twenty miles already, he thought, *and it's not even daylight.*

It would be pointless to go into work now. Morning start-up times for the CDF's firefighting aircraft were just as rigidly prescribed as evening cutoffs. Serabia and his air attack fleet couldn't arrive at the fire any earlier than thirty minutes before sunrise. Today that meant they couldn't fly until 6 a.m. He went back to bed and tried to cram in another hour or two of sleep. He knew he'd need it later. But his mind wouldn't cooperate, and he finally gave up. A little after four, as Serabia pulled into the Ramona Air Attack Base, he noticed the security lights glinting off something out on the tarmac. He looked closer and saw the silver tail fins of two twin-propeller Grumman S-2Ts, the air tankers he so desperately needed. Serabia felt a surge of hope, the first good feeling he'd had since sighting that thin column of smoke near Cedar Creek.

Thank you, Lord, he thought.

With so many other fires burning throughout Southern California, Serabia wanted to be sure he could keep the pair of tankers at Ramona. He called the Monte Vista Interagency Command Center for an update. The same chief who'd taken Serabia's initial report of the fire again answered the phone. Immediately, he referenced Serabia's bold prediction that the fire could reach 20,000 acres overnight.

"You underestimated," he said, and both men forced a laugh.

"So where's it at now?" Serabia asked.

"Well, it hit Barona sometime after midnight. Then Wildcat Canyon. Muth Valley. Everything's burned from there to Cedar Creek. Plenty of houses. And we've got confirmed casualties in the Wildcat Canyon area."

"Oh man." Serabia felt his gut tighten. "Was my order placed last night for ten air tankers and five helicopters?"

"Yeah, it was. But I don't know that you're going to get them. We've got another fire at Valley Center. Started around 1:30. The Paradise Fire."

"Great. How big is it?"

"Twenty-thousand acres," the chief said. "Structures gone, we don't know how many; possible fatalities."

"Well, I've got two tankers sitting here."

"Yeah, they came back from San Bernardino yesterday," the chief said. "They had a restriction on the use of aircraft up there because of the winds, but a no-divert because they were losing houses, so they're still assigned to San Bernardino."

"Are they going back to San Bernardino?"

"I don't know."

"Well, I need them. If all you can give me is two, then give me these two. If there's something we can do, we're going to try to do it."

"OK," the chief agreed. "I'll see what I can figure out."

There was no guarantee. Under the rules of mutual aid, units committed to a fire outside their own districts can't leave until the incident commander releases them, despite emergencies on their home turf. But Serabia lucked out. The two tankers based in Ramona remained at his disposal.

By 5 a.m., the air base came alive with the personnel Serabia's colleague, Shari Lee, had lined up the night before, including the retardant contractor and his team, the pit crew of aerial firefighting. When an air attack really gets rolling, a good retardant crew can pump 1,200 gallons of the red stuff into an S-2T and send it off within six minutes. Over the next three days, a dozen air tankers would fly out of Ramona, making 560 flights in all, 215 that first day alone. Until then, Ramona had launched only 169 flights the entire year.

Each takeoff would depend on the wind. Too much wind speed makes it too dangerous to fly. Sitting at his desk, consulting maps, making calls, and pulling together all the information he could ferret out, Serabia worried about the winds still screaming outside, well above the thirty-five-mile-per-hour threshold for grounding an air attack. Yet the radio sputtered out a litany of requests for help from ground crews stretched as thin as onionskin. "If we can get a copter drop in here at daylight . . . if we can get an air tanker . . ." Meanwhile, to the north, the lightening sky revealed huge clouds of smoke boiling up over Valley Center.

We've got to try, Serabia thought over and over. *We've got to try something.*

Ultimately, it was up to the pilots. Three came in that morning: tanker pilots Billy Hoskins, a thirty-year veteran, and Lynn McGrew, one of the first women to fly commercial airliners and the CDF's first female tanker pilot; and David Gregg, who manned the OV-10A Bronco lead plane. A turboprop designed and used for light attack and observation during the Vietnam War, the OV-10 served as Serabia's aerial reconnaissance and command center. By the time all three pilots arrived, Serabia had gathered as much data as possible to inform their decisions: the weather forecast, a map showing power lines and other aerial hazards, the radio frequencies they'd be using, their contacts on the ground, resource deployment, and the fire's recent progress. Another piece of news: Winds were still too high to fly in San Bernardino; all aircraft there remained grounded. No chance anybody would be cut loose and redeployed to San Diego now.

Man, Serabia thought, *we're really on our own.*

Hoskins arrived first, bringing his breakfast with him. Gregg and McGrew came in soon after. They gathered around tables in the briefing room, a tiled utilitarian space that doubled as a kitchen and dining hall.

"OK," Serabia began. "We got one helicopter, two air tankers, and the OV-10. I have eight more air tankers and four more helicopters on order, but we can't count on them. So here are our options. We can sit here today at the base and say it's not safe, we're not going to go, because the wind gusts exceed thirty-five miles an hour on the ground.

"But here's what we're looking at. We've got fire south of Ramona; we've got a fire north of Ramona. People have already been killed, and homes have already burned. The chances of those two fires meeting and taking everything—your house, my house, everybody's houses, whole communities—are great.

"I'm a firefighter; I want to do something," Serabia continued. "But you're the pilots. You guys have to fly the airplanes under these conditions. It's going to be dangerous. We're going to have downdrafts; we're going to have updrafts. But if we can save a handful of homes, will it be worth the effort?"

"Yeah," Gregg answered. "We're going."

"I'm in," Hoskins said.

Serabia turned to McGrew.

"Lynn, we're pushing the envelope. We're on the edge. I need your opinion as a pilot. Are you in? Do you want to go or not?"

McGrew didn't hesitate.

"We're going as a team," she said.

From there, things moved into high gear. Serabia punched up the usual safety briefing, and at 5:30 a.m. the pilots moved out to the tarmac to preflight the planes. Serabia went with Gregg. They'd worked together for a year and gotten to know each other pretty well, well enough for Serabia to make a suggestion.

"Dave, before we get in this airplane, we need to pray."

Standing together by the plane, the men dropped their heads.

"Heavenly Father," Serabia prayed. "Whatever happens today, your will be done. Whether we're successful or not, at least we're going to try. Be with us and guide us. Watch over us, protect us and everyone on the ground. In Jesus's name, amen."

"Amen," Gregg added.

Serabia felt a little lighter after that. Both men climbed into the plane and buckled in. Gregg locked down the cockpit, started the engine, and taxied to the runway.

Later, angry citizens and media reports would claim no aircraft flew against the Cedar Fire that Sunday morning, October 26, 2003. But a camera installed at the Ramona Air Attack Base as part of a university research project documented Gregg and Serabia's takeoff into uncertainty at 6 a.m., with Hoskins and McGrew following close behind in the tankers.

From the air, Serabia and Gregg took a quick look around to see what they were up against. Neither could quite believe what he saw. The fire stretched out beneath them in all directions, a vast charcoal canvas, dabbed everywhere with red embers and framed to the west by a ragged line of orange flames. Even with all their years of experience, both men lapsed into shock at the extent of land burned since Serabia's call to Monte Vista barely twelve hours before. Serabia estimated the footprint of the fire at 100,000 acres, easily five times his original prediction. He'd never heard of such a rapid rate of spread.

They started by flying east toward the fire's point of origin, the spot firefighters call "the backdoor." Typically, firefighters take a stand here, establish an "anchor point" they can hold and work from. Serabia knew if his tankers didn't deal with this trailing edge of the fire now, there'd be hell to pay as soon as the Santa Anas died away. The usual onshore winds would blow back from the Pacific and shoot the fire into unburned territory to the east. But he couldn't justify looking that far ahead, not with houses burning and lives in jeopardy along the fire front. Plus, he needed to scout out the rest of the perimeter. So Gregg turned the OV-10 around and flew back over Ramona along the fire's northern flank. Looking west, Serabia could see smoke pluming all the way to the coast and far out over the ocean, testimony to the wind's relentless drive. Scanning south, he saw that fire had reached San Vicente Reservoir and even the island at its center.

"Dave, would you look at that," Serabia said over his helmet radio. "The island in the lake is on fire; most of it's burned already. That's some wind to blow embers over all that water."

Beyond the reservoir, Serabia saw fire skipping through the Lakeside community of Eucalyptus Hills. Equally alarming, wind-blown embers had started a spot fire on the next ridge to the west, near a massive gravel pit. From there it was a straight shot to San Diego's city limits, across undeveloped parkland heavy with old chaparral.

The way the wind is pushing this thing, Serabia thought, *it's likely to burn all the way to the ocean.* In his mind he could see the progression. Sycamore Canyon. Scripps Ranch. Miramar. Mount Soledad. La Jolla. Thousands upon thousands of homes and businesses along the way. He got on the radio and tried to raise a San Diego city dispatcher, but no one answered. He tried multiple county frequencies—County Red, County White, County Green—plus half a dozen mutual aid frequencies. Still nothing. CDF and Cleveland National Forest dispatchers were busy, too. Over and over he called. At times he could hear conversations, but he couldn't get anyone on any channel to answer him. Every frequency was overloaded. He'd just have to hope that somebody else had gotten through. In the meantime, Serabia had a big decision to make, and it was all his. What good could two air tankers do against a world of fire?

He ticked through his options methodically. He had to think in terms of triage. *Who needs the most help right now? Who's in danger right now of losing their lives or their homes? Where can I be most effective? Where can I fight the fire and make it stick?* Attacking the westward head of the fire in Eucalyptus Hills or above the gravel pit would put his tanker pilots in too much danger. Heavy smoke and poor visibility would make it tough to gauge a drop, to come in low enough to do any good while maintaining the ability to pull out safely. Not to mention avoiding electric wires, cell towers, and other aircraft.

Ultimately, Serabia chose targets fairly close to the Ramona air base, minimizing the turnaround time to reload the tankers with retardant and rush back to the fire. In particular, he'd noticed fire on a hill above the equestrian center in San Diego Country Estates. From that point, flames could easily spread into the heart of the community. He'd also noticed the vegetation there looked younger and not as dense, offering the fire less fuel than most of the surrounding chaparral. Even without troops on the ground to finish off the flames, Serabia figured he had a decent chance to stop this finger of fire from edging down to the streets below. If he got really lucky, maybe he could hold the fire's opposite edge in check too, keep it from spreading north, at least until more resources arrived.

As Gregg again turned the OV-10 back toward Ramona, Serabia briefed the tanker pilots on their targets. Once in position over the equestrian center, Gregg circled high above the two heavier planes, giving Serabia a wide-angle view of the whole operation. Hoskins went in first in Tanker No. 70, his plane jumping around a bit in the gusts, and laid a nice line of retardant. McGrew positioned No. 71 to tie into Hoskins's drop, but it was still so early, the sun still so low in the sky and the shadows so heavy, that she couldn't see it despite the chemical's distinctive red color, intended to make it more visible.

Gregg made a suggestion. "Let's go down and check the target," he said, "locate Billy's drop, and Lynn can just follow us in and make her drop."

Serabia agreed. "Billy," he called over the radio, "how bad was it?"

"Not bad headed right into the wind."

Sounds optimistic, Serabia thought. He'd watched the retardant when Hoskins dropped it, streaming straight back out of the plane like a windsock in a storm. Still, he was game.

"Let's go, Dave," he said, and Gregg started down.

The closer to the ground, the greater the turbulence. By the time they reached the drop zone, the ride got jaw-jarringly rough. Serabia tightened his shoulder harness and seatbelt.

"Are you all right, Dave?" he shouted across their radio connection.

"Yeah, I'm fine," Gregg answered. "A little bumpy, huh?"

"Like driving a car fifty miles an hour over a plowed field."

Behind them, McGrew brought her big tanker in and laid a second line of retardant. On the turnaround Serabia took a critical look at their handiwork and saw to his relief that the red stuff was holding.

For the next half-hour, the air tankers traded off dumping fresh loads of retardant until the blaze settled down to a smolder. But even concentrating their combined efforts on that one spot, they couldn't completely kill the fire. As Serabia watched, a gust of wind blasted embers into a big pile of mulch and manure behind the equestrian center. By this time, he could see engines stationed nearby. He tried to raise them on the radio but couldn't access their frequency. Before the engine crews noticed the fire and finished it off, flames had spread to a barn and consumed several RVs parked in a storage lot next door.

Long before that, Serabia realized he had to shelve his frustration and move on. A CDF helicopter pilot had now joined the air attack. Serabia directed him to a couple of ponds within the Country Estates golf course and watched him save six or eight evacuated homes by dropping water on fires in adjacent woodpiles or landscaping. Yet all around them, Serabia could see that dozens of houses had burned overnight, many belonging to people he knew. They'd want to know why no firefighters showed up to save their homes. What was he going to tell them? How could he ever explain the enormity and speed of this fire?

CHAPTER 18

SAN DIEGO CITY LIMITS

TAKING PHONE CALLS AT ALL hours had become routine for Geoff Patnoe, part of his job as chief of staff to San Diego County Supervisor Dianne Jacob. At 5:30 a.m. on Sunday, Geoff rolled out of bed to talk with the San Diego County Office of Emergency Services (OES), calling to report a wildfire near Ramona. Fires in the backcountry were pretty routine, too, especially in Dianne Jacob's second supervisorial district. By far the largest of the county's five jurisdictions at 2,000 square miles, East County encompasses six cities, but most people think of it as San Diego's backyard, where town centers, subdivisions, and office parks give way to sparsely populated canyons and foothills, green mountains, and, beyond them, endless desert. As supervisor since 1992, Dianne Jacob was the region's only elected representative at the county level, a responsibility she relished. After only six months on the job, Geoff Patnoe already knew his boss would want to be informed about fires. In fact, she would probably want to be at the command center, to facilitate whatever help the county could offer. He did his best to shake the sleep out of his head and gave her a call.

There wasn't a lot to report. A wildfire threatening thirty or forty houses in Ramona. Evacuations underway. That's all the county's top emergency officers knew. It was old news, of course. More than six hours old. No one yet knew the real extent of the situation: that twelve people had been killed; 100,000 acres burned; hundreds of homes destroyed; and that a forty-five-mile line of fire was galloping unchecked across the heart of San Diego County faster than fire engines could drive. But the outdated OES report was enough for Dianne Jacob.

"OK," she said. "Come get me."

The sky had begun to lighten now, enough that Geoff could see ashes blasting past the windows in a stiff wind, ashes even dusting the ground. When his wife, Christy, woke up and took their Corgi outside, she could see their footprints. Geoff couldn't imagine that ashes from a fire in Ramona, almost an hour's drive from their townhouse in the city, could travel all that way. But then he'd never seen the sky snowing ashes. It made him uneasy enough to gather a few valuables by the front door—books, papers, a photo of him as a Congressional page shaking hands with President Richard Nixon.

"If you have to leave for any reason," he told Christy, "there's a couple of little things right here to take with you."

Driving home from a charity function a little before midnight on Saturday, San Diego Fire-Rescue Chief Jeff Bowman heard a late-night radio news report about a small vegetation fire way out toward the Cuyamaca Mountains. He made a mental note of it, despite its considerable distance from the city limits where his jurisdiction began.

Around 5:00 a.m. Sunday, long after his department had dispatched two battalion chiefs and four engines to help protect the San Diego Country Estates,[32] Bowman got a call from one of his staff, reporting that the fire had spread to Ramona.

"Where's Ramona?" Bowman asked.

He was a relative newcomer to San Diego, eighteen months into the job, which he'd taken shortly after retiring as chief of the Anaheim Fire Department near Los Angeles. Jeff Bowman would be the first to tell you he had no idea what he was getting into coming to "America's Finest City." San Diego's municipal fire department was in dire straits—drastically underfunded, underequipped, and understaffed. All this in a region threatened by the most extreme fire risk Bowman had seen in three decades of firefighting. Once he had the full picture, he tried to sound the alarm, but no one wanted to listen. San Diego was in the midst of an unprecedented financial crisis, overextended and grossly in debt. When he submitted his first budget request, Bowman told me, he was ordered not to voice concerns about his department's shortcomings to the city council. The new chief was flabbergasted.

"All right, I'll do this much," he said. "I won't say anything. But if anyone asks me a direct question about it, I'm not going to lie."

The seeds of Bowman's frustration didn't sprout overnight. In Pulitzer-winning breaking-news coverage of San Diego County's catastrophic 2003 fire siege, the *Los Angeles Times* pointed to a history of "drastic underfunding and poor organization of firefighting efforts" as an ominous backdrop to the Cedar Fire.[33] Over the preceding quarter-century, a period

---

[32] City of San Diego Fire-Rescue Department. *Cedar Fire 2003 After-Action Report.* June 2004, 2.

[33] Tony Perry, Stuart Pfeifer, and Jennifer Oldham, "San Diego Was in No Shape for This Fight," *Los Angeles Times*, October 31, 2003.

when the population of San Diego County nearly doubled,[34] a succession of San Diego municipal fire chiefs and fire marshals had warned of acute fire danger, especially in communities bordered by wildland chaparral, such as Tierrasanta and Scripps Ranch. At least one chief had resigned when his pleas went unheeded.[35] And yet, the *Times* reported, during this same period, voters had defeated thirty-two of fifty ballot measures intended to increase funds for fire protection. Even after San Diego's great trial by fire, voters remained stalwart in their opposition to new taxes. In a March 2004 election, with thousands of fire survivors yet to rebuild, four of seven fire-protection initiatives failed at the ballot box.[36]

Fewer dollars in the budget meant fewer firefighters, about 35 percent fewer per thousand residents than the nationwide average for big-city fire departments. Equipment suffered, too. As he settled into his new job in San Diego, Bowman had been appalled to discover his engine fleet included vehicles that failed to comply with the very regulations he'd helped instate as a leader of the National Fire Protection Association. As for firefighting aircraft, the *Times* noted the Los Angeles Fire Department owned six helicopters; San Diego, zero. Nor could San Diego depend on a centralized county fire agency, as did California's six other largest counties, because there was none. Faced with such a stark situation and no hope of support from the city council, Bowman took his concerns to San Diego Mayor Dick Murphy, pulling no punches about the dangers he foresaw.

"This county is primed to burn," Bowman told the mayor. "It could all go, from the desert right down to the beaches."

---

[34] US Census Bureau

[35] Tony Perry and Joel Rubin, "San Diego Fire Warnings Were Repeatedly Ignored," *Los Angeles Times*, November 15, 2003.

[36] Tony Perry, "4 Fire Protection Measures Rejected," *Los Angeles Times*, March 4, 2004.

In mid-2003, the *Los Angeles Times* noted, a county fire protection task force released a study that backed up the chief's warning. "Almost half the vegetation in San Diego County's wildland is over fifty years old," the report stated. "Another 30 percent is over twenty years old. This means that 80 percent of wildland areas in San Diego will burn explosively under typical periods of high fire danger."

On Sunday morning, October 26, 2003, when Bowman learned the wildfire in the Cleveland National Forest had spread to Ramona, he asked the staffer who'd called him a crucial question: "Is it threatening the city?"

"No, doesn't seem to be."

"If it even looks like it's coming near the city, let me know," Bowman said. "Do you understand?"

"Yes, sir."

With that the chief went back to sleep.

Dianne Jacob knew firsthand how devastating wildfires could be. A San Diego native, she'd seen plenty of them, including the historic 1970 Laguna blaze. She'd never forgotten how quickly it moved across East County, covering thirty miles in twenty-four hours. Eight people died; 400 homes went down; 175,000 acres burned. And it happened in the district Dianne Jacob now represented.

Yet only a few years after the Laguna Fire, San Diego's supervisors started talking about canceling the county's contract with the California Department of Forestry and Fire Protection (CDF)—the arrangement that paid the state's fire agency to serve also as the county's official fire department. The idea worried Dianne Jacob, then a schoolteacher living in the rural East County community of Jamul. She even attended a supervisors' meeting to voice her opposition to the proposal.

But the board didn't budge. Citing the need to cut costs, the supervisors voted to end the CDF contract and get out of the firefighting business. As the state's official firefighting agency, the CDF units in the San Diego region would remain responsible for local protection, but without any particular obligation or additional staff. If called to incidents elsewhere in the state, San Diego-based CDF crews would answer as needed.

The supervisors' decision left fire-prone San Diego County without the protection of a centralized firefighting force. Individual communities, many scattered across the most remote—and flammable—reaches of the county, had to provide their own fire protection.

After her election to the board of supervisors, Dianne Jacob continued to voice concern about the county's extreme fire danger, so heavily concentrated in her own district. More often than not, fire protection improvements lost out to competing budget priorities. Still, she told me proudly about a number of positive steps taken over the years. By far the biggest was an $84 million investment in the mid-1990s that funded a countywide 800-megahertz communication system, intended to enable emergency responders from various jurisdictions to communicate with one another. At about that same time, the county convened an emergency services task force, which Supervisor Jacob chaired, and the Board approved $400,000 annually to purchase fire trucks and other essential equipment for agencies in unincorporated areas. What Dianne Jacob really wanted to see was consolidation of the county's fragmented fire protection network. But even beyond the funding issue, it was a tough sell convincing individual fire jurisdictions to give up their autonomy. Still, she tried to keep attention focused on fire protection.

Like any politician, Dianne Jacob had her supporters and her detractors. After the Cedar Fire, people would say she hadn't done enough. I was among them. Why was the county so unprepared for a catastrophic fire? When I checked her record, though, I realized Supervisor Jacob had tried. Tried to boost fire protection budgets, unite fragmented departments, and sound the alarm among her tax-averse constituents. Ironically, the September 2003 issue of her newsletter—the last issue before the Cedar Fire—featured a front-page story urging East County residents to prepare their properties for fire season.

Early Sunday morning, as Bob and I and the Newfoundlands settled into our room at The Bristol Hotel downtown, daylight found its way back to San Diego. But it would be no ordinary day in "America's Finest City," not a good day for the beach or the zoo or SeaWorld. Outside our third-floor window, palm trees and skyscrapers stood shrouded in a muddy haze. The sun, when it rose into view, looked sick and shrunken, not golden as the tourists expect, but red as blood.

Our first task was calling our families. We wanted to talk with them before they saw or heard the news. But what I had to say would change their worlds, and just the thought of that made me feel sick. Neither of our daughters answered, so I left messages, doing my best to swallow the stress in my voice and sound reassuring: "Hi baby, it's me. Just wanted to let you know we're OK. There's a big fire down here, though, and, uh, we probably lost the house. But we're fine. Call when you can. We love you very much."

The incoming calls began around 6:20 a.m., the first from Nancy Wolf, our hostess in the land shark costume at the Halloween party the night before. Had it really been only eight hours since we'd left our silly company of dog lovers?

"Come stay with us," Nancy said. She'd smelled the smoke, seen the brown sky to the east, and figured we were in trouble. But I knew the Wolfs and their big Newfy boy, Onslow, lived in a one-bedroom condo in Tierrasanta.

"Oh, Nancy, thank you so much, but you don't have room for all of us."

"We'll make room. Just come."

"No really, we're fine where we are for now."

I told her about The Bristol, how welcoming they'd been to the dogs, and she finally relented. Nancy's invitation was the first of probably twenty such offers that day. Friends, coworkers, even the most casual of acquaintances wanted to help us, begged us to come stay with them, offered to take the dogs. Thank you, we told them all, thank you so much, but we're OK. Yes, the dogs would appreciate some outside space soon, but for now we all needed to be together. Just looking at Terra and Charter kept me from focusing on what the fire might have taken from us. We'd escaped with everything that truly mattered.

Driving to work around 7:30 a.m. on Sunday under skies dark with smoke and ash, San Diego Fire Captain Billy Davis feared the worst. He was right. By 8:30 a.m., he and his crew were laying hose lines in Scripps Ranch, an affluent community at the eastern edge of San Diego's city limits, where street after street of expensive homes lay in the path of the firestorm. Already houses were burning. Dispatched barely ahead of the flames, Davis could do little but wait for the fire front to blow through and then try to mop up. Only an hour earlier, he figured, he could have laid backfires to eliminate fuel ahead of the fire, which might have protected whole sections of Scripps.

Still, Davis and his men were able to save a few homes, and they were starting on another one when headquarters ordered them out of the area. Before he left, Davis gathered photos from the doomed house and left them wrapped in a jacket on a corner of the lawn for the owners to find when they returned. After that, Billy Davis was done with dispatchers.

For the next twelve hours, he made his own decisions, did what he knew he could and should do, pushing himself and his men beyond the point of exhaustion to do it. No one ever showed up to relieve them.

Maybe it was poor situational awareness—nobody could see the big picture. Or maybe it was San Diego's serious shortage of vehicles and equipment. After the Cedar Fire, Davis was frustrated to learn that scores, perhaps hundreds, of city and volunteer firefighters, responding to the city's attempt to recall off-duty personnel via media announcements, sat idle at a staging area Sunday for lack of trucks and engines.[37]

As Billy Davis was driving to Scripps Ranch, Geoff Patnoe and Dianne Jacob left her home near El Cajon, his trunk filled with bottled water for any firefighters they might come across. Driving into a brown murk, it was hard even to find the sun. They headed first to the Lakeside Rodeo grounds, site of an impromptu staging area. On the way, the supervisor started making phone calls—first to the Office of Emergency Services for an update, next to the county's top administrative officer. With more accurate reports now available, detailing the devastation and continuing threat to other communities, Dianne Jacob asked him to declare a countywide state of emergency, the first step required to request state and federal declarations.

The rodeo grounds overflowed with emergency vehicles, trucks, and horse trailers. Geoff Patnoe remembers lots of people, lots of horses, lots of smoke. He and the supervisor spent an hour or so gathering information and trying to calm worried evacuees before moving on to the Cedar Fire command center in Ramona. A CHP escort, Public Information Officer Brian

---

[37] The City of San Diego Fire Rescue. *Cedar Fire 2003 After-Action Report.* 2004, 26-27.

Pennings, led them north on California Highway 67, past police barricades and into a smoldering wilderness. At one point they had to stop while Pennings checked a wire that had fallen across the road, making sure it was dead. Still, Geoff held his breath as they drove over it. He tried to absorb the surreal scenes flashing by in the haze outside the car windows. The orange flickering of still-burning trees and houses. Charred remnants of guardrail posts. A glowing junkyard pile of old cars.

"Look at all these code violations being resolved," he commented. Gallows humor, falling short.

Ramona seemed an oasis, the main part of town still untouched, blue sky overhead. All they could see behind them was smoke, and in front, to the north, more smoke— huge, boiling clouds rising from the Paradise Fire in Valley Center, filling the sky. At the command center, Dianne Jacob conferred with the fire chiefs and continued to make phone calls, coordinating with the American Red Cross, and contacting other government officials. She left a voicemail for Congressman Duncan Hunter Sr., who didn't answer the phone at his home in Peutz Valley, near Alpine. Later she learned he was in Washington, trying to find a way around antiquated laws to marshal military firefighting resources for San Diego, even as his own house burned to the ground.[38]

Later that day, at the request of San Diego Mayor Dick Murphy, California Governor Gray Davis declared a state of emergency in Southern California. On Monday, President George W. Bush followed suit, an action that authorized the Federal Emergency Management Agency (FEMA) to assist those affected by the fires. Murphy worked with FEMA Director Michael Brown—who would later draw criticism for

---

[38] In 2003, a number of inconsistencies between military and firefighting air assets, including training and communication, also prevented firefighters from accepting offers of military assistance. Since then, those issues have been resolved; specifically trained military pilots can assist in fire agency air attacks.

his perceived mishandling of the Hurricane Katrina disaster—
to accelerate the setup of a help center in Scripps Ranch. Later
in the week, President Bush capped the parade of dignitaries
who visited San Diego to confer with leaders, thank the
firefighters, and tour devastated neighborhoods.

In the meantime, the Ramona command center on that
early Sunday morning, October 26, reminded Geoff Patnoe
of a Hollywood war-room scene. Uniformed officers, maps
tacked to the wall, urgent phone calls, and two words written
on a chalkboard: resources, communication. No one had
nearly enough of either. Unbridled lines of fire still threatened
thousands of homes and businesses across San Diego County,
but with most of the state's firefighting resources already
concentrated between Los Angeles and San Bernardino, the
closest remaining reinforcements would have to come from
Northern California, a good day's drive away. Meanwhile, not
even the top fire officials in San Diego County had anywhere
close to a bird's-eye view of the situation, just bits and pieces
of information, and all of it changing as quickly as it came in.

"We had no idea," Geoff told me later. "We were with the
fire guys, but we had no idea anybody had died or how many
homes were lost."

For a while, continuing new reports of fire in nearly every
part of the county led these veteran chiefs to think a rash of
new blazes had kicked up. Even given their combined decades
of experience and knowledge of fire history, not one could
imagine Sergio Martinez's tiny signal fire had spread so far
so fast. Voices volleyed back and forth, trying to pin down
locations. Where were the flames now? Where were they
headed? Did they have any crews that could be redirected to
intercept them? Already dealing with the unthinkable, the
top chiefs now had to accept the fact that things could get
even worse. Geoff Patnoe and Dianne Jacob listened as the
fire officers laid out the grim possibilities. The Cedar and
Paradise Fires could merge, destroying everything in between.

The continuing Santa Anas could push the Cedar Fire down California Highway 52, a wide-open east-west corridor thick with chaparral and ridgetop city neighborhoods, including Tierrasanta, where Geoff and his wife lived.

Shit, we can see 52 from the house, he thought.

"All the way to the ocean if this wind doesn't stop," someone said next. The 52 corridor led straight into the famed seaside village of La Jolla, long revered as "the jewel" of San Diego. The specter of losing La Jolla to wildfire seemed inconceivable, and yet, somehow, it had suddenly become possible. Everything depended on the wind.

Joe and Susan Lee and their young family lived on an idyllic suburban street in Scripps Ranch, directly across from the neighborhood tennis courts and about a block away from the edge of the development, where backyards meet open canyons. Waking up around 8 a.m. on Sunday morning, the Lees thought it looked a little foggy out. Then they turned on the news and heard about a fire in East County. That explains it, they thought. We're seeing the smoke from that. Looking again, they noticed a red glimmer behind the smoke to the east, but they assumed it was simply the morning sun. Less than fifteen minutes later, a neighbor phoned with alarming news. Her husband had just called from the canyon at the end of the street, where he could see flames headed their way. This doesn't look good, the woman said. We've got to evacuate.

Evacuate? Joe Lee had a hard time taking his neighbor's suggestion seriously. How bad could it be? They'd seen smoke from wildfires before. Just a few weeks ago, in fact, a spot fire started in the canyon, but firefighters jumped on it right away, and it hadn't amounted to anything. Still, they decided to play it safe. Taking only a safe box of important papers, Joe and

Susan, their two daughters, ages eight and ten, and the family dog headed for the garage. On the way out, Joe picked up their movie video rentals, so he'd be able to return them on time even if police closed the neighborhood for a while. Outside, however, the urgency of their circumstances became clear. The entire neighborhood seemed in motion. Everyone was packing cars, driving out. The smoke had gotten thick now. And just as they pulled away, the Lees saw fire cresting the ridge at the end of their street, burning down into their neighborhood.

No one called San Diego Fire Chief Jeff Bowman with an update on the fire in Ramona, allowing him to enjoy a leisurely Sunday morning. It was around eight when he got up, threw open the window coverings to let the sun in, and discovered a brown sky full of ashes flying on a wild Santa Ana wind. In a heartbeat, he realized his worst fears had come to life. Within hours, Bowman was briefing Mayor Dick Murphy, California Governor Gray Davis, and Governor-elect Arnold Schwarzenegger. Shortly after that he escorted Murphy on a helicopter tour of the unfolding disaster, flying above a fire front fifty miles long.

"This is just what you told me could happen," Murphy said.

"Yes, sir," Bowman said." This is it."

Tierrasanta is a pleasant master-planned community of 30,000 situated just inside the eastern edge of San Diego's city limits.[39] Surrounded by undeveloped public land, it's known as "the

---

[39] City-Data.com

island in the foothills." Only three roads lead in and out of the area, giving it a cozy, small-town feel. Geoff and Christy Patnoe liked that. And they loved their townhouse, an upstairs end unit, perched on the edge of a canyon with a broad view to the north. They'd bought it just a little over a year before, their first home together as newlyweds.

All morning, Geoff checked in with Christy by phone whenever he had a minute. So he knew she was OK and watching the fire news on television. Around 10:30 or 11:00 a.m., she buzzed him to say she could see flames in the distance. A few minutes later, she called again to tell him she was leaving; police were evacuating the neighborhood.

Dianne Jacob and Geoff Patnoe didn't leave Ramona until Sunday night. The supervisor rode with an out-of-town fire captain who'd volunteered to escort them back through the burned area. Geoff followed in his own car, white-knuckling it all the way. Around him the darkness glowed red and orange, marking whatever was left of trees, houses, and vehicles. After seeing Supervisor Jacob home safely, the captain asked for directions to his next stop, the Office of Emergency Services.

"It's complicated," Geoff told him. "I'll just take you there."

Besides, Tierrasanta was on the way, giving him an opportunity to check on his townhouse. By the time they'd negotiated the check points, driven the eerie, empty freeway, and pulled into Geoff and Christy's complex, it was close to midnight. To Geoff's huge relief, everything seemed fine. But then he caught sight of a fire hose lying on the ground. Around the next corner, the air got smoky.

Shit, he thought.

Except for a couple of garage doors standing open, though, his building looked OK. Geoff got out for a closer look and started up the stairs to his front door. Then he realized: Where he should have been seeing walls and a roofline, there was only a starless sky. The rest of the building was gone. The fire captain helped him salvage a few boxes from the garage. Boxes full of mementos. His high school diploma. A few favorite pictures. Christy's wedding dress. Oh god, how was he going to tell her this was all they had left? She and the Corgi had taken refuge in Dianne Jacob's downtown office, camping out for the night with a few blankets and pillows. He remembers walking in, saying hello, trying to gather his thoughts.

"Do you think the house is OK?" she asked.

"No."

"What do you mean?"

"I saw it."

She took a long moment, trying to find the words to express it all. In the end, she could come up with only three.

"My new couch," she said.

As bad as things looked when they left Scripps Ranch Sunday morning, with flames skipping in from the canyon at the end of the street, Joe and Susan Lee never thought they'd lose their house. They weren't immediately next to open land after all. If they'd had any idea, they might have grabbed the big box of photos and videos of their girls, the irreplaceable original Chinese paintings Susan's father had given them, their wedding photos, and probably Susan's wedding dress, too.

Traffic choked Pomerado Road, the only thoroughfare leading in and out of Scripps Ranch. Yet everyone who evacuated reached the freeway safely. It would be Tuesday before they were allowed to return home. Family groups, clusters of neighbors, couples holding hands, friends supporting one another—they all walked in from Pomerado Road together. Scripps Ranch returned en masse through the lingering smoky haze, an army of stoic survivors, uniformed in borrowed clothes, red bandanas, and surgical masks.

The Lees already had been told that their house was gone. The news came in a phone call from a community leader who'd been allowed to assess the damage. Nearly 350 families, plus fifty-four more in neighboring Poway, received similar calls. So Joe and Susan Lee knew. Still, it was too much to believe. Surely someone must have mistaken another house for theirs. And then, walking home with their neighbors, they turned onto their street and saw it. A mound of ashes sandwiched between the still-standing homes of both next-door neighbors.

"When we got back, and we saw the rubble, that was a surprise to us," Joe told me. "To the very last minute, it was a surprise to us."

As they came closer, Joe and Susan noticed a jacket lying on the ground in a corner of their front yard, still lush with green grass. *Someone must have dropped it when everyone was leaving,* Joe thought. But it was folded. In the next moment, the Lees recognized it as one of their daughters' jackets. When Joe picked it up, they discovered it was wrapped around several of their framed family photos. Someone, somehow, in the midst of the fire, had done this for them. Someone had saved these precious remnants, made sure the Lees would have something to come home to after all. And in this second surprise, they found the strength to accept the first.

CHAPTER 19

HOMELESS

Downtown at The Bristol Hotel, Bob and I rested for a while between phone calls, and then decided to drive to San Carlos for breakfast. We knew of a restaurant near our old house where we could take the dogs and eat on the patio. About halfway through our meal, one of the first friends who'd called that morning walked up to our table and joined us. It felt good to see a friendly face. When we'd finished eating, he opened his business in the shopping center across the street, even welcoming Terra and Charter inside, so we could use his phone to make more calls and return the ones we'd missed.

One of the calls I made was to Mike Pratko, our Bible-believing tree trimmer. "If our house is still standing, it's because of all that brush you cut," I told him in a voicemail, "because that fire rolled right over us last night."

What I didn't say, what I couldn't bear to think about myself, was what Bob had told me, describing his final moments in the house. Just as he grabbed Chelsea out of her cage, huge, white-hot flames crested the knoll just outside the family room and jumped to the windows, not even pausing at the wide buffer of bare soil and rock Mike and his crew had cleared just a month before.

"All of a sudden," Bob said, "everything outside the window was on fire."

Mike called back and seemed glad to hear from me. He told me how he and his wife had watched from their home in nearby Santee as the fire's glow advanced down Wildcat Canyon.

"I asked her, 'Isn't that where the Youngers live?' and she said yes, and we both hit our knees right then."

"Oh, Mike," I said. "Thank you. What time was that?"

"About three or so."

Exactly the time Bob and I were waking up to flames in the canyon outside.

After finishing our phone calls, we drove past familiar landmarks barely visible through a brown haze to the street where we'd lived for nineteen years before moving to Terra Nova, just seven months earlier. For the next hour or so, we watched television news reports with our closest neighbors, John and Judy Pilch. We flipped from channel to channel, trying to piece together what was happening. No one yet had a grasp on the full extent of the fires, but clearly San Diego was in the midst of a full-fledged disaster. Television news reports, mostly from Scripps Ranch, showed whole blocks of houses ablaze, and every update reported fire in new locations.

Spurred onward by the wind, the Cedar Fire had traveled west more than twenty-five miles overnight, jumping freeways up to fourteen lanes wide, blasting into the city of Poway and San Diego proper, from Scripps Ranch to Kearny Mesa, a largely commercial community in the heart of the city. All in all, the fire had consumed about 100,000 acres since exploding out of the Cleveland National Forest less than twelve hours before, an astounding rate of spread. Along its southern front, east of Lakeside, flames were advancing down the San Diego River drainage toward El Capitan Reservoir. From there, fire would soon overwhelm parts of Alpine, surge south across Interstate 8, and devastate the rural communities of Harbison Canyon and Crest, flattened three decades before by the historic Laguna Fire. In North County, the Paradise Fire was burning out of control near Valley Center, taking dozens of houses there.

As we sat tethered to John and Judy's television, phone calls kept coming from concerned friends and family. One coworker drove over with a bag of clothes for me to borrow. She sat down and watched the news with us for a while, until an update added her neighborhood to the evacuation list. Since she lived alone and had no one to help her pack, Bob and I herded the Newfs back into the Acura and followed her home to help. It felt good somehow to be loading a car, almost like finishing a chore we'd left undone.

By now we'd also gotten in touch with Jeri Deneen and Jon Powell, the friends we'd first called when we reached the bottom of Wildcat Canyon. Caught in San Francisco on business when the fires broke out, they'd tried to rush home, but found all flights to San Diego had been canceled. At least Jon and Jeri could rent a car and drive home. Elsewhere, in airports all over the country, travelers on their way to San Diego sat stranded. Another friend later told me that he and his family found themselves grounded in Orlando after a Disney World vacation.

"What do you mean nobody's flying to San Diego?" he asked the gate agent. "Why?"

"San Diego's on fire," she said.

It certainly seemed that way to us. A third major blaze, called the Otay Fire, had now erupted near the Mexican border. It would go on to injure a firefighter, destroy one home and burn 46,291 acres.[40] Every section of the county felt threatened; nothing seemed impossible anymore. Jeri and Jon lived well inside the city, insulated from the fires by several residential miles. Still, Jeri worried about her animals—two cats and a tiny zebra finch—and I couldn't blame her. "We'll go get them," I offered. She told me where to find a key hidden outside the house, and we took off, Bob and I and both Newfs again shoehorned into my little white car.

One of the cats sauntered up to us when we opened the front door. We boxed him into a carrier we found in the garage. Jeri had warned that I might have to search for the other cat, and she was right. I poked my head into each room, calling his name, looking under beds and behind furniture. Finally, I found him, totally unperturbed, tucked away deep inside a bedroom closet. We had found only one cat carrier, so now we had to improvise. Checking the garage again, we discovered two plastic laundry baskets and a roll of duct tape. We plopped the cat into one basket, roofed it with the second one, and taped them together. Our design worked beautifully but made an unwieldy package that took up most of the trunk, leaving no space for the second kitty. With Terra and Charter filling the backseat and the finch cage still to go, I had to squeeze the carrier into the footwell behind my seat. The cat's bitter complaints sent both Terra and Charter to the opposite side of the car, where they sat smashed together, casting wary glances toward our unhappy passenger. Bob was driving now. I squeezed in beside him, holding the birdcage on my lap.

Jeri had arranged for a coworker to meet us at her office and take custody of the cats, leaving us pretty much where we'd started the day, with two Newfs and a bird. Just then my cell phone rang again. It was a coworker of mine who happened to live nearby.

---

[40] California Department of Forestry and Fire Protection, *Otay Fire—Final Update*, October 27, 2003.

"I just heard," she said. "Is there anything we can do?"

"Well, can you take a bird?"

Jennifer Zweibel not only took in Jeri's finch, she cleared her kitchen counter of snacks and freshly baked pastries. Keeping none for her own family, she packed everything in a neat parcel for us to take back to the hotel. A heartfelt thank-you was all I had to offer in return, and it didn't seem nearly enough.

We arrived downtown again at around four in the afternoon and found a big sheet of yellow legal paper taped to our room door. Its scribbled message, including a room number down the hall, was signed "Love, Nancy and Eric." Just a few hours after Nancy Wolf's call that morning, inviting us to stay at their condo in Tierrasanta, they'd been evacuated, too. Because we'd reported that The Bristol was dog friendly, the Wolfs decided to join us there with their furry guy, Onslow. They weren't alone. Over the next day or so, the hotel's third floor, specially set aside for pets, turned into a sort of Noah's ark. The once-empty hallway filled with exuberant children and wiggling dogs; the dawn hush that first greeted us gave way to conversation, laughter, woofs, meows, and even an occasional squawk.

We spent the evening with the Wolfs in their room, a little larger than ours. Terra, Charter, and Onslow tussled happily for a while, enjoyed a quick dinner, and then collapsed for the night, carpeting nearly every square inch of the floor in thick black shag. Meanwhile, Eric, ever the perfect host even under duress, opened a bottle of expensive red wine, the only kind he ever drank or served. It was a blessing to be with good friends that Sunday night, when we got a call confirming that our home was gone—and again two days later, when we finally learned that theirs had been spared.

Back in our own tiny room, Bob and I couldn't tear ourselves away from the nonstop television news reports. Still burning out of control on all sides, the Cedar Fire had taken out random canyonside homes in Tierrasanta and broad swaths of Scripps Ranch—hundreds of houses in all.

The screen filled with maps of the hardest hit areas, and newscasters read off the names of streets overrun by flames. Semillon . . . Kingspine . . . Grainwood.

"Oh no!"

"What?" Bob asked.

"That's where the Blakes live. That's their street. They live on Grainwood."

Steve Blake was another friend we'd met through our dogs. A holistic veterinarian and acupuncturist, he ran a consulting business from his home in Scripps Ranch. The television coverage suddenly switched to on-the-street reporters interviewing shell-shocked homeowners, and there he was with his wife, Charene. They looked stricken yet resolute, his arm wrapped firmly around her shoulders, her face reflecting both grief and strength.

"Yes," Steve was saying. "We've lost our house and our business."

It was agonizing to see them in such pain, to know that they, too, were wrestling with the same flattening sense of loss and bewilderment we felt. The day's flurry of phone calls had brought a mixture of worrisome news and rumors about other friends' homes lost, or thought to be lost. Worst of all, news reports confirmed that several people in Wildcat Canyon had died in the fire. Our neighbors? We had no way of knowing. The depth of San Diego's tragedy, the context of destruction all across Southern California, left us feeling at once traumatized and comforted. Tens of thousands of people were suffering, yet we'd all been thrown into the same lifeboat, creating a ready-made support group for the difficult times ahead.

Exhausted as we were, Bob and I found it hard to sleep that night. We cuddled together, but the downtown sounds of traffic and sirens made us flinch, and a flickering red neon sign outside our window, eerily reminiscent of the flames we'd driven through only hours before, seemed to be mocking us. More than anything, my mind returned again and again to that first glimpse of the fire through our bedroom window, so wild and brilliant against the night.

"Wasn't it beautiful, though?" I whispered, and Bob understood.

"It was spectacular," he said.

Sometime later during those dark hours, I remembered my writing. Thirty years of newspaper and magazine clippings, my laptop and backup disks. All my files, everything, both paper and digital. It was all gone.

"Bob," I managed to choke out, "I've lost my writing."

"Oh, Cutes," he said, and pulled me closer.

And then, finally, the tears came.

CHAPTER 20

RIGHT BEHIND ME

AFTER DOING ALL HE COULD in Wildcat Canyon and Eucalyptus Hills, Lakeside Division Chief Andy Parr redeployed his meager troops ahead of the fire front as it somersaulted south toward Alpine, a community of 13,000 bisected by Interstate 8. Hoping to hold the flames at the built-in firebreak the freeway provided, Parr and the engine crews waited there. Meanwhile, the fire raged toward them through the yawning canyon that contains El Capitan Reservoir, normally a picturesque northward glimpse from vehicles speeding by on the freeway. But again the Cedar Fire had its own ideas. As firefighters watched in dismay, Santa Ana winds drove the flames through the narrow canyon corridor at fifty miles an hour, concentrating the fire's enormous energy into a blowtorch that blasted up and out of the rift and effortlessly leaped all eight freeway lanes.

"The longest flames I'd ever seen in my whole life, and they crossed Interstate 8 like it wasn't even there," Parr told me. "Four lanes plus a center median and shoulders. The fire jumped all the way across, onto the hill on the other side, headed toward Crest."

At the same time, flames followed the shoreline of the lake and jumped into the chaparral on either side, hitting the entire length of the adjacent Peutz Valley residential area with a wave of heat and flames. Witnesses said the whole community, fifteen square miles, ignited within ten minutes. Embers from that enormous conflagration shot south on the wind across the interstate and set off spot fires on the southwest side of Alpine.

"Some of those fires we were able to pick up kind of small, like a couple of acres," Parr said. "And then we had one section where we had a spot fire that hit about twelve houses in the middle of Alpine."

But it was the southbound head of the fire, charging full tilt along the same path the Laguna Fire had taken thirty-three years before, that did the most damage. From the huge hill where Parr first saw the surging flames take hold after jumping the freeway, the blaze charged into the rural neighborhood of Harbison Canyon, home to 3,645 people.[41] Tornadoes of flames all but destroyed the community, taking nearly 300 homes, along with its fire station, its only church, and its only restaurant.

"In Harbison Canyon, they had a true-blue firestorm," Parr said. "People say that all the time, but this was a real one."

Rachel Tsosie woke up around 10 a.m. on Sunday to the sound of wind clawing at her bedroom window. She got up, brushed her long, dark hair, and dressed as usual, yet couldn't help but sense something weird about this new day. The sky seemed off-color—gray, not blue. The air, swirling with dead leaves, smelled odd. And then her mother called to her.

---

[41] 2000 US Census, US Census Bureau.

"There's a fire down the road. Let's go check it out."

Rachel jumped into the family minivan with her mother and sisters. When they came to the end of their road they could see it, a fire far off on the other side of Interstate 8, probably a good ten miles away. Although another cluster of Harbison Canyon residents gathered nearby seemed concerned, Rachel and her family judged the flames too distant to be dangerous and returned home.

Rachel climbed back into bed and considered how to spend her day off. Do her laundry? Listen to CDs? Suddenly she heard sirens from the fire station down the street. She went to her window to look for the engines, trying to determine where they were heading, and saw a truck approaching on her street, its speaker blaring.

"There's a fire. This is a voluntary evacuation call."

Rachel walked out to the living room to confer with her mother and sisters. They all agreed. They'd seen the fire; it was miles and miles away. It's not going to make it here, they decided. But half an hour later, the sirens sounded again. A second warning.

Maybe it's closer now, Rachel thought. *Maybe I should do something.* Her mother had left to visit her parents, but soon she was back.

"Hurry!" she said. "Start packing!"

Rachel ran into her room, her mind a jumble. She'd never had to evacuate before. What should she take? She started throwing clothes and shoes into a bag. She grabbed her photo albums, the pictures hanging on her wall. She could hear her mother and sisters screaming. Grab this. Grab that. With the minivan finally loaded, mostly full of pictures and suitcases, the family drove to Rachel's grandparents' home a few blocks away and rushed to help them evacuate, too. A cousin and his friends showed up and pitched in, tossing whatever they could fit into a trailer and spraying the house with a hose. Within fifteen minutes, they were all on their way out. Rachel drove her grandmother's car. Soon they'd joined a long line of evacuees, and time seemed to slip into slow motion. In her side mirror, Rachel saw fire shooting up from behind the nearest mountains like a huge, red hand, reaching out to destroy everything within its grasp. The sky had turned black now, obscured by vast, billowing clouds of smoke. *I'm in a horror movie,* Rachel thought. She had never been more scared in her life.

The cars in front of her were barely moving, and behind her vehicles had stacked up in a seemingly endless line. Meanwhile, in the rearview mirror, she saw flames rolling up and over the mountains. Cars began passing her. Law enforcement officers on the scene had opened the entire road, including oncoming lanes, to exiting traffic. Soon Rachel and her family had gathered at the home of another sister in the city. From a hilltop high school nearby, they watched a line of flames march across the landscape they'd just traversed, consuming everything in its way.

Nearly a week passed before Rachel and her family were allowed back into their neighborhood to learn the fate of their house. But somewhere deep inside, Rachel already knew it was gone. When the time finally came, they started up the familiar hill toward home hoping to see their neighbors' houses along the way, just as they'd always been, just as they should be. But only three still stood. Three houses on a road once filled with life, now transformed into a barren and charred battlefield. Smoke still rose from a few hot spots. Gunmetal gray hulks of vehicles slumped in front of gutted houses. Pulling into their own driveway, Rachel and her family encountered only a mound of ashes. Everything they'd owned was gone.

How could this happen to us? Rachel wondered. *Why didn't our house survive like the ones across the street?*

So many questions, but no answers.

Along the top of the next ridgeline, residents of the tightly knit community of Crest began watching the fire burning to the north early Sunday morning. By midafternoon a long line of vehicles stretched down the mountain, streaming out of the village. Those who waited for sheriff's deputies to announce official evacuations, between 3:30 and 4:30 p.m., had little time before the Cedar Fire sheeted up the mountain from Harbison Canyon and arrived in a huge ember storm, igniting row after row of structures. In the end, Crest lost 290 of some 1,100 homes, plus its community center.[42]

Crest residents Don and Barbara Halte had lived in the ridgetop community since 1966. Just beyond their property, a wildland canyon plunged down the mountain. When the record-breaking Laguna Fire roared up that natural chimney in 1970, the Haltes' home narrowly survived, but flames hot enough to melt cast iron destroyed the rental house they owned next door. They rebuilt it, moved in, and turned the older house into the rental.

The day the Cedar Fire retraced the Laguna Fire's path through San Diego's backcountry, Don Halte was coming to the end of a long and happy tenure as a teacher and football coach for El Cajon Valley High School. He'd been in L.A. that weekend, attending his forty-five-year Whittier High School reunion. When he arrived home Sunday afternoon, he found Crest veiled in a thick curtain of smoke and its main road choked with bumper-to-bumper traffic coming up and over the mountain from Harbison Canyon. Don stopped and talked to a crew of firefighters who'd just been through the firefight below.

"We felt like ants," one told him.

Arriving home, Don checked the house and its surroundings. Although things seemed in order, he walked around back to peer down into the canyon below. That's when

---

[42] Crest (California) Historical Society, "The October 26, 2003, Cedar Fire."

he felt it—the same eerie phenomenon he'd experienced just before the Laguna Fire exploded into Crest.

"All of a sudden the wind stopped for a minute," he told me later, "and then it started blowing the opposite direction. I knew then that the flames were very close and coming fast. The fire was feeding itself, pulling the air toward it."

Don called to Barbara, and they both ran for their vehicles, taking their two dogs with them. Within minutes, they'd joined the line of cars, now four lanes wide, pushing down the opposite side of the mountain toward El Cajon. As they left, around 4:15 p.m., they could see flames flaring up behind them.

Days later, the Haltes, their daughter—who'd lived in the next-door rental—and hundreds of neighbors returned to find their homes leveled. Crest's path to recovery would be especially long and torturous, complicated by insurance headaches and litigation. Unlike many residents, however, the Haltes eventually rebuilt and returned to their beloved mountaintop.

"Why?" people asked them. "Why did you come back a second time?"

"Because," they said, over and over again, "this is our home."

Despite the devastation and heartache in Crest, it was below, in Peutz Valley, overlooking the long blue sliver of water that is El Capitan Reservoir, where the fire did its worst. Peutz Valley Road is an asphalt roller coaster, winding, rising, and dipping through mostly undeveloped chaparral on the northwest side of Alpine. It's a good road for the first three miles or so, a comfortable two lanes edged with guardrails on the west side, where the terrain drops toward the reservoir. Eventually the asphalt gives way to dirt and gravel. Even so, and despite a truck trail leading out the other end of the community, Peutz

Valley Road is the only good road connecting its residents with the outside world, creating yet another one-way-in-and-out backcountry community.

Residents said mandatory evacuation orders came late, only minutes before the fire. Most people made it out on the twisting road to the freeway ahead of the flames, but some were trapped, forced to stay and defend themselves against the fire. A few others, armed with chainsaws and a backhoe, chose to stay. Once the fire caught, it burned nonstop for hours, destroying ninety-one structures in all, displacing fifty-one families. Worst of all, Peutz Valley lost a neighbor, the thirteenth victim of the Cedar Fire.

Christy Seiler-Davis was a bold yet gentle spirit, an artist, a speaker of French, an animal lover, and a horsewoman. She loved living in the backcountry. At forty-two, she had just returned to college to pursue a business degree. She planned to learn enough about computer processing to start a home business from a property she'd bought way out in the boonies of Colorado.

Christy had last talked with her mother, Marcia, late Sunday morning, as the fire approached Alpine.

"Don't stay too long," Marcia warned her.

"I won't," Christy promised. "And if I have to evacuate, I'll come to your house."

But she never came, never called. When Marcia tried to reach her again around noon, she couldn't get through. Eventually she heard from a neighbor who said he'd seen Christy as he left.

"She said she'd be right behind me," he told her.

On Monday, Marcia and her two other daughters, Tracey and Susan, started searching for Christy. They couldn't yet get into Peutz Valley without proof of residency, so they made phone calls, and Susan spent all day driving from one end of the county to the other, personally checking hospitals and emergency shelters, without success.

On Tuesday, the family reported Christy as officially missing, but no one came to help them look for her, so they persisted on their own. The barricade still blocked Peutz Valley to everyone but those who lived there. They had to find someone who knew the backdoor truck trail to lead them to the rubble of the house where Christy had rented an upstairs apartment. The blackened shell of her loaded pickup truck sat nearby, the driver's door open, and they found her keys in the dirt beside the driveway. Marcia and her daughters talked with a few neighbors who had returned to check on their homes. One gave them the good news that Christy's dog, Poncho, had been found, injured but alive. A friend was caring for him. But there was no sign of her cat, Tipper. Or of Christy herself.

The Seiler family refused to give up hope. If anyone could have made it out of this, even on foot, it would be Christy. They searched adjoining properties, too, wandering through the crumbling black and gray landscape, dodging still-smoldering stumps, calling her name. They could hardly believe that one nearby house stood completely intact, garden and all—surreal evidence of the fire's capricious bent.

"She said she'd be right behind me."

The neighbor's words haunted them.

On Wednesday, Marcia, Tracey, and Susan started searching through the ruins of the house where Christy had lived, moving fallen beams, buckled pipes, whatever was left. And then Tracey saw the teeth.

"Is this what I think it is?" she asked.

Looking further, the three women found a full skeleton, Christy's skeleton, lying straight out, face up, among the charred remnants of her front porch.

But Christy's story does not end there. Marcia and her daughters later learned that she had taken precious time after the initial evacuation warnings to ensure the safety of a woman who lived next door. A nurse who worked the night shift, she was deeply asleep until Christy knocked on her door, a warning that no doubt saved her life.

CHAPTER 21

BACKDOOR BURNING

Monday, October 27, dawned beneath an apocalyptic sky. The sun—when it could be seen at all through a dense, amber haze—burned blood red, and a shroud of ash smothered the entire county. Across the backcountry and edging into the city, some 200 square miles of blackened, smoking wasteland stretched to every horizon. Hundreds of homes and numerous businesses lay in rubble. Broad expanses of the county untouched by the fires suffered from power outages and contaminated tap water. Meanwhile, tens of thousands of anxious fire evacuees crowded into friends' and relatives' homes, hotel rooms, evacuation centers, Navy ships, and a huge impromptu camp at Qualcomm Stadium, where the San Diego Chargers and Miami Dolphins were scheduled to play a nationally televised game that evening. Monday Night Football moved to Tempe, Arizona, instead. But by far the worst news came from Valley Center and Wildcat Canyon, where officials had confirmed eleven casualties, with more fatalities expected as inspections of the burned areas continued.

Cooler weather and an overnight lull in the winds had given San Diego city firefighters a chance to set backfires and corral sections of the fire front. But elsewhere, all three San Diego County fires—the Cedar, Paradise, and Otay incidents—still raged, and few reinforcements had arrived to spell exhausted fire crews. Officials requesting additional state and federal aid had been told they'd have to wait until at least Tuesday.

In the meantime, Bob and I needed clean underwear. Our supervisors had assured us not to worry about work, and the entire university where I was employed had declared an emergency shutdown for the first time in decades. Our Newfoundland club friends Eric and Nancy Wolf kept Terra and Charter for us at the hotel while we tried to do a little shopping. The air quality was so bad, the smoke so heavy and toxic, that San Diego Mayor Dick Murphy had done his best to shut down the city, closing schools and municipal agencies, asking employers to let their workers stay home, and urging everyone to "stay calm." Motorists who ignored the mayor's request to stay off the roads, leaving them open for emergency vehicles, were forced to use their headlights at midday to cut through the smoky gloom, and most of us who found it necessary to venture outside for any reason wore surgical masks. Bob and I got ours on the street in front of The Bristol from a random do-gooder who was handing them out free to passersby. With several major freeways closed and few stores open, we ended up at Kmart, an OK place to buy sneakers, jeans, and sweats. But the lingerie selection disappointed me.

"Bob, I don't want Kmart underwear."

"Just get something," he said.

I ended up with white cotton grandma briefs.

We were still shopping when the store started closing around us, forcing us back to our hotel room, where we fielded more phone calls and watched more news reports. That afternoon we heard from our neighbors Randy and Sue Fritz, who'd cut short their visit with relatives in Missouri and rushed back to California. They called to say Wildcat Canyon Road had been reopened. Bob left immediately to meet Randy on the mountain. I wasn't ready. It was bad enough looking at the photos he brought back. When I first saw those images of ashes and tortured metal heaped where our beautiful house should have stood, something inside me flew apart, as if I'd just stepped off the edge of the world.

Fire officials map every wildland fire they fight. When you overlay these maps to create a composite, you get a good idea of the fire history of an entire region. A year or so after the Cedar Fire, I looked at the fire maps of Wildcat Canyon and discovered nearly every inch of it had burned at least once during the past seventy years or so, since record-keeping began—all except for a small oval of land that happened to include our own five acres. *My god,* I thought, *Terra Nova was sitting atop its own funeral pyre.* No wonder the surrounding chaparral had been so tall, so impenetrable that we couldn't explore our new land beyond the cleared area circling the house. Randy Fritz told us he'd never made it to the farthest corners of the property in the nine or ten years he owned it. Looking at that tiny unburned oval on the map, I realized the timing of our arrival at Terra Nova couldn't have been worse. For at least seventy years, maybe a century, our special spot in the chaparral sat untouched by fire. And then, only seven months after we moved in, the worst wildfire in memory hit the heaviest fuel in Wildcat Canyon, with Bob and me sound asleep right in the middle of it. Terra Nova never had a chance, and our escape had been nothing short of miraculous.

The firefighter who showed me those maps was CDF Division Chief Randy Lyle, a thirty-two-year veteran and one of the chiefs who'd gathered on Boulder Creek Road near Pine

Hills when the Cedar Fire began to help coordinate the initial attack. As flames blew out of the Cleveland National Forest late Saturday night, responsibility for managing the fire transitioned from the Forest Service to unified command. Lyle became a joint incident commander, working first with Forest Service Division Chief Carlton Joseph, and the next day with Cleveland National Forest Fire Chief Rich Hawkins. By Monday morning, Lyle had gone forty-eight hours without sleep. So when the CDF dispatched an incident management team to the Cedar Fire, he was happy to brief the new IC, CDF Division Chief John Hawkins, and stand down.

Monday's weather forecast had called for a shift in the winds. Sure enough, as the day wore on, the Santa Anas weakened and died, and San Diego's normal onshore breezes resumed. As all the chiefs had expected from the beginning, this reversal halted the Cedar Fire's fearsome westward march down the California Highway 52 corridor toward La Jolla, while whipping its lazy opposite edge, some fifty miles distant, into full eastward gallop. Firefighters call this trailing edge the "backdoor" of a fire. Best case, they try to snuff it out early to prevent precisely the situation those battling the Cedar Fire now faced—a wind shift pushing a long line of fire through the backdoor into new territory. Fire commanders responded by splitting the firefight into two zones, leaving the western side of the fire under CDF control, with John Hawkins in charge, and establishing a second command post for the eastern section of the fire, led by Forest Service incident commander Mike Lohrey.

When Randy Lyle returned to work on Tuesday morning, October 28, his assignment was to contain that eastern edge, from the community of Descanso in the south to Santa Ysabel in the north near the fire's point of origin. It was an immense area—more than 100,000 acres—that included all of Cuyamaca Rancho State Park and the historic mining village of Julian. The fire commanders placed Lyle there for a reason. He'd lived in Julian for eighteen years. Now the future of Randy Lyle's former home, one of San Diego's favorite mountain retreats, would depend in no small measure on how well he did his job.

Lyle started the day by attending an early-morning briefing for firefighters held at Viejas, an Indian casino and shopping complex near Alpine. From there, Lyle headed north toward Julian, stopping in areas of major concern, including Descanso. He felt heartened to find the local forces there included CDF colleagues Acree Shreve and Rick Marinelli, plus a couple of savvy Forest Service battalion chiefs—all guys he'd known for ages and all Descanso residents. They, too, would be fighting for their home turf. Lyle tried his best to bolster their spirits with a pep talk. With resources so thin, he knew encouragement would probably be all he'd have to offer them.

Fortunately, the Descanso men proved more than capable of defending the community on their own. As flames feasted on the mountain, Shreve and Marinelli commandeered a couple of bulldozers, cut firebreaks, and led a Herculean firefighting effort that saved the commercial center of the village and most of its homes. Forty-three houses burned that day in the Descanso area, but fire officers had worried they might lose hundreds.

After leaving Descanso that morning, Lyle continued north, up California Highway 79 toward Julian, under a high green canopy. A thick forest of centuries-old conifers made Cuyamaca Rancho State Park a majestic place, beloved by San Diegans from one end of the county to the other. Lyle felt lucky; he drove this road almost every day. It was his usual route to work. But he'd never see it like this again. Within hours a tsunami of 200-foot-high flames would sweep through the park, obliterating the village of Cuyamaca and the park's historic headquarters buildings, gorging on bug-killed timber and reducing San Diego's treasured old-growth forest to a towering sylvan cemetery, each blackened tree its own tombstone. Even the earth beneath the canopy, a seedbed for the future, lay scorched in the wake of the fire's tremendous heat, causing foresters to worry about whether Cuyamaca Rancho State Park could ever recover its former grandeur.

Colin Wilson, a fire chief from Northern California working in the area the day Cuyamaca burned, later described the sight of the approaching fire as "biblical."

"In truth, I don't have words in my vocabulary that would express the massive, raw, unrestrained force that was about to descend on the town," Wilson wrote in a personal essay about his fire experience. "It felt like we were so inconsequential and so pitifully weak in the face of the monster closing in on us as to be completely ridiculous to even consider attempting to stand in its path.

"What had been forest," Wilson wrote of the aftermath, "looked for all the world like a huge city with all the lights on in hundreds of buildings. In reality, it was hundreds of acres of burned-over forest and buildings with glowing embers and burning snags everywhere."

Continuing his drive to Julian, Randy Lyle passed the park's headquarters, a complex of historic buildings erected by the Depression-era Civilian Conservation Corps. Just beyond, Lyle saw a few spots where fire had already bumped and even crossed the highway. Even more alarming, a line of flames was working down the eastern slopes of Middle Peak and North Peak, two of the park's highest points. Lyle was stunned to realize the fire had already traveled so far. *Even three days into this thing,* he thought, *and we've got no real intelligence to draw on, no real handle on this fire.* It was just too big, he told me later, moving too fast, keeping him and all the other chiefs scrambling from crisis to crisis. Nobody could cut loose long enough to put together an overall view. Instead, they'd been ad-libbing—relying on seat-of-the-pants, bump-and-run tactics for days.

"We could have done a lot of good by firing California Highway 79 all the way through the park," Lyle said, referring to the tactic of creating or widening a natural firebreak by burning off enough surrounding fuel to starve the oncoming fire front. "If we'd had the resources, we probably would have had a good chance of holding it there, or at least holding it longer."

But they didn't have the resources.

"You can't just say, 'Hey, send me some fire trucks,' when they don't exist," Lyle said. "They're not sitting around in fire stations. Everybody had been out working for days without a break. Guys were starting to drop from exhaustion."

There weren't enough firefighters available to put in front of the fire line edging down the mountains, Lyle reasoned, and not enough aircraft to attack it, leaving him no choice but to drive on. Downtown Julian had to be his biggest priority. Save the commercial center, he figured, and the rest of the community would grow back. Lose it, and historic Julian would be done. Lyle parked behind Julian High School and worked out of his truck. Units and strike teams began showing up from all over, following the shift in the wind and ready to reassemble along the fire's new front. As each crew came in, Lyle organized and deployed them to various areas of the battle line. By the time the flames reached Julian that afternoon, 125 fire engines and crews stood positioned around the village center.

First out of the chute was Harrison Group, two strike teams (ten engines and forty-three firefighters) assigned to protect the densely wooded residential community of Harrison Park. Pine Hills Group took charge on the other end of town, in the neighborhood closest to the Cedar Fire's point of origin. From the start, Lyle worried about Harrison Group. Harrison Park was high risk, and every local firefighter knew it. High-density homes, heavy fuel, narrow roads, all-around bad fire juju. Lyle tried to convey the extreme need for caution when he briefed the group.

"I'm sending you to a really tough place," he told them. "I don't want anybody getting hurt. So be careful. Find somewhere in there to hunker down first thing in case that's all you can do."

Before long Lyle got the call he'd been dreading. It came from an out-of-town CDF chief assigned to Harrison Group.

"We're trapped," he said.

"Are you OK?" Lyle asked.

"Yeah, we're OK, but we can't get out."

"Call me again in five minutes."

Five minutes later, Lyle's phone rang again.

"We're still trapped, and we're getting some spot fires in our area. We're still OK, but we lost one of our engines. It died. It didn't burn up, but it just died."

Lyle felt his heart drop. Sitting in his command post, miles from the heat, he knew the best he could do for Harrison Group was to stay in contact, let them know they weren't alone. Experience had taught him an outside link can make all the difference in a crisis.

"OK," he said. "Hang in there. Call me back in five. Make it regular. I want you to call me every five minutes, you understand?"

The stream of incoming engine crews kept him busy for a while after that, making it easy to lose track of time. Far more than five minutes had passed when Lyle realized he hadn't heard back from Harrison Group. So he called them. No answer. He tried again and again. Thirty, forty minutes went by, and still he couldn't reach the stranded strike teams. Finally, he asked for radio silence, in case someone had been talking over them. Still nothing. They just weren't there. Lyle couldn't wait any longer. He recruited two or three engines and led the way south in his chief's truck, through the twists and turns of California Highway 79, until he found a vantage point above Harrison Park. What they all saw below grabbed them by the throats.

"I see this indescribable fire storm swirling," Lyle told me later. "I mean big fire. Just the wind from the fire itself, from the combustion, is actually tearing branches off of trees, ripping little ones out of the ground, destroying highway signs."

Lyle knew there was nothing anyone could do for Harrison Group.

"Look," he told the would-be rescue crews. "This is my territory. This is where I come from. I know where they are. I know what it's like down there. There's no point in us going down there and getting stuck, too. They've already felt this thing. If they're still alive, they're still going to be alive. If they're dead, we're not going to fix it. Let's go."

Randy Lyle liked going to fires, liked the challenge of beating them back. He'd liked it for thirty years, since the day after high school graduation when he snipped off his hippie ponytail and joined the CDF. He'd been in a lot of tough spots since then, tackled his share of hard assignments. He'd even been burned a couple of times. But never anything like this. This fire was different. He hated this fire.

Just as Lyle got back to Julian, he heard the radio crackle. "Branch three, branch three, this is Harrison Group," a voice said.

A beautiful voice.

"We're all OK."

Later, when Lyle finally made it home for a few hours of sleep, his wife asked him whether a group of engines had been trapped in the fire.

"Yeah," he said. "How'd you hear about it?"

"I didn't," she said. "I had a dream last night. I saw a bunch of engines all parked together, with fire everywhere around them. And then an angel came and spread its wings over all the engines until the fire passed by."

Mysterious and terrifying, the Harrison Park incident presaged the way the whole battle for Julian would go.

"Heavy, hairy stuff," Lyle called it.

By late Tuesday afternoon, after its run at the east end of Julian through Harrison Park, the Cedar Fire was also closing in from the southwest. Determined to hold the flames at California Highway 78/79, the main corridor running through town, Lyle ordered his crews to "fire out" along the road, widening the asphalt firebreak by eliminating fuel on both sides. He aimed to create "a black line" west of Julian between Pine Hills Road and Santa Ysabel, a distance of about seven miles. The operation lasted all night. By 6 a.m. on Wednesday, October 29, Randy Lyle's black line extended all the way to the Inaja Fire Memorial, just a mile short of Santa Ysabel. Shortly before 7 a.m., however, a sudden wind shift drove the flames up out of an adjacent canyon faster than anyone expected, forcing the strike team manning the firing operation to shut it down.

At about that time, CDF Battalion Chief Ray Chaney showed up to relieve Lyle as branch director of operations in Julian. Mostly, Lyle could report, the firing operation had gone as planned. But at the very end of the line, near the Inaja Fire Memorial, where crews had been forced back, the main fire had reached the highway. In the next few moments, a vanguard of flames leaped across the road, bit into the dry vegetation on the other side and took off running—exactly the scenario Lyle had hoped to prevent. Now it would take an air attack to stop the Cedar Fire and save Julian.

All in all, hundreds of homes and vacation cottages burned near the little mountain town. For Julian-area firefighters, the losses quickly became personal. Randy Lyle told me story after story about colleagues who lost their own homes—or those belonging to close friends or family members—while fighting to protect the property of others. Similar stories played out across the county as emergency responders forced themselves to focus on the task at hand, even as the fires forced their families to pack up and flee. Many, like us, eventually returned to ashes and rubble. Just as I still wonder if we might have saved our house by closing the garage door, they must wonder whether they could have saved their homes if only they'd been there to do what they did best.

Retired fire chief Jim Baker, a trim, grandfatherly figure in blue jeans, a plaid shirt, and suspenders, can answer that question.

"I felt so prepared for the Cedar Fire," he told me later, "I had a fire pump and a 5,000-gallon reservoir. I felt confident. But I want to tell people you can lose that thought pretty easy."

Before retiring to Pine Hills, Jim spent a career fighting fire, beginning as a rookie on the infamous Inaja incident and eventually settling into a long and fulfilling stint as chief in the seaside town of Del Mar, next door to La Jolla. "Bake," as his firefighters called him, fits so naturally into the backwoods, where he delights in watching curious deer wander right up to his windows, that it's hard to imagine him hobnobbing with the trendy citizens of Del Mar. In fact, Chief Baker was such a popular man about town that when he retired, the city threw a huge party and presented him with a gold-plated fireman's ax. It now hangs in a place of honor over the front door of the handsome brick house in the woods Jim and his wife built themselves.

The night Sergio Martinez lit his signal fire off Eagle Peak Road, four miles south of Pine Hills, the couple were enjoying a dinner party with neighborhood friends. When fire engines started rolling by, Jim followed them to the rendezvous point where the chiefs in charge met to scope out the incident.

"What's happening?" he asked.

"Just a little fire," someone said. "It's not going anywhere. We're probably going to get after it tomorrow."

Jim wondered about the nonchalant attitude, but he agreed the fire seemed benign enough at that point.

"It didn't look threatening at all," he told me later.

Still, Jim kept his eye on the blaze, driving occasionally to Fletcher Point, a nearby viewpoint where he could see all the way to Ramona, some eight miles to the west. When he finally went to bed, the wind had picked up a bit. By early the next morning, it was screaming through the surrounding pines. Toward Ramona, smoke boiled across the sky. The residents of Pine Hills watched the fire's progress hour by hour, all day Sunday and well into Monday. At times, up to a hundred people gathered at Fletcher Point. And then the Santa Ana winds stopped blowing.

Here it comes, Jim Baker thought.

From the start, he'd told his wife he planned to stay and defend the house once the winds shifted. So in the predawn hours of Tuesday morning, with San Diego's characteristic onshore breezes pushing the Cedar Fire back toward its point of origin four miles south of his home, Jim watched his neighbors—and his wife—pack up and evacuate. Soon he was by himself on the mountain, with the fire front closing in.

"It was lonely," Jim admitted, "and the loneliness scared me."

Hoping to get a read on the fire's progress, he hiked about a quarter mile through heavy smoke to a vantage point, and arrived just in time to see flames blast into Pine Hills. The house where he'd enjoyed dinner with friends on Saturday night was the first to burn. Four or five others followed within moments. All around, propane tanks began venting in the heat; the escaping gas squealed and shot blue fire into the darkness.

"It was very scary, and I was very concerned," Jim said. "All my confidence had gone to hell."

He'd also told his wife that he'd know when to leave. This was it. Jim turned and sprinted home. He made it all the way to his driveway and then passed out. When he regained consciousness, he found it hard to breathe. He'd never felt more afraid in his life, not even as a young Marine in Korea. Somehow he got up, climbed into his truck, and drove out to the main road and down the mountain. He figured he'd been overcome by smoke, but later he learned he had a treatable heart condition that caused his pulse to occasionally drop through the floor.

Despite his scare, Jim Baker returned to Pine Hills on Wednesday, after the main fire had blown through, and found his home intact. He teamed up with a local game warden and canvassed the neighborhood, taking note of houses destroyed and saving two others by pouring bottled water—all they had—over hot spots on the roofs. At about the same time, a strike team from Northern California moved into the area and extinguished lingering fires that threatened numerous other homes in the area.

"I know they saved at least seven houses," Jim said. "Still, we lost forty-two houses in Pine Hills."

On Wednesday morning, October 29, after watching the Cedar Fire make its end run around his carefully laid "black line," Randy Lyle left Julian in Ray Chaney's hands and went home to sleep off his exhaustion. But only four or five hours later, his wife woke him. Something about Wynola, he heard her saying. Orchard Lane.

"What happened?" he asked.

"A firefighter was killed."

CHAPTER 22

FIVE HUNDRED MILES FROM HOME

Here is what I know about Steven Rucker, a Novato Fire District engineer, who died in the Cedar Fire trying to keep someone's home from burning—someone he didn't know, someone who lived 500 miles from his own home just north of San Francisco. He was thirty-eight, a husband, a father, and an all-around good guy, the kind of guy known for helping anyone who needed it without being asked, and a guy who loved firefighting. Once, on a family trip to Los Angeles, Rucker took his wife, Cathy, and their two young children to see the fire station where the 1970s television show *Emergency* was filmed. As a boy, Rucker had idolized Johnny and Roy, the firefighter/paramedic stars of the show. Cathy remembered that her husband got as giddy as a kid at Christmas seeing the site of Johnny and Roy's imaginary workplace.

That last week of his life, Steve Rucker had been off duty and riveted to news about the Southern California fires. He even added a Los Angeles news channel to his satellite TV menu to follow the situation more closely. But Rucker was a doer, not a watcher. So when the Novato Fire District requested volunteers to join the battle against the Cedar Fire in San Diego, Cathy Rucker knew better than to try to talk her husband out of signing up.

"I let him go, and I don't regret it," she later told the news media. "If I hadn't, it would have broken his spirit."

San Diego's plea for resources reached Novato on Monday evening, October 27. The district already had sent two engines and seven firefighters to Southern California, one crew each to the Grand Prix and Old Fires burning near San Bernardino. Yet Novato had a fresh crew to spare. Rucker and three colleagues—Captain Doug McDonald, engineer Shawn Kreps, and firefighter/paramedic Barrett Smith—had just reported back to work that morning after four days off.

At around 9:30 p.m. on Monday, the four men climbed aboard Engine 6162, a Type 3 or brush truck, for the long ride south. Novato Fire District encompassed 60,000 people, spread across seventy-one square miles, plenty of it the typical California wildland-urban intermix of buildings and highly flammable native vegetation. So Novato equipped and trained its firefighters for both structure protection and wildland firefighting, experience they'd need to battle the fires devouring San Diego County.

After leaving Novato Fire District Station 4, the crew of Engine 6162 joined three other Northern California crews in a convoy headed south. They drove all night, taking turns behind the wheel so each man could sleep as much as possible along the way. About 11 a.m. on Tuesday, thirteen hours and 528 miles from Novato, Rucker and his colleagues pulled into the firebase that had sprouted up seemingly overnight at El Cajon's Gillespie Field and reported for their first assignment. They spent the afternoon and evening protecting homes and other structures near Alpine. Back at Gillespie by 10 p.m., the Novato men enjoyed the luxury of a full night's sleep and woke up Wednesday morning feeling rested and in good spirits. They had breakfast, attended the usual briefings and equipment checks, and then Engine 6162 and the rest of the task force took off for a second day of fighting the Cedar Fire, this time near Julian.

They arrived at Santa Ysabel around 9:15 a.m., just minutes after the fire front leaped the highway at the end of CDF Division Chief Randy Lyle's black line. As the Novato crew watched, the "slop-over" fire spotted into light grass and flashed up the next ridge to their left. Engines ahead of them began backing down the highway to escape the heat. The strike team that had been firing out along the highway to prevent this exact turn of events gave chase, but the fire behavior proved too erratic, forcing the firefighters to pull out and causing traffic to hold on the highway for an hour before it was safe to continue. Barrett Smith took a souvenir photo of the flames lighting a smoky sky orange and white.

Soon the air attack arrived to slow the fire's progress, and bulldozers began carving a new firebreak ahead of the flames. Working together, three air tankers made good progress protecting structures on the north side of California Highway 78/79. The winds weren't that bad now, only five to seven miles per hour. If the air tankers could buy enough time to reposition enough resources, the chiefs in charge figured, they might be able to make a new stand and contain the slop-over before it slammed into the tiny community of Wynola and moved on from there into downtown Julian. But just after requesting helicopters to double-team the flames, air attack officer Ray Sauceda called off the assault, saying he couldn't contact fire crews on the ground. By the time air tankers were able to return to the fire front, it was too late to stop the Cedar Fire from hitting Wynola. CDF investigators later attributed Sauceda's decision to "a perception that the frequencies assigned for air-to-ground communications were incorrect" and cited the withdrawal of air assets as a contributory factor in the fatal incident that followed.[43]

Among the teams assigned to protect Wynola was the group from Northern California, now known as Task Force 2005A. Command dispatched the group to Orchard Lane, a narrow gravel road running along a low ridgeline. As the convoy of five engines lumbered into the neighborhood, with Engine 6162 bringing up the rear, crews toward the front saw fire at the far north end of the road. Immediately, all the engines turned around and waited, poised to make a quick escape if necessary. Helicopter crews working the area at the time noticed the flames, spot fires from the bigger blaze, and hit them with a few water drops. Two bulldozers rumbled cross-country from the highway to finish the copters' work.

With the spot fires knocked down, Task Force 2005A redeployed. Battalion Chief James Watkins of the Lawrence Livermore National Laboratory, the task force leader, bore the responsibility of deciding how best to defend Orchard Lane. He had to write off the house at the far north end of the road, closest to the spot fires. Narrow access and heavy vegetation made it too dangerous to defend. The third property down the ridge also looked dicey. A closely grouped campus of unique free-form buildings nestled into chaparral and scrub oaks, it housed a colony of painters and sculptors headed by renowned artist

---

[43] California Department of Forestry and Fire Protection. *Engine Crew Entrapment, Fatality, and Burn Injuries, October 29, 2003, Cedar Fire*, 57, 65.

James Hubbell. But the house in between, 920 Orchard Lane, looked salvageable. Watkins assigned it to the crew from Novato.

Kreps backed the engine up the long curving concrete drive to the house as Smith and Rucker cut back overhanging oak and manzanita branches to make room for the big vehicle. Meanwhile, McDonald walked on ahead to assess the situation. Halfway up the driveway the captain got a bad feeling. So much fuel so close to the house. Was this place really defensible? He radioed Watkins to express his doubts. "Then get out," Watkins responded. McDonald agreed, but before giving up on 920 Orchard Lane altogether, he took one last reconnaissance walk around the house. Smith and Rucker joined him. On the backside of the property, facing west, they discovered brush had been cleared for 150 feet or so downslope, providing the defensible space McDonald was looking for. He called Watkins back and told him it looked like Engine 6162 could save the house after all.

The Novato crew couldn't see much to the southwest, where an impenetrable stand of mature chaparral grew twelve feet high. But they weren't too worried about that. They'd already seen the head of the fire passing north of them, just beyond the end of Orchard Lane. What they had to watch for now was the flanking fire—a wedge of flames spreading out behind the front like the wake of a boat—coming at them from the northwest. They could see it already, grazing in short bursts toward the bottom of the canyon below, where it would likely pick up speed and scramble uphill toward their position. McDonald intended to be ready for it.

He briefed Kreps, Smith, and Rucker on his plans and reminded them to take key safety precautions. In particular, he ordered them to suit up in full protective equipment— heat-resistant shirts, pants, and jackets, plus gloves, goggles, and helmets with shrouds wrapping around the neck and face. Kreps added a structure hood—an extra layer of protection covering his head like a ski mask underneath his helmet and shroud; McDonald and Rucker put on face shields. The crew also agreed on an emergency escape plan: Worst-case scenario, if things blew up, they'd take shelter inside the house.

Then everyone got busy laying out and charging the hoses, one in front of the engine, two behind; placing an axe near the backdoor of the house; leaning a ladder against the roof in front; and tossing stacked firewood away from the structure. McDonald put Rucker in charge of burning a nearby pile of brush cuttings, using one of the hose lines to keep the flames under control. Meanwhile, Kreps and Smith fired the grass in the cleared area behind the house, plus a ring of vegetation beyond that.

Just before 12:30 p.m., McDonald saw a pickup truck marked with the CDF logo pull up the driveway of 920 Orchard Lane and park near the detached garage. A firefighter got out. From his helmet and gear, McDonald identified him as a CDF captain. The men didn't speak, but McDonald later reported he felt pretty sure they'd both seen each other. Approaching 920 Orchard Lane a few minutes later to check on Engine 6162, task force leader Watkins saw a CDF truck emerging from the driveway. He recognized the driver, a CDF captain, from the morning briefing.

John Childe had been fairly vocal when Division Supervisor Dan Runnestrand laid out his strategy for the day. To Watkins, it seemed the captain got pretty aggressive, volunteering advice on how he thought the supervisor should be fighting the fire. When Watkins stopped his truck in front of 920 Orchard Lane, Childe started grilling him, too.

"Why don't you have a unit up there?" he asked.

"We do," Watkins shot back.

In the meantime, McDonald had asked Kreps to go talk with the CDF captain and find out if perhaps they could work together to better protect the house. But when Kreps got to the garage, Childe had already left. Kreps noticed a grassy area nearby was burning. *Must be the flanking fire arriving as expected,* he thought. But the flanking fire was still some 300 yards to the north. McDonald could see it plainly, edging down a ridge under a clear sky toward the bottom of the canyon behind the house. Later the Novato team would learn that Childe had taken it upon himself to burn out the vegetation around several structures on Orchard Lane in an attempt to buffer them from the approaching fire.

The Cedar Fire incident commander, CDF Division Chief John Hawkins, told me he and his fellow CDF division chief Bill Clayton had given John Childe a different assignment.

"Bill Clayton and I that morning told Childe at the incident base: 'Your job is to be a field observer and go out and determine if the Paradise Fire will join the Cedar Fire,'" Hawkins said. "And then Childe went out and did what we know he did."

When Kreps returned, the Novato crew regrouped near Engine 6162. They'd done all they could to protect 920 Orchard Lane in advance of the flanking fire's arrival. Now their job was to stand by, ready to fight any flames that might breach the blackened buffer they'd carved out around the house. Kreps revved the engine to high idle, making sure the pump was engaged to keep the hoses charged and ready, and then rejoined his team outside the vehicle.

The four men watched the fire repeatedly flare up and die down as it worked its way toward them through the chaparral. Soon it would bump up against the black and falter for lack of fuel. They'd hit it with the hose lines, and that would be it. Kreps took a moment to fish his camera out of a jacket pocket and grab a photo—all orange light and smoke beyond the tail of Engine 6162, and in the shine of its red paint, reflections of tall flames to the south and southwest, where McDonald had thrown the final flares to complete their firing operation. It was a scene worth recording, Kreps thought. Everything was going just as planned. He could've been standing there in shorts and a T-shirt and felt perfectly safe.

Suddenly, Rucker yelled at him to "get back" behind the engine. Within fifteen to twenty seconds, blue sky gave way to orange twilight, followed by smoky darkness. A red meteor shower of embers shot past in a sudden stiff wind. The air thickened with the noise of fire blasting through brush, and a surge of searing heat boiled upslope from the canyon. Smith grabbed the front hose and began spraying embers landing in a tall hedge of juniper and boxwood behind them, next to the house; Rucker took one of the rear lines. Kreps covered his mouth with a gloved hand and told himself to take quick, shallow breaths to keep from inhaling the killing air.

In the next moment, the hedge ignited, and suddenly everything was on fire. McDonald yelled for everyone to take cover inside the house as planned. Smith led the way, leaping up the steps to the patio and sprinting through waist-deep flames before disappearing around the corner. Following close behind, Kreps tripped and fell on the steps. For a moment he found himself completely engulfed in fire. *Don't breathe,* he told himself again, *that's what's going to kill you.* Insulated from the flames by his multiple layers of protective gear, he popped back up and quickly joined Smith on the backside of the house. Using the axe they'd placed by the door, the two men broke it open and stepped inside.

McDonald was right behind them, until he sensed Rucker wasn't. Looking back, the captain saw him still standing near the rear of the engine.

"Steve, c'mon, let's go!" McDonald shouted.

But Rucker didn't respond. He seemed disoriented, even turning toward the flames, as if he were about to walk into them. McDonald yelled again, cupping his hands around his mouth to be heard over the roar.

"Steve, c'mon, let's go! We've got to get in there."

Finally, Rucker started toward him, took two steps, and fell heavily. He got up slowly, on hands and knees at first, and then rose and took another few steps toward McDonald.

"I'm burning," he said, and fell again, this time into the flaming hedge.

McDonald leaped to grab him, helped him up, and steered him to the patio where Rucker fell for the last time, to his knees and then face down on the concrete without even attempting to brace his fall. McDonald struggled to lift him, but Rucker had gone limp. The captain next tried to call for help and found he couldn't hang on to his radio. It was too hot. He could feel his own skin burning now; he knew he should already have taken shelter. But he had a man down, and he couldn't make himself leave. Once more McDonald grabbed Rucker, twisting head-on into the heat and flames this time in an effort to yank the fallen man to safety. He shouted for Smith and Kreps to come help, but the noise of the fire swallowed his voice, and the heat of it closed in on him. He had no choice now. Looking back once as he staggered toward the corner of the house, he saw Rucker's body on fire.

Kreps and Smith stepped inside the building only long enough to realize MacDonald and Rucker weren't immediately behind them. Bursting back out, they saw a solid screen of fire shooting past the corner they'd just rounded. In the next moment, McDonald materialized out of the flames, burned and dazed, his jacket scorched and smoking.

"Steve's down," he told them. "We've got to go get him."

"No way," Kreps said. "If Steve is still out there, he's dead. We can't go back or we're all gonna die."

Still, McDonald turned around as if to lead the way back. Kreps and Smith had to grab him and pull him inside. The web belt and harness carrying the captain's gear had melted, dumping all his equipment onto the patio, yet he searched momentarily for his radio before he realized he no longer had it. Kreps and Smith didn't have one either. They'd given their second unit to Watkins, the task force leader, who'd gone to pick one up that morning at headquarters only to discover they'd run out.

The Novato crew were on their own. No one else was going to rescue Rucker. They tried opening the front door to the patio, slowly, carefully, but a blast of intense heat forced them to slam it shut. After a few minutes, Kreps tried again, made it outside, and found Rucker's body lying in the middle of the patio, burning. Somehow, Engine 6162 still stood intact, still running on high idle just as he'd left it. Grabbing the closest hose, Kreps opened the nozzle in Rucker's direction, but the burst of water lasted only a few seconds. The fire had burned through the other two hoses; the 500-gallon tank had pumped dry.

Another surge of heat sent Kreps into the backseat of the engine cab. He thought about staying, deploying the fire shelters stored there, but decided against it. If he didn't return, Smith or McDonald might come after him. Taking a deep breath, Kreps jumped out of the cab and sprinted back through the heat to the house, arriving just as Smith opened the door to look for him.

The three men sat for a while longer on the floor by the front door, until the rear of the house began to burn, smoking them out and back to the engine. Knowing for sure now that Rucker was past help, they had to attempt an escape. Kreps inched the big truck down the driveway through dense black smoke, following the pale edge of the concrete against the dark earth. A timely gust of wind cleared the murk just long enough for him to avoid a tree where the driveway curved. In the meantime, McDonald got on the engine's radio. His voice was clear, his message concise. "Firefighter down." He made a second call, this one to request additional units. When Engine 6162 reached Orchard Lane, its crew emerged from the smoke into bright sunny daylight. Before they reached the highway, however, McDonald told Kreps to stop, then opened the door and climbed out of the engine cab, perhaps in a last attempt, despite his own injuries, to save his engineer. Smith and Kreps were quick to bring their captain back into the vehicle and drive on.

Watkins had seen the fire's sudden charge from his position closer to the highway, and had tried to raise Engine 6162 by radio, but no one answered. When McDonald's distress call came in at 1:05 p.m., the task force leader immediately requested emergency airdrops and a medevac helicopter, then launched a rescue attempt. The entrance to 920 Orchard Lane, where the Novato engine had just emerged from the flames, was still burning so fiercely that Watkins and his crew couldn't punch through right away. When they finally did reach the house, they found only a burned body. There would be no rescue. Up and down the fire lines, radios crackled with the code no firefighter wants to hear. 11-44. Possible fatality.

When CDF incident commander John Hawkins heard the news, he took it personally.

"One of my professional goals is to never kill or injure a firefighter in the line of duty," he later wrote about that day. "I had failed and knew it. I sat on a curb outside the command post and cried, cried damn hard."

Engine 6162 by now had made it out of Orchard Lane and parked at the highway. When an ambulance arrived, Smith and Kreps, both paramedics, climbed in with their captain and used their own medical supplies from the engine to start an IV line before McDonald was airlifted to the hospital. Suffering from second-degree burns over 28 percent of his body, he faced a long and excruciating recovery. Barrett Smith and Shawn Kreps escaped serious injuries; they were treated for minor burns and released the following day.

Although Engine 6162 sustained the only casualties on Orchard Lane, two other crews in Task Force 2005A came close to disaster when John Childe's firing operation temporarily cut off their escape routes. Another of his fires spread too far, too fast, and had to be contained by a helicopter drop. Task force leader Watkins also was trapped for a time by Childe's operations, blocked by his pickup parked in a driveway. The freelancing captain had never contacted the division supervisor, Dan Runnestrand, to advise him of his operations.

"I didn't even give it a thought to call the division because I didn't really have a lot of time to try," Childe later told investigators.

Representatives from multiple agencies pored over the Rucker incident for months, but none could say for sure why the man died or what kept him from sprinting with his crewmates toward the shelter of the house at 920 Orchard Lane. The CDF report noted that a hose pack was missing from Engine 6162. Although no evidence confirmed that Rucker had taken time to strap on the pack, two bundled one-hundred-foot-long hoses were found on the patio near his body. Had he perhaps hoped to establish a protective link to the engine's water supply—a tactic sometimes used when firefighters must shelter in place? An autopsy found high levels of carbon monoxide in Rucker's body. Was he standing too close to the revving engine's exhaust? Or did he just breathe in too much smoke, thick with pollutants, carbon monoxide among them? Did a deep breath of superheated air damage his airway—a possibility his wife, Cathy, and crewmate Shawn Kreps consider most likely—or, since fire devours oxygen, was he simply oxygen deprived? Any of these scenarios, investigators noted, could impair judgment or incapacitate a person.

Much speculation centered on the fact that Rucker was mildly asthmatic and sometimes used an inhaler. But the condition had never before affected his performance. In fact, just two months before his death, during a required physical exam, Rucker had aced a breathing test even without medication. Autopsy results indicated he hadn't used the inhaler he carried with him the day he died either, indicating that he hadn't felt the need to. So investigators ruled out asthma as a causative factor in Rucker's death.

In the end, investigators pinned the cause of the accident on external factors—the decision to defend Orchard Lane and especially the house at 920, a ridgetop location in the path of the fire but without a clear view of its progress; the sudden wind shift just as the fire reached the bottom of the canyon and started upslope, sending a horizontal blast of heat through the crew's location; Rucker's and McDonald's delay in taking shelter in the structure; and, finally, the lack of a designated lookout to keep an eye on the fire.

The uncompleted segment of Randy Lyle's firing operation along California Highway 78/79 and the loss of air support also made the list of factors contributing to the incident. So did CDF Captain John Childe's unauthorized, unannounced firing operation. Review teams concluded Childe's maverick march down Orchard Lane endangered both property and lives, trapping crews and necessitating a water drop to protect a house he was supposedly trying to save. Fire behavior models showed that flames from Childe's firing operation south of 920 Orchard Lane, coming from an unexpected direction not visible to the crew, may have drawn enough air toward itself to accelerate the flanking fire's arrival by as much as two minutes—"a minor but potentially significant decrease in the amount of time available to react to the changing conditions." More than enough time, in other words, for McDonald and Rucker to have reached the safety of the house.

Later that Wednesday afternoon, after the tragedy on Orchard Lane, CDF Captain Ron Serabia, the man who reported the Cedar Fire minutes after it sprang to life and then led the initial air attack against it, stepped up to end the monster's wild run toward Julian. With Serabia choreographing the aerial assault, six air tankers and assorted helicopters, plus ground crews cutting lines around the air attack's tightly targeted drops, intercepted the flames at the foot of Volcan Mountain, preventing the fire from reaching central Julian. Elsewhere along the fire line, the Cedar Fire's eastward run faltered when it hit territory denuded just the year before in a major incident called the Pines Fire. Similarly, a recent controlled burn protected the town of Pine Valley.

When Randy Lyle next reported for duty at the Julian CDF station, the winds had stilled, the humidity had spiked, and the weather had turned cold. *Finally,* he thought, *this thing is just about done.* He lit a cozy fire in the wood stove he himself had installed years before and got to work directing the mop-up operation. On Saturday, November 1, the first drizzles of San Diego's annual winter rainy season at last gave firefighters a real advantage over the Cedar Fire. Fire activity settled down to creeping and smoldering, punctuated by occasional flare-ups in stumps and snags.

On November 5, the incident commanders declared victory—100 percent containment—and California's infamous Cedar Fire crashed into fire history. Corralling the runaway beast had taken the herculean efforts of 4,275 firefighters over ten days at a cost of nearly $30 million. Fifteen people lost their lives, as did countless pets, livestock and wildlife. More than 273,000 acres burned, along with 2,232 homes, 22 commercial buildings, and 577 additional structures.

Elsewhere in San Diego County, the Paradise and Otay fires had also surrendered to firefighters' relentless efforts, but not without taking two more human lives, 222 homes and 102,671 additional acres. If measured as a single complex incident, as many subsequent fires have been, San Diego County's great 2003 fire siege would have hit the record books at a stunning 375,917 acres, with suppression demanding the efforts of 6,635 firefighters and costing more than $43 million in 2003 dollars.[44]

---

[44] CDF, Cal OES and USDA Forest Service, *California Fire Siege,* 72, 74-5.

Beyond all the numbers, the deepest impact of the fires played out in the hearts and minds of those who survived—civilians and responders alike. No one who lived through the terror of that time will ever forget it, or the years that followed—years spent rebuilding our homes, fortifying our firefighting capabilities, and mending our shaken souls.

Looking at a map of the fire's enormous footprint, you can plainly see the protective notch firefighters worked so hard to carve around downtown Julian. Almost everything beyond that area, including at least 600 structures, burned in the cataclysm. But, as Randy Lyle had hoped, the heart of the village survived, giving residents a place to come home to and start over. On the same map, just north of Wynola, a ragged spike in the fire's perimeter juts up like a pounded thumb. If time and conditions had allowed firefighters to complete Lyle's black line, the Cedar Fire's footprint likely would have ended on the south side of the highway, almost exactly at the Inaja Fire Memorial. In that case, no firefighters would have been needed to protect the homes on Orchard Lane. And Steven Rucker would not have died. Instead, visitors to Julian now see a new tribute to a fallen firefighter. A 15-mile stretch of California Highway 79—from Santa Ysabel through the heart of Julian and past Harrison Park—today is known as Firefighter Steven Rucker Memorial Highway.

CHAPTER 23

THE KINDNESS OF STRANGERS

O N WEDNESDAY, THE DAY STEVE Rucker died, San Diego International Airport reopened, and our twenty-five-year-old daughter, Lauren, arrived from Seattle toting an enormous suitcase. Hugging her felt like the first breath of air after swimming up from a deep dive. Just that morning, our friends Eric and Nancy Wolf and their Newfoundland boy, Onslow, had been allowed to return home to Tierrasanta, leaving us on our own at The Bristol. To better accommodate our Newfoundlands and now Lauren, the hotel management promptly moved us into the Wolfs' larger room. Lauren walked in, set her bulky bag on the floor at the foot of the beds, and flipped it open.

"Wait 'til you see what I brought!" she said. "Mom, I've got clothes for you."

I felt awkward taking charity from my own daughter.

"Thanks, baby, but I have a few clothes."

Lauren looked at me and raised an eyebrow at my ensemble, a navy blue sweat suit I'd grabbed that first day at Kmart.

"Oh, I brought you way cuter clothes than that."

She'd gone through her own closet, choosing pants, tops, and sneakers she thought would fit me. I tried on a pair of her fashionably low-rise jeans, and we laughed at the broad expanse of white Kmart underwear rising above the denim waistband. Lauren dug into that suitcase again and again, pulling out more clothes, including shirts for Bob and a denim jacket I wore for years, all donated by friends of hers, most of them people we'd never met. Next came a flurry of pastel envelopes, each containing a touching message, many folded around gift cards for Home Depot, Eddie Bauer, or Circuit City. In response, Bob and I could only manage a few shaky "oh wows."

"OK, Mom," Lauren said next, "this is going to make you cry."

She reached into her magical suitcase one more time and handed me two framed photos, photos I'd seen on her own dresser and bookshelves. One was an Easter Sunday shot of two adorable little girls in pink ruffled dresses and straw hats— Lauren and her sister, Kendall. The second was a freeze frame of Epic, my first Newfoundland water rescue dog, suspended like Superman between boat and lake in his typical zeal to save me from drowning.

I did cry, of course, but not for all the jeans and sweaters and Nikes I'd have to replace, not for my lost writing or the images collected by Bob's camera over our three decades together—words and images we would never see again. I wept instead at the wonder of those two precious images rising from the abyss of hopeless loss. I wept at the miracle of the young woman who'd brought them to me, once a child in ruffles and lace, totally dependent on our care, now a responsible adult taking care of us. And I wept in gratitude for the stunning and unfathomable kindness of strangers. Even Lauren's presence with us was a gift from people we didn't know. Her employer had given her emergency leave, and a friend's father, a Delta pilot, had arranged complimentary round-trip flights.

During those first weeks and months after the fire, Bob and I often found ourselves in tears, but never because of what we'd lost. What moved us most was the care and generosity, proven through countless surprises, of those who rallied to our aid—family, friends, and a multitude of strangers. The house we rented was offered to us by a couple we knew from the Newfoundland dog club, who had a rental available and figured we'd have a hard time finding accommodations elsewhere with two enormous dogs in tow. Nearly every day's mail brought a new stack of cards and checks, each one an expression of concern and support. And for days, my cell phone barely stopped ringing. While I was talking with one person, two or three others would leave messages. People wanted to know if we were OK, if we needed a place to stay, a yard for the dogs, anything at all. Some wanted only to hear our voices and express their relief that we'd made it. Our friend Jenni Lott from Oregon left four or five messages before we finally connected.

"Sandra, you're alive," she said. "You're alive! You're alive!"

It's true that adversity can bring out the best in people. Nearly everyone across San Diego County experienced some sort of trauma during that horrific week of fire. With three major blazes destroying 2,454 houses overall, thousands of us suddenly became homeless. Tens of thousands more frightened residents either evacuated or packed their vehicles full of pets, photos, and computers, ready to leave if necessary. Schools and businesses everywhere shut down, giving most San Diegans plenty of time to worry about the news reports, the brown sky, the orange glow, the rain of ash, the eerie pallor of a world burning down around them.

Yet on every side, everyday people helped each other through our shared tragedy. In thousands of ways, people rallied to restore what the fires had taken. They did whatever they could, offered whatever they had, from bulldozers and helicopters to shampoo and styling gel. Costco and Walmart sent pallets of bottled water to firefighters on the lines; department stores gave special discounts to fire survivors; and a local mortuary covered funeral arrangements for the fire's victims. Radio show hosts raised over a million dollars, even as donations cascaded into the American Red Cross and other nonprofits leading the recovery effort. Churches, corporations, and community groups provided cash, goods, and services. And grassroots organizations sprang up in the hardest-hit areas as fire survivors banded together to recuperate and rebuild. Thousands of people volunteered to staff impromptu shelters and emergency aid centers, to house homeless family members and friends, to help neighbors sift through ashes and rubble in the sad search for anything salvageable. It was the same all over the county, in every community. Just as we'd all fallen prey to the fire's reckless cruelty, in its wake we all shared the balm of uncommon kindness.

Our neighbors, Dave and Leslie Nunez, who took refuge from the fire at Barona, told us how a guard at the casino thrust $25 into Leslie's hand.

"This is half of everything I have," he said. "I want you to have it."

"No," Leslie said. "We'll be OK."

"But I want to give it to you," the man protested, "and I hope you will do the same for somebody else sometime."

It did feel strange, suddenly being an object of charity. At first, like Leslie, I fought it. I wanted to send everything back. I wanted to say, "We're fine. We have insurance. Please, help someone who doesn't." For years I'd written checks to charities, sponsored impoverished kids in Africa, and schlepped boxes of outgrown clothes and toys to Goodwill. I thought of myself as a giver, not a beggar. But now, bereft of everything we'd owned except a Nikon and a laundry basket full of photos, it was hard to deny that we were the ones in need. I found it an awkward and embarrassing adjustment until a psychologist friend gave me the perspective I lacked.

"Sandra," she said. "Right now, your job is to be a grateful recipient."

People wanted to help us, she explained, but more important, they needed to help—some because of innate compassion and generosity, some to fulfill their values or religious beliefs, some to work through their own fire trauma, and some, simply because their homes didn't burn, to appease a sense of survivor's guilt. I had plenty of opportunity, over those first post-fire months, to practice the humility my new job required. The calls; the checks; the gifts; the loans; the donations of clothes, sheets and towels, lamps and furniture—they all kept coming. Some people reached out with more unusual acts of kindness—returning framed prints of Bob's photographs, leaving a basket of cookbooks at our doorstep, mailing us a signed children's storybook about the famous Newfoundland dog, Seaman, who crossed the country with explorers Lewis and Clark. I declared it the first of a new collection replacing Lauren and Kendall's favorite childhood storybooks, books I'd hoped to someday share with my grandchildren.

Often, the creativity and thoughtfulness of our bene-factors amazed us. Friends who owned a grooming shop called us during those first days at The Bristol and invited Terra and Charter to come for a spa day. I took them in grimy, smelling like smoke, and they came back clean and gleaming, sporting jaunty Halloween neckerchiefs. Later that afternoon, room service brought up a huge basket of dog food and treats, compliments of those same dog-loving friends, plus a bottle of wine and a platter of cheese and crackers for Bob and me.

As the holidays approached, we sometimes found canisters of home-baked cookies on our porch. One day the mailman brought a tiny potted pine tree, bedecked with doves and angels—an early Christmas gift from my father and his wife. My coworkers threw a special holiday party for me, an ornament shower. Each person donated a bauble from his or her own collection, along with a note explaining its significance. Handmade ornaments, heirloom ornaments, favorite childhood ornaments, and, from my Jewish friends, brand-new ornaments, the first they'd ever bought, they told me.

"They really do get it, don't they?" I said to my friend Coleen Geraghty, the woman who'd masterminded the shower. "They really do understand that we lost everything."

"Yes," she said, "they do," and gave me a hug.

I was just as touched by a group of friends beyond our Newfoundland community who arranged for a local surf shop to fit me with a new wetsuit so that I could return to water rescue training with Terra and Charter. "We thought it would be therapeutic for you to get back in the water with your Newfs," they told me. And my sister, Karen, knowing how much I'd cherished a quilt made by our great-grandmother (we each had one), insisted on giving me hers.

Bob's coworkers chipped in to replace his cherished Marine Corps officer's sword and then presented it with full pomp and circumstance at a surprise party billed as a routine happy hour. When Bob arrived, he found his military friends resplendent in dress blues. Our friend Scot Miller, a Navy captain, told the story of the original sword, the coveted ROTC award presented by Admiral (retired) Elmo Zumwalt at Bob's commissioning into the Corps in 1975. And then a Marine colonel we didn't even know handed Bob a brilliant silver scabbard containing a new blade engraved with his name.

"Captain Younger," he said. "You were a Marine; you are a Marine. The honor once bestowed is never relinquished. It is my honor to return to you your Marine officer's sword."

The thread that ran through everything, all the emotions, the monumental going and coming of stuff, was how little any of it meant in and of itself. It was the sentiment behind the gifts that triggered our tears, the love of those who cared enough to share not only their material wealth, but their spirit and energy, too.

Beyond that, we lived each of those first chaotic post-fire days acutely aware and grateful for the simple gift of life itself.

If you had seen us that night in my little white sports coupe, inching through a nightscape opaque with smoke and possessed by flames; if you had pulled back in a helicopter shot until the Acura became a tiny white pinball careening through a red and orange maze of fire, you would have thought, and rightly so: *They'll never make it; there's no way they'll ever find their way out of that.* And yet we did. Somehow, for some reason, Bob and I, Terra and Charter, and even Chelsea the brainless cockatiel, came through the flames untouched. As the news filled with the names and locations of the fire's first victims, twelve of them in Wildcat Canyon, our friend Jenni's mantra kept running through my mind. "Sandra, you're alive! You're alive!" Compared to that, nothing else mattered. Nothing.

Bob had been back to Wildcat Canyon several times by now. On Monday, just thirty-six hours after our desperate departure, he'd met there with Randy Fritz, our neighbor who'd designed and built our house for his own family before selling it to us eight years later.

I'd asked Bob to give Randy a message: "Do you remember how you built it?"

And I liked the answer Randy sent back: "Tell Sandra I could build it without the blueprints."

Standing between the heaps of ashes that marked the Fritzes' home and ours that first day after the fire, Bob and Randy shook hands, and we had our contractor.

The only real topic of discussion was mathematical: the ratio between rebuilding costs and insurance payouts. Bob and I had given serious thought to the insurance issue when we'd first moved to Terra Nova. We'd asked Randy how much it would cost to rebuild the house. His answer was a number significantly higher than what we'd paid for the entire property—the house and five acres. Wow, we wondered, could we even afford that much insurance?

"Well," I remember saying, "if something did happen, I certainly wouldn't want to be underinsured."

Bob agreed. He'd long been influenced by his father's attitude toward insurance: "It always seems expensive until the day you need it."

So we'd set our policy limit exactly as Randy advised, an amount verified a few weeks later by an independent appraiser. Yet after reporting our loss to our insurer, USAA, I couldn't help but worry. What if something had gone wrong? What if the bank had somehow flubbed our automatic payments? What if we got a call saying, "Sorry, you don't have any homeowners insurance after all"? We'd lost everything—except responsibility for a thirty-year mortgage on a pile of ashes. What would we do? How would we reboot our lives?

Two or three days after the fire I did get a call—from a compassionate USAA representative, assuring me that we did have insurance, enough to replace the Suburban and rebuild Terra Nova down to the last detail. I called Bob with the good news, and we both choked up.

"So the bad news is that we have to start over," he said, "but the good news is that we can."

We had good reason to feel grateful, even blessed. Most of those who lost their homes in the fires would find themselves underinsured, and many had no insurance at all. Wrangling with insurance companies, often to the point of litigation, proved another ordeal for many fire survivors. Some told me they found their insurance headaches more painful than the loss of their home and possessions—a bitter pill indeed.

By the end of the week, with the fires waning, the air quality in San Diego improved enough for our daughter Kendall to join us. She'd wanted to come sooner, but she had asthma, so we'd urged her to wait. It had taken me all that first week to muster enough courage to view the remains of Terra Nova in person. Now, with both Lauren and Kendall in town to accompany me, it was time. On our way, we stopped at a military surplus store to buy black Army boots and pack shovels. Bob had advised us we'd need them. When we reached the bottom of Wildcat Canyon Road, the flat stench of ashes seeped into the car and caught in my throat. I pulled over onto the shoulder.

"I think we need to pray," I said, and neither daughter objected. There wasn't much to say—be with us, help us be strong—and then we drove on.

As far as we could see in any direction, Wildcat Canyon had shriveled into a desert of death. Where green chaparral had softened the mountains on either side of us, enormous granite outcroppings and boulders now stood naked and scorched, some split and flaking from the fire's heat. In between those prehistoric rocks we could see nearly every inch of earth. Hidden before by vegetation, it stretched out in patches of brown and black, a macabre and crusty quilt. In places, where scrub oaks had grown thick, a field of charcoal spines twisted up from the burned ground, as if even the trees had died in agony. Most people who drove through the fire areas soon after the flames shared our dismay, struggled to find anything at all familiar short of the horizon. Many described San Diego's burned backcountry as a lunarscape. True enough, it no longer resembled any place on Earth. But I have seen pictures of the moon, and from what I could tell, the moon looks better.

Wildcat Canyon appeared more like a war zone, the result of malicious destruction. Between the bare rocks, occasional mounds of debris and sometimes an isolated chimney marked the former homes of canyon neighbors. Near many of these ruins, the colorless metal shells of vehicles sat slumped on their axles, tires burned away, wheels dissolved. Bob's beloved Suburban looked exactly like that. It sat in the driveway where we'd been forced to leave it, flanked by blackened earth and brown withered trees marking our once verdant front yard. Underneath, a crater in the concrete confirmed that Bob had recently filled the gas tank. Tiny pieces of engine—springs and seals mostly—lay scattered yards away, and shiny silver rivulets of aluminum snaked from empty sockets. All four wheels had melted. Just past the truck, where Bob and I had last seen our beautiful home standing tall, proud, and defiant against a high breaking wave of light and heat, there was nothing. Nothing but a whitened, powdery heap of ashes and gypsum, the stuff of wallboards, punctuated by a single chunk of sagging exterior wall and a few blackened pieces of twisted metal—the carcass of a refrigerator, a dog crate, and my grandfather's iron bedstead, fallen from an upstairs bedroom when the floor beneath it disintegrated.

The heat in a burning house is unimaginable. Stacks of hardened aluminum drops marked the slow melt of cookware. Porcelain glaze had run and pooled at the bottom of a cast-iron bathtub. Chunks of granite countertop, turned white and porous, crumbled in our hands like packing foam. Glass had softened and re-formed into thick abstract chunks. Here and there we found recognizable remnants of things. A broken dish. A melted camera lens. A pile of blackened coins from a jar where we kept loose change. A glob of yellow metal. Could it be gold? Even the jeweler I consulted thought so at first, but it turned out to be only brass, probably the base of a lamp.

We fool ourselves, really. We pluck elements from the earth, transform them into building blocks, cobble together shelters, craft furnishings, accumulate clothing and keepsakes, collect books and art. We trade our time for things, spend our lives spinning cozy cocoons to make us feel safe from a dangerous world. It all seems so substantial, so indestructible. I wonder if ants feel the same about their carefully crafted tunnels and mounds of dirt, or birds, their nests of twigs and grass, even though, in truth, it doesn't take much to erase all evidence of their efforts. Or ours.

After the fire, people asked me, "Did your whole house burn?" Yes, yes it did. "Were you able to salvage anything?"

No, not really. Except for the gas grill on our back patio, which survived with its propane tank intact—astonishing evidence of the fire's capricious nature. We did try to find more. We climbed all over the mound of ashes, the gypsum sticking to our black surplus boots, and we excavated here and there where we guessed something important—my jewelry box, my mother's sterling silver flatware—might have landed when the house collapsed.

Where the dining room had been, we found half a box of tissues unburned and dampened, proof that the automatic sprinkler system had worked, at least for a while. That unlikely discovery made me wonder if somehow another piece of paper, my mother's wedding portrait, might have survived. We dug deep into the corner where the photo had sat atop a chest of drawers until we found a corner of its metal frame—enough to satisfy my wistful curiosity. But nothing more.

The one remarkable find from our private archeological dig came the day I stayed behind with the dogs at the hotel, too sick of the wreckage to face it again, while Bob and the girls tackled the ash heap on their own. When they returned, Kendall walked over to me holding out a closed fist.

"This is all we found of the Christmas decorations," she said.

I held out my hand, and my daughter dropped into it a tiny ceramic figure of the Virgin Mary, the lone survivor from my childhood nativity set. She was bleached white of her painted features, but unbroken—a portent even for a Protestant, a reminder of forces greater than fire.

Some survivors sifted ashes for weeks in a determined and thorough search for such treasures. Some found a few—a teapot, a college ring, a scrap of an old letter. But after three or four attempts to salvage remnants of our former belongings, we were done with the past. We laid down our shovels, took off our boots, and called a demolition crew to haul away the debris. It was our first step in rebuilding Terra Nova.

CHAPTER 24

WE BURIED THE VICTIMS

W HEN YOU'RE CAUGHT IN A catastrophe, either personal or shared, right away you're labeled. From that point forward, in the eyes of the world, you become a victim. After the fire, in both media reports and private conversations, all of us who'd lost our homes heard ourselves branded as "fire victims." For Bob and me, the label never seemed to fit. We'd escaped the worst part of the biggest fire most Californians could remember. We'd driven down a mountainside through smoke and flames yet emerged physically untouched. How could we possibly think of ourselves as victims?

One of our neighbors expressed our feelings succinctly.

"We buried the victims," she said. "The rest of us are survivors."

Even by that definition, so many of our fellow survivors had lost and suffered so much more than we had. We thought often about the families and friends of those killed in the fire. By now, with the discovery of an unidentified male body in an open area near Miramar Air Station, thought to be the remains of an unauthorized immigrant, the fire's human toll had risen to fifteen. Adding the two Paradise Fire fatalities, San Diego had lost seventeen people in the fire siege. How do those left behind adjust to such terrible loss? How do they keep from thinking about the way those beloved lives ended, what their final moments must have been like? Poet Jim Milner's haunting lines about the death of his wife, Galen Blacklidge, offer a glimpse into his nightmare.

> My wife, Galen, dead now nine months—
> consumed at night by the light of fire—
> her hair brittle as dried leaves,
> on her back, beginning bridge pose,
> full face to a burning sky. . . .
> When I found her body, I placed one
> hand on her forehead, another
> on her chest
> and tried to say goodbye;
> I stood, stumbled and
> dropped, shoving my hands
> into still-warm earth
> blackened with ash,
> screaming her name
> over and over
> as if I could call her from
> out of this burnt ground.[45]

We thought a lot about those who came even closer to death than we, more than a hundred people burned by the flames, twenty of them seriously injured. I ached especially for Allyson Roach, full of faith and confidence despite losing her home, her sister, and her fingers in the Paradise Fire; spending four painful

---

[45] From "Exuviating Light" by Jim Milner. Reprinted with permission.

months in the hospital; and undergoing dozens of surgeries. We thought, too, about those who'd lost their animals. Jeff Fritz, our neighbor Randy's brother, took precious seconds as the flames arrived to open a corral gate and give his wife's two horses a chance to outrun the fire. And yet they stayed and perished, while the Fritzes' home survived.

"I told Jeff I would've traded the house for my horses," Judy Fritz told me later, and looking at my two beloved Newfoundlands, I knew I would have felt exactly the same. Bob and I would always carry the fire in our memories, but these fellow survivors would be reminded by grief and physical scars. When we thought of them, how could we ever consider ourselves victims?

And then there was Sergio Martinez, the reviled lost hunter whose desperation led him to light a signal fire that exploded into a natural disaster. Many affected by the fire blamed him for their losses; many felt cheated when he managed to avoid a prison sentence. Others found a way to forgive him. Still others saw his role in the drama as peripheral, or even superfluous. He may have started the fire, they reasoned, but he could hardly be blamed for its unprecedented spread and unimaginable consequences.

After the fire, a grand jury weighed all the evidence and concluded that Martinez should be indicted, charged with setting an unauthorized fire on federal land and lying about it to a federal official. At first he pleaded not guilty, claiming he didn't remember how the fire started. But faced with a maximum possible sentence of ten years in federal prison, plus the evidence of a marijuana pipe discovered near the rock pile where he'd been rescued, the lost hunter eventually agreed to accept a plea bargain.

When I first set eyes on Sergio Martinez, in a federal courtroom the day he pleaded guilty to starting the Cedar Fire, I saw a broken man, stooped-shouldered with worry and remorse. It struck me then that Martinez was also a victim of the fire he'd started. He, too, had lost more than money or time could restore. A couple of wrong turns in unfamiliar territory, an empty canteen, a desperate decision, and his life had changed forever. From that point on, everything else he'd ever known or thought or been or hoped sank into a sea of anxiety and regret. Bob and I could look forward to rebuilding our lives. Martinez had to live his life knowing his actions had led to immeasurable loss and tragedy.

But despite how we saw ourselves, almost everyone else saw us as victims. People changed when they found out we'd lost our house in the fire. Their faces fell slack; their voices thickened in sympathy.

"Oh my god," they'd say. "I'm so sorry."

Some people, when a conversation circled close enough to raise a question in their minds, would ask outright.

"Are you a fire victim?" Or: "You're not a fire victim, are you?"

Some even introduced me to others by my new status: "This is the lady I was telling you about, who lost her house in the fire."

And then the cycle began again. "Oh my god; you're a fire victim; I'm so sorry."

No one meant to offend us. People felt genuinely stunned and concerned. For most, just thinking about losing their home and everything they owned was jarring, unimaginable. They had no idea how to respond, no way of understanding that Bob and I couldn't afford to dwell on our loss; we had to focus on the future. I tried explaining our mindset to a few friends.

"If I'd lost just my college ring, I'd be sick," I said. "Or our family videos. My favorite jacket. Any one of those things. But when you've lost everything, you can't be that sick. You have to be something else."

As Bob and I saw it, one word summarized that "some-thing else" attitude: survivor. Raised in the South, I'd grown up steeped in a culture that prizes manners and civility. Yet after the fire, whenever anyone dropped the "V" word, I challenged them.

"I like to think of myself as a survivor," I'd say.

Sometimes I even stopped people in mid-sentence: "Not victim. Survivor."

I wrote letters to publications that used victim terminology: "Thank you for your coverage of those of us affected by the Cedar Fire, but please don't call us victims. We aren't victims; we're survivors."

Looking back, it all seems a bit militant, but at the time it felt critical to press the point. The "victim" label implied that the fire had conquered us, but it hadn't. By the grace of God we had escaped the flames, and in the same way we would meet the challenges of rebuilding our home and our lives. Sometime during those early days I came across the words of Austrian psychiatrist and philosopher Viktor Frankl, a Holocaust survivor who emerged from that terrible crucible with a great lesson to share.

"Everything can be taken away from a man but one thing," Frankl wrote, "the last of the human freedoms—to choose one's attitude in any given set of circumstances, to choose one's own way."

I thought of the choice the fire forced upon us in an allegorical sense, like finding a bridge leading to a lush world of unimaginable potential. But when I started across the bridge, an ogre popped up and demanded that I pay a heavy toll: everything I owned. Who wouldn't step back at that? Who would choose to pay such a price, no matter how enticing the possibilities? But what if the awful decision had been made for you? What if the toll had already been paid? Would you still turn away? That's exactly how it seemed to me. The fire had taken so much, and without my consent. But now I could choose—I could remain "that lady who lost her house in the fire," lamenting all I'd lost, or cross the bridge and trust that fortune would somehow spring from misfortune. It was heartening that so many other fire survivors made the same choice. So many comments, shared in person or published in the media, echoed a familiar theme: "We are so grateful to be alive, to have our family, our friends. Everything else is just stuff."

Of course, we all mourned the loss of cherished family photos and heirlooms, anniversary gifts and kids' art projects. But in time we discovered that these treasures, too, were "just stuff," touchstones to people or experiences held forever safe in our hearts. Because I had forced so many family photos on friends and relatives over the years, we recovered dozens of our favorite images of Lauren and Kendall growing up. As for the rest, I eventually realized they'd simply joined the many special moments never caught on camera. One woman I met, who had rebuilt her Julian home after a house fire only to lose it again in the Cedar Fire, passed along a similar thought I found helpful.

"I visited my favorite things in my mind from time to time," she told me, "until gradually I was able to let each of them go."

Some survivors found the sudden loss of all their possessions strangely liberating. Scripps Ranch resident Joe Lee, whose family lost everything but the photographs saved by San Diego Fire Captain Billy Davis, was one of these individuals.

"I tell a lot of people it's kind of a cleansing experience actually," he said. "You reset your priorities. You realize there's no point in storage. All that stuff we had stored away; it's useless. These days I live very minimally—a few shirts, a few pants, enough to get by for work, and that's it. We have our family and our health; that's all that matters."

I understood Joe's perspective. There was so much I didn't have to worry about anymore: All those unpacked boxes in the garage, those piles of unfiled papers in my office, those stacks of books and magazines I meant to read. Not to mention the cat scratches on my grandfather's Victrola or the stain I couldn't get out of the kitchen counter. It reminded me of a line from a

1960s rock song: "Freedom's just another word for nothin' left to lose."

Inspiring us all, many of those most affected by the fire moved ahead with spirit and optimism. The family of forty-two-year-old Christy Seiler-Davis, who died when the Cedar Fire hit her home in Alpine, celebrated her life by traveling to places she had loved and leaving a little of her ashes in each spot. A little of Christy tossed to the wind here and there, even from the top of the Eiffel Tower. For the Seilers, there was no temptation to hunker down in grief. Christy wouldn't have wanted that, they all agreed. Instead, they established a college scholarship fund in Christy's memory to support other midlife women returning to school as she had.

John and Lori Roach, who lost their Valley Center home, their sixteen-year-old daughter, Ashleigh, and very nearly her sister, Allyson, in the Paradise Fire, created two foundations in Ashleigh's memory, both intended to turn evil into good. One raises scholarship funds for students sharing her passions—music, dance, and sign language. The other teaches hospital and emergency workers best practices in caring for serious burn victims. Allyson Roach went on to become a motivational speaker, dedicated to honoring her sister's memory by sharing her own story of hope and healing.

"The fire took so much," Lori Roach told me. "We will not let it take any more—not our joy, not our future."

But not everyone affected by San Diego's fire siege responded in the same way. Some did consider themselves victims. Many voiced anger toward Sergio Martinez, the firefighters, or their supervisors. The CDF, in particular, drew criticism for bungling the initial attack on the Cedar Fire, even though the Forest Service was in charge at that point. I saw Kelly Zombro, the CDF battalion chief who first met the fire head-on in the Country Estates, shouted down while trying to explain the firefighters' challenge to a town hall meeting of fire survivors.

"The flames were moving so fast, and our resources were spread so thin," Zombro began.

"We know how fast it was moving," an audience member interrupted from the back of the crowd. "We were in it."

A roomful of voices and clapping seconded the protest.

One citizen stood up in a post-fire public meeting and said firefighters should have done whatever it took, regardless of the risk to their lives, to save homes from burning. Such harsh sentiment weighed heavily on those who'd fought heroically to end the fire siege and lost one of their own in the effort. After the fire, veteran CDF chiefs told me they'd never seen agency morale sink lower.

Among the most vocal critics of the fire leaders' performance were Mussey Grade neighbors Diane Conklin and Art Bale, key members of an ad hoc citizens' group called the Committee for Full Accountability on the Cedar Fire. In various public meetings, a query to the regional US district attorney, and eventually an unsuccessful $236 million class-action lawsuit, group members claimed government and fire officials had failed to prepare for an inevitable fire catastrophe, botched the response once it happened, and attempted to cover up their failure.

"I don't think we've been told the truth, and I'm beginning to have my doubts that we ever will," Art Bale told me. "I thought they would have an investigation. Fifteen people died. I thought they would sit people down on their sworn testimony and pull out the records."

The committee produced signed statements by individuals who claimed they'd called 911 an hour before the first official report of the fire shortly after 5:30 p.m. on October 25. They couldn't produce records of those calls, however, and they dismissed their absence from multiple agencies' 911 logs as either error or deliberate deception. From their perspective, it had taken more than an hour for firefighters to respond to the fire. Why, they wanted to know, especially with Santa Anas in the forecast? Why didn't anyone dispatch the air tankers? Why did they turn away the sheriff's water-dropping helicopter?

I understood their outrage and bewilderment. Bob and I initially shared the same emotions, the same questions. We, too, had been incensed by early media reports about aircraft turned back from the flames, and hundreds of firefighters bedded down at Pine Hills, waiting for the fire to burn its way to a road. Why hadn't they attacked right away? Why had they given the winds time to surface, the fire time to spread? Why did so many homes have to burn? Why did so many people have to die? It all came down to Bob's single, agonized question that night we abandoned Terra Nova in a blizzard of red embers and brilliant firelight: "Where is the fire department?"

Our anger cooled once we learned more about the scope of the fire and the paucity of available resources, once we realized there simply weren't enough fire engines and squad cars to go around. In a widespread disaster, there never are. But still, we wondered, why hadn't anyone warned us the fire was coming? Why did Bob and I, and so many of our neighbors, have to wake up to fire outside our windows? We were among a contingent of Wildcat Canyon residents who posed that question when a local television reporter came to our charred community to interview "fire victims."

"Nobody should've had to die," I said. "Somebody should've warned us."

"Even an old-fashioned siren or factory whistle would've helped," Bob added.

It certainly didn't help that the county's emergency alert system, designed to trigger warnings via local radio and television stations, was never activated during the fires. After investigating this omission, the *Los Angeles Times* reported that neither the sheriff's department nor firefighting agencies considered it their job to request an emergency alert. The Forest Service countered that they'd considered it but found the system "impractical" because it couldn't accommodate the long list of communities in the fire's path, and few people would be watching television or listening to the radio at such a late hour anyway.

Amid all the controversy, few of us who woke up to the fire on our own had any idea how many firefighters and law enforcement personnel risked their lives in the attempt to warn us. Sheriff's Commander Robert Apostolos, whose assigned territory encompassed fire-ravaged East County, told me he did his best to anticipate the fire's path and begin evacuations well ahead of the flames. Still, dozens of deputies later received medals for breaching walls of smoke and fire to warn or rescue residents during the emergency, which San Diego County Sheriff Bill Kolender called "the biggest challenge in the department's 154-year history."[46]

Firefighters, too, had stretched beyond limits to save lives and defend homes and businesses, with remarkable success. While public attention focused on the staggering number of structures lost, after-action reports estimated that 85 percent of homes threatened by the fires survived. In terms of sheer numbers, California's 2003 fire siege triggered the largest mobilization of firefighting resources in the state's history, with a total of 14,000 personnel engaged against fourteen major incidents spread all across Southern California. In San Diego County alone, the firefighting forces peaked at 5,203 individuals, 722 engines, twelve air tankers, forty-six helicopters, thirty-eight bulldozers, and fifty-six water tenders. Many firefighters worked forty-eight hours, even seventy-two hours, at a stretch, and often without food. With no backups

---

[46] San Diego County Sheriff's Department. *2003 Year in Review.*

to replace them on the fire lines, they simply didn't have the luxury of stopping for meals or sleep.

"I was proud of my guys," said CDF Battalion Chief Ray Chaney, who single-handedly saved hundreds of lives with his decision to lock down the Barona Resort complex. "Going days without food or sleep, eyes bleeding, falling down from exhaustion, still getting back up and saying, 'Where to next, Chief?'"

San Diegans were effusive in their praise and gratitude for these heroic warriors, many of whom, like Novato's Steve Rucker, came hundreds of miles to help. Handmade thank-you signs sprang up all over the county—on front lawns, in store windows, on freeway overpasses. Firefighters who did finally catch a break and make it out to a local restaurant, if only on their way home at the end of the siege, became the beneficiaries of free dinners and impromptu hugs from restaurant managers and ordinary citizens. Motorists honked and flashed thumbs up at every passing fire vehicle.

The government officials and citizens who complained about the firefighters' response directed their criticism toward the top decision makers in the fire agencies. Committee for Full Accountability on the Cedar Fire member Art Bale focused on the lack of air support during the initial attack. Long after the fire, when we sat down to talk in his rebuilt home on Mussey Grade Road, he showed me four time-stamped snapshots he said were taken by residents of the Country Estates. Spanning a period of a few minutes beginning at 5:45 p.m., just after the first 911 calls, each showed a distant, grainy ring of flames.

"You can see it's definitely still daylight," Art pointed out. "So we shouldn't hear excuses like 'inaccessible' or 'after cutoff time.' I refer to this picture, and I say, 'You couldn't put that out? You couldn't get a drop of water on that thing?'"

I liked both Art Bale and Diane Conklin. I appreciated their concerns and respected their intelligence—enough to fully investigate their claims. Their most troubling accusation was the charge that firefighters took an hour to respond to initial reports of the fire. So I kept asking questions until I'd found multiple witnesses in multiple locations who'd seen the fire's earliest moments. Each of them corroborated Ron Serabia's 5:39 p.m. time frame. So did a ranger standing watch in a lookout tower in the Cuyamacas, whose log notes "wispy white" smoke visible near Pine Hills at 5:45 p.m.

It's not that I disbelieve those who say they called 911 at approximately 4:30 p.m. that Saturday. They struck me as sincere. Perhaps they'd simply set their clocks back a day ahead of the transition from daylight saving to standard time, which occurred at 2 a.m. on Sunday. In any case, I hope all who doubted the first responders' concern for their welfare eventually found satisfying answers to their questions, just as I eventually found mine.

The more I read and the more people I talked with, the more I understood what had happened that first night of the Cedar Fire. When Bob and I hiked out to the fire's point of origin, an up-and-down half-mile into the chaparral from the narrow gravel passage of Eagle Peak Road, I could see why chiefs in charge didn't send 350 men and women all that way, cross-country through thick, dry brush, with no safety zones or escape routes, under shifting wind conditions, to meet flames they couldn't have seen until they got close enough to feel the heat.

Forest Service Division Chief Carlton Joseph, calling the shots as the initial incident commander, was especially aware of the danger. For his entire life, he'd carried the name and the memory of his father's best friend, Carlton Lingo, lost with ten other firefighters in the historic Inaja Fire tragedy of 1956. All eleven men died only a ridgeline or two away from the rock pile where deputies Rocky Laws and Dave Weldon found Sergio Martinez. I thought about all this as I sat on those same rocks, contemplating the rugged ravines that funnel into the thousand-foot-deep cut of the San Diego River Gorge, and Kelly Zombro's maxim pounded through my head: "It's not acceptable to kill firefighters."

At first, as I struggled to make sense of the unexpected turn our lives had taken, being a survivor felt all encompassing, and the philosophy served me well. But the time came when somehow that label, too, seemed inadequate. Gradually, Bob and I realized that survival was only the first step in the long process of healing and reordering our world. Eventually we learned that if we paid careful attention, we could uncover opportunities in the ashes.

It would be difficult to find anyone affected by the Cedar Fire who'd say they're glad it came into their lives, that they'd do it all again. No one I know would pass up an opportunity to travel back through time and pluck Sergio Martinez out of the chaparral before he became so desperately lost. But many I know would say the fire held a profound lesson: Great loss can lead to greater clarity, greater depth of spirit, greater peace. And some might even say the fire gave more than it took.

Chapter 25

Forgiveness

AFTER ALL THE MEDIA COVERAGE, all the public vitriol, and all the personal upheaval, seeing Sergio Martinez for the first time was like catching sight of a celebrity, and just as surprising in its ordinariness. Nearly a year and a half after the fire, on March 10, 2005, I sat among a tense crowd of spectators in a sleek, wood-paneled courtroom several floors above the streets of downtown San Diego and listened as the famous lost hunter pleaded guilty to the felony charge of setting fire to timber on federal land without authorization.

Many of the people packed into that modest gallery would have much rather seen Martinez tried for murder or manslaughter, or for destroying 2,232 homes, or at least for illegal possession and use of marijuana. But the plea bargain struck by his attorney limited the charges and reduced the maximum possible prison sentence from ten to five years. When the lawyers finished discussing the technicalities of the plea, the defendant emerged from the gallery—he'd been sitting among us, in the back row between his sad- and worried-looking parents—and took his place at a podium alongside his attorney to face Judge Roger T. Benitez.

Sergio Martinez in the flesh was short and heavy, his bronze face round and somber, his dark hair freshly buzzed. He stood slump-shouldered, hands shoved deep into the pockets of slate gray chinos. His blue short-sleeved shirt hung untucked, and there was no shine to his plain black work boots. So here he was, the man who lit the fire that killed my neighbors, took my home, and changed my life, and he did not look at all notorious. He looked scared to death.

Judge Benitez, whose lean, bespectacled face seemed to float atop a billowing black robe, began with solemn warnings about the ramifications of pleading guilty to a felony. Felons cannot vote. They cannot seek or hold public office, although these basic civic rights may be restored. They cannot serve on a jury for seven years. They cannot possess firearms and may lose professional licenses or permits.

"Do you understand?" he asked the defendant.

"Yes," Martinez answered. His voice sounded small and soft, barely audible.

"Do you waive your right to a trial by jury?"

"Yes."

Martinez's lawyer, an African-American man of similar height and even heavier build, looked pristine in a dark suit and serious tie. He laid a paternal hand on his client's shoulder, leaned in, and whispered something into his ear.

"Yes, your honor," Martinez responded.

"And to all your other rights except the limited right of appeal regarding criminal intent?" the judge continued.

"Yes, your honor."

"Do you understand?"

"Yes, your honor."

And then Judge Benitez asked for more than "yes" or "no" answers. Then he asked the question all of us affected by the fire had wanted answered from the beginning.

"What happened?"

Martinez was succinct in his reply.

"Got lost," he said. "Got completely dehydrated. Set the fire. Put it out with my hat. Set it again. Couldn't put it out. Too late."

Twice. He'd set the fire twice. I felt a stab of emotion—part astonishment, part anger.

"How do you plead?" Benitez asked, "and bear in mind that it does not matter one iota to me whether you plead guilty or not guilty."

Martinez paused for a long moment before speaking again. "Guilty."

It was over quickly after that. Benitez scheduled the sentencing hearing at the end of the summer, to give the lawyers time to gather witnesses and statements, and to give himself time to solicit input from fire survivors and victims' families. Not until then would Martinez tell his whole story, how it was that day at Kessler Flat, what drove him to his fateful decision.

Outside the courtroom, I was surprised to see all the media representatives huddle around the lawyers while Martinez broke away and walked alone to a windowed wall overlooking the green courthouse lawn and soaring cityscape beyond. He set his arms on a wide railing running chest high through the glass and stared out with swollen eyes. Sergio Martinez, now a confessed felon, from whom no one had been able to wrest a word in the sixteen months since the fire, stood alone and unprotected amid a sea of reporters.

He looked forlorn and broken, so much so that I felt suddenly flooded with the conviction that someone needed to do something for him. Someone needed to throw this man a life ring before he sank any deeper. And then it occurred to me that perhaps I could do it. I took a deep breath, made myself move forward, and walked gingerly toward the window until I was standing beside him.

"Excuse me," I heard myself say, quietly, tentatively.

Martinez didn't respond.

"Excuse me."

He turned his head slightly for a moment, a bare acknowledgment. I took another breath and stumbled on.

"I just want you to know that I forgive you. I lost my house in the fire, and I forgive you."

"Thank you," he said without emotion, still staring straight ahead.

"I know you didn't mean to hurt anyone."

Suddenly, unbelievably, words began pouring out of him.

"I pray every day for the people in this fire. I pray every day. That's why I did this today—because the man upstairs told me to."

I reached out and touched his arm.

"I believe he forgives you, too."

He nodded slightly.

"That wasn't me out there; that was a dying man," he said. "I'm in good shape. I work out every day. Every day. I know I don't look like it, but I do. Nobody knows what it was like out there."

People were approaching us now. Diane Conklin from the Committee for Full Accountability on the Cedar Fire walked up, stood over Martinez's shoulder, and addressed him in a consolatory voice.

"Sergio, we don't blame you," she said, and he nodded again, still without shifting his gaze.

In the next moment Martinez's lawyer arrived and whisked his client away. I stepped back from the window, stunned. All this time without a word to anyone, and Sergio Martinez had opened up to me. We ended up crammed side by side in the same elevator, Sergio and I, plus his lawyer and several other courtroom spectators. An awkward silence oppressed us as the car descended to the lobby. Outside, on the lawn, the media waited en masse, their news vans lining the curb behind them. Martinez exited the building flanked by his parents and his lawyer, who escorted him up to a bank of microphones. The lawyer spoke first, and then Martinez made a halting statement that topped the news that night, repeating almost word for word what he'd already told me.

I spoke with Sergio Martinez once more after that, at an interim hearing leading up to his sentencing. He'd hired a new attorney by then, a distinguished Hispanic man whose silver-gray suit complemented his wavy hair. During a break in the proceedings, I approached the lawyer and Martinez in the hallway and asked why the defendant had switched representation. Neither man wanted to say outright, but both hinted that Martinez had come to regret his guilty plea. He'd been scared of prison and hoped a plea bargain would spare him that fate, or at least shorten his sentence, while saving his parents the costs of a trial—they'd already mortgaged their home to post his $100,000 bail. Toward the end of our conversation, Sergio Martinez looked me straight in the eyes, managed an embarrassed half-smile, and said, "I'm sorry about your house."

"Thank you," I answered.

And that was that.

The last time I saw the lost hunter was Thursday, November 17, 2005, at his sentencing hearing. He had dressed up for court this time—brown trousers and a sport coat over a crisp white shirt and tie. When Martinez took the witness stand, he talked for an hour, expressing his remorse and explaining in detail how and why he'd become desperate enough to light a signal fire in a tinder-dry sea of fuel.

Afterward, sitting with his attorney at a table facing Judge Benitez, Martinez had no choice but to listen as more than fifteen people affected by the Cedar Fire got up to speak. Most were angry, if not at the man who started the flames, at the firefighters who couldn't stop them.

One of the first speakers to take the podium said he'd called 911 at 4:37 p.m. the day the fire started, a full hour before the first officially recorded report, which he disputed. He couldn't understand why the water-dropping helicopters he'd expected never responded.

"Martinez should be held accountable," he said, "but it's not right for him to be blamed for the holocaust that followed. That responsibility appears to lie with the leadership of the fire agencies."

Diane Conklin backed him up, saying she knew others who claimed to have reported the fire an hour or more before the first documented call. Representing the Citizens for Full Accountability on the Cedar Fire, Diane lamented that Martinez's guilty plea preempted the trial her group had hoped would uncover the truth about the fire agencies' initial response.

Marabeth Lis, who lived at 920 Orchard Lane in Wynola, turned the spotlight back on Martinez. She reminded Benitez that firefighter Steven Rucker had died trying to save her house from the flames, and also reported that an eighty-year-old neighbor had taken his own life two months later because he had no insurance to help him rebuild his home. Yet another victim of the Cedar Fire, Marabeth pointed out.

"This was not the act of nature," she said. "It was the act of a man. Sergio Martinez started the fire; he's responsible."

Another woman pronounced Martinez guilty of murder and suggested "the punishment should fit the crime." She threw a hunter's whistle in Martinez's direction, barely missing his attorney. It landed with a clatter on the table in front of them both.

"Walmart. $2.98," the woman said, spitting out the words. "Next time you get lost hunting, try walking west, and when your feet hit salt water, blow that."

A couple of speakers seemed more injured than angry; their comments broke my heart. One young mother cried through her entire statement, saying she could hardly take care of her family because of lingering trauma from the fire. As she spoke, Martinez's shoulders shook, and his lawyer patted his back in a fatherly way.

"I forgive you," the young woman told Martinez. "I forgave you a long time ago. But you're an adult, and you were unprepared. I believe you should get the maximum sentence. Five years is one day for each house you burned."

One of the last speakers, a polished young man in suit and tie, had been sitting beside me throughout the proceedings, typing away on his Blackberry. He was angry, too, and he made a point of shooting a venomous glance at Martinez before speaking.

"This is a teachable moment, a critical opportunity for the court to send a message," said Geoff Patnoe, County Supervisor Dianne Jacob's chief of staff. "I am a victim of this crime, and I urge a significant sentence."

It wasn't until much later, when I got to know Geoff, that I learned he'd led the efforts to help countless constituents affected by the fire who'd come to their elected official for help—all while rebooting his own life. It was their grief and frustration, added to his personal loss, right down to his treasured Nixon photo, that fueled his bitterness in court that day.

Finally, after everyone else had had their say, it was Judge Benitez's turn to speak. The gallery bristled with energy, the same question vibrating in each person's mind. Would he send Martinez to prison?

"I wish I could reverse the course of time," Benitez began, "but the reality is we're not like God. And I'm not here to decide about [fire] agencies. My job is to impose a sentence."

It had been a tough case, he admitted, and he'd struggled for months over his eventual ruling.

"If I thought Mr. Martinez acted with malice, five years in prison would not be enough," the judge said. "Nothing is going to bring loved ones and property back; nothing is going to heal those wounds."

After all the deliberating, Benitez concluded, two factors emerged as indisputable: "One, this was a terrible tragedy. Two, Mr. Martinez was lost."

Paramedics confirmed he'd been distressed and thirsty enough to consume one hundred ounces of liquids within an hour of being rescued, the judge noted.

"It appears that while engaged in a lawful use of public lands, the defendant got lost and ran out of water and food," he said. "It was going to get dark soon, and he was distressed."

So Sergio Martinez did what he'd been taught to do in hunter safety courses, Benitez continued. He lit a signal fire.

"We might look back and ask if he acted responsibly, but he did exactly, exactly, what he was supposed to do, what was recommended that people do in precisely the circumstances he was in, which, I might add, worked.

"Contrast that with people using firecrackers, throwing cigarettes out car windows, walking away from a campfire. If Mr. Martinez gets five years in prison, what would I do with that kind of egregious behavior? The law doesn't lack compassion and a concern for understanding how things happen."

In the end, noting the defendant's clean history, Benitez sentenced Martinez to five years of probation; six months of community confinement, enabling him to keep his job; 960 hours of community service, rebuilding homes and reforesting open areas lost in the fire; and restitution of $150 a month for five years, totaling $9,000. Because of concerns raised during the investigation about Martinez's possible use of marijuana, he was also to seek substance abuse counseling.

After the sentencing, Sergio Martinez again met the media and their cameras outside the courtroom. Visibly relieved, he even managed a smile, which a newspaper photographer caught, editors showcased on the front page, and some readers interpreted as a remorseless smirk. The media also reported that after the press conference, a couple of angry spectators heckled Martinez and his parents, forcing them to retreat into the courthouse and sneak out later through a side exit. Sergio Martinez had escaped prison, but the consequences of his actions would likely dog him forever.

Forgiveness can be unpredictable—sometimes sprouting overnight; sometimes only after a long, fallow season of healing; other times never germinating at all. Some people think of it as an innate human trait; some believe no forgiveness is possible without divine intervention. Who can say for sure? I don't know why some of us touched by the fire could forgive Sergio Martinez while others could not. I don't know if my forgiving him helped him heal. I only know that it helped me.

Chapter 26

A New Season

THREE MONTHS AFTER THE FIRE, Bob and I bought an Airstream travel trailer and started spending weekends at Terra Nova. We parked it in front of the empty concrete pad where our house once stood, with the window over the bed facing east. Waking up again to the pink and golden glow of sunrise in the canyon soothed the ragged places in us. Something about the morning air, cool and clean, hinted of hope. And that view we so loved, stretching down the cut between the mountains, though scorched and drained of color, still caught our breath and buoyed our spirits. Terra Nova had always been more than a house. Standing in the midst of our "new land" after the fire, our hands and clothes smudged with ash, Bob and I still felt at home, still found ourselves reminding each other, this time with grit more than wonder: "We live here."

We could walk the entire property now, exploring for the first time the bare ground between the boulders. Rocks we'd never seen thrust up through the earth or lay piled together as if tossed aside by giants. Under all the vegetation, we realized,

Terra Nova was defined by primeval chunks of granite. Exposed like this, so empty, so quiet and still, it seemed almost a land before time, certainly a land before life. Where once birdsong and coyote choirs reverberated across nearby ravines, the air hung heavy with silence. So many animals had lived all around us in the chaparral. Where were they now? Surely some must have survived, at least a pair or two of each species to repopulate the world after our flood of fire. Yet for the longest time we didn't see a single creature, and hardly a sign of former life— only occasionally scraps of fur and bone that once belonged to a hapless cottontail, or a chain of ribbed vertebrae and shriveled skin, remnants of a snake that didn't find a gopher hole in time.

If you had seen Wildcat Canyon in those first weeks after the fire, a blackened valley of rocks, ruins, and withered trees, you would not have believed that Terra Nova could ever again grow fruitful and verdant. You would not have expected ever again to hear the chatter of birds, to catch a rabbit nibbling your grass, to surprise a tiny tree frog in your garden. Yet over the next two years, as Bob and I rebuilt our home in the chaparral, we saw the land rush back to life with amazing speed, greening and blossoming after the first winter rains, maturing season by season, and gradually drawing all of its creatures home. At first, we saw only ravens and squirrels, and then songbirds, rabbits, and coyotes. We hung a beautiful copper wall fountain, an anniversary gift from Lauren, just outside the front door of the new house, and within weeks, a family of tree frogs took up residence on our porch. We'd find them perched on the lip of the fountain at night or flattened to the wall behind it during the day. How did these tiny water-lovers come back from the fire? We couldn't imagine. But we knew that if they could do it, so could we.

And then, one day, neighbors told us they'd seen a bobcat.

I'd thought often about the creature that leapt in front of my car the night of the fire, keeping us on the road during our frantic escape from Terra Nova. What were the odds that a wildcat, so elusive, so totally unexpected, would cross our path at exactly the moment we most needed it? Only a flash really, a blur, materializing out of the smoke barely long enough to be seen.

"Honey, I've been thinking about your bobcat," my father said when I flew back to North Carolina to see him a few weeks after the fire. "God sent one of his wildest creatures to lead you out of danger."

Even normally skeptical family and friends interpreted the story of a wildcat coming to our rescue as more than coincidence.

"I don't want to get religious here," commented our friend, Scot Miller, the Navy captain who'd helped replace Bob's Marine officer's sword. "But that cat . . ."

Scot shook his head.

"Something was going on there."

I asked my Wampanoag friend Marla Bingham, who'd foreseen the fire, what significance the bobcat held in Native American lore. She referred me to the Medicine Wheel, a symbol of the natural world and its animal inhabitants, which offered two intriguing explanations. First, because of the bobcat's secretive nature, encountering one means that people will tell you their confidences, and you must honor their trust. Second, the bobcat is a sign that something is stalking you, and the cat, being an excellent protector, has come to lead you to safety—just as my father believed.

Our friend Henry Large, the realtor who'd driven me out to Wildcat Canyon for my first look at Terra Nova, seconded the rescue idea, but with a twist. Having played such a crucial role in our move to the backcountry, Henry felt especially disturbed by how things had turned out a mere seven months later. He kept in close touch after the fire and came out now and then to visit us in the Airstream. One weekend Bob, Henry, and I crowded around the trailer's tiny dinette table, opened a bottle of wine, and settled in for an evening of Henry's legendary storytelling. But that night our normally expansive friend seemed more philosophically inclined. Somewhere between his second and third glass of Chardonnay, he leaned across the table, his faded brown hair a little tousled, his eyes bloodshot yet intense.

"That cat," he said, "what if it jumped to your car on purpose?"

"What do you mean?" I asked.

"I mean cats can see in the dark, but not in the smoke."

Henry leaned closer, so earnest now that his expression turned a little wild.

"Maybe he saw the light from your car and jumped to it thinking it might be a way out, a way to escape the fire. Maybe you were helping each other, Sandra. Maybe you helped him as much as he helped you."

Could it be that a wildcat blinded by smoke, charged with fear, running just ahead of a killing heat, may have found its bearings in the sliver of asphalt illuminated by my headlights? I'd certainly like to think so.

I hadn't questioned the bobcat's leading. I'd simply known to follow it. In the same way, Bob and I never wondered whether to rebuild Terra Nova. From that first day after the fire, when Bob shook hands with Randy Fritz amid the ashes, we started the long process of re-creating our oasis in the chaparral. Building a house is a massive project, a curious amalgam of excitement and anxiety, decision and indecision, celebrations and setbacks—and it seemed to take forever.

In the meantime, except for our weekend visits to the Airstream, we were stuck in the suburbs again, living in a house owned by someone else, surrounded by someone else's furniture, often wearing someone else's clothes, and yearning all the time simply to go home. We'd gotten off to a fast start, not having to shop for a contractor or haggle with our insurance company as so many other rebuilders did. Still, it took nearly two years before Terra Nova once again stood complete, looking as if it had grown in place, its stucco echoing the color of canyon earth, its window frames repeating the sage green of returning chaparral, its tile roof blending the slate and silver of surrounding boulders.

Long before, we'd begun planning a grand welcome-home party. Randy estimated construction would be finished in March 2005, so we set the date for our gathering at the end of May, over Memorial Day weekend. It would be a multiple celebration—an open house and dedication of our new home, our thirtieth wedding anniversary, and our daughter Kendall's twenty-fifth birthday. Adding icing to the cake, our Newfy boy, Charter, would turn three that same weekend.

We invited nearly everyone we knew, including all the workers who helped us rebuild, from the framers to the kitchen designer, and people responded from across the country. Friends would be driving in from all over the state. Bob's mother, sister, and brother-in-law would be coming from Arizona. Two couples would be flying from the East Coast.

What we hadn't counted on was Southern California's first really wet winter in six years. Throughout January and February, storm after storm soaked our half-built house, each time forcing Randy and his subcontractors to wait until everything dried out before resuming work. Despite Randy's best efforts to make up for lost time, it began to look as if his crew wouldn't be able to finish before the big celebration.

"Don't kill yourself," I told him. "It doesn't matter if the house is done for the party or not. We've come back from nothing, and everyone knows it. Wherever we are, we'll have plenty to celebrate."

But Randy didn't let up. That final week before the open house, workmen swarmed in nearly every room, and the dusty air reverberated with the pop of nail guns and the whine of power tools. The last planks of rich brown hardwood flooring were set into place the day before the big event. It would be another month before we "finaled," passing the last inspection, allowing us to move into our beautiful new home. But when our guests arrived to celebrate that impending milestone, no one minded the unfinished details, the unpaved driveway, or the unplanted landscaping. No one complained about the stacks of leftover lumber in the yard, the rented folding chairs and tables in lieu of real furniture. Terra Nova rocked that day with joy and laughter, and with the love and good wishes of more than a hundred family and friends who braved the twists and turns of Wildcat Canyon Road to share our celebration.

Many brought cards, flowers, and gifts to fill the empty rooms. One friend presented us with a framed spoon, one of our own she'd mistakenly taken home with a potluck dish shortly before the fire. She'd labeled the mat inside the frame with a single word: "Luck." We returned that lucky spoon to our kitchen with gratitude, not tucked away in a drawer this time, but hanging in a prominent spot on the wall.

We'd also invited several of the firefighters who battled the flames in our area to join the party. Kelly Zombro, the CDF battalion chief who first met the Cedar Fire head-on in San Diego Country Estates, arrived with his wife and children, and brought a gift.

"It's not much," he said as he handed me a plain paper bag, "but, well, you'll see."

I reached in and pulled out a matchbook-size fire engine and helicopter, both marked with the CDF logo.

"How perfect!" I said. "Thank you so much."

I glanced up, and Kelly Zombro met my eyes with a somber gaze.

"I just wish I'd had them to send you that night," he said.

Before the festivities began, our good friends and former pastors Steve and Cinda Gorman, who'd come all the way from

Cincinnati, Ohio, helped us mark our return home with a brief dedication. We all stood in a circle in the new family room, its rock fireplace, grand windows, and hickory floors every bit as beautiful as before. Steve and Cinda expressed thanks that Bob and I had survived the fire and been able to rebuild. Lauren and Kendall, through tears, read aloud the names of the seventeen people lost to the flames. And then we dedicated our new house to God, asking his blessing and protection through all the years and fires to come.

"To everything there is a season." I'd borrowed that well-worn scrap of Scripture in writing the invitation to our celebration. "A time to tear down, and a time to build up . . . a time to weep, and a time to laugh, a time to mourn and a time to dance."

That day at Terra Nova, we welcomed a new season.

The Cedar Fire came and went in a rush, a mere flash in natural history, but it was years before I'd read enough reports, attended enough meetings, and talked with enough people to tell the whole story of the fire and distill some sort of meaning from it. After all that, here is what I know:

Fire is a paradox. Both terrifying and splendid, polluting and cleansing, demonic and holy. Sometimes it acts as servant; sometimes tyrant; sometimes midwife; sometimes murderer.

Fire gives and fire takes. It can light our way forward; it can erase our past. Neither creature nor creator, it is physics only, a scientific phenomenon, unliving, unfeeling. Yet fire breathes; it moves; it grows; it reacts. And in the end, it dies.

Fire cast abroad is like a horse unbroken. It may be corralled, even gentled. But ease up on the bit, and it will bolt, gallop where it wills, with the wind at its back laying on the whip. Once loosed, it cares for no one, needs no one. All that

it touches turns to fodder, and the more it consumes, the faster
it runs. Everything normal, everything known can fall beneath
those hoofbeats. And the trail they leave is marked by smoke
and tears.

Sometimes it seems the wildest fires run with purpose, but
whether malevolent or capricious, who can tell? One house is
spared; another crumbles into ashes. A young girl disappears in
the flames; an old couple emerges untouched. It even seems,
sometimes, that fire does us a favor, burning away all that is
false, revealing all that is true and good and essential, all that in
normal times we mistake for miracles. And sometimes, digging
through the ashes of what has been, we find not what we hoped
to find (a relic intact, however small), but something better. A
touchstone to what could be. A key waiting to be turned.

Acknowledgments

I HOPE THE BOBCAT ESCAPED THE flames, too. Leaping into my headlights and showing me the road I could not find in pea-soup smoke, it likely saved my life the night the Cedar Fire destroyed my home and killed twelve of my neighbors. I will always be grateful for that wild creature, and to God, who sent it my way at just the right moment.

I knew soon afterward that I had to tell the story of the Cedar Fire—not just my piece of it, but the whole story. As both a fire survivor and a journalist, how could I not? So I set out to research and write a thorough, fair, and accurate account of that historic event, which terrorized a metropolis of three million people and helped redefine the world's expectations of wildfire behavior. At the same time, I worked to give all those affected by San Diego's 2003 fire siege some piece of story they can relate to, something that enables them to say, "Yes, that's exactly how it was." To anyone whose perspective I inevitably missed, I offer my sincere apologies.

It has, indeed, taken a village to nurture this manuscript through a long and sometimes dubious gestation to completion. Nearly every person I know encouraged me along the way, and I'm grateful to each one. I'm indebted also to my long-ago teachers, Genella Allison, Walter Spearman, John Keats, and Bill Glavin, who taught me how to write.

The incomparable Judy Reeves, founder of San Diego Writers, Ink, and my brilliant colleagues in her Wednesday night critique group helped me complete and polish an initial manuscript. My sister, Karen Millers Allen, the world's greatest grammarian, combed through a later draft. Master photographers Dave Gatley, Dan Megna, Eric Millette, and

Bob Younger enabled me to assemble a jaw-dropping visual supplement to this story. My thanks to each and all.

I cannot begin to express, only acknowledge, my gratitude for the unfailing love and encouragement of my family in this and every venture of my life. I could not have written this book without the strong foundation provided by my parents, Art and Lucille Millers, or the loving encouragement of my daughters, Lauren and Kendall. My "Younger mother," Margaret, and sister, Terri, have also been stalwart supporters. Most of all, I thank my extraordinary husband, Bob, who never once in the nine years it took me to finish this manuscript suggested that I go out and get a real job. "Cutes," he said, "we're on this journey together; don't give up on your dream." Bottom line, his constant love and support made this book possible.

Finally, I offer my deepest thanks to the many firefighters, law enforcement officers, fire survivors, and family members of those killed in the Cedar and Paradise fires, who trusted me, often through tears, with their fire stories. I hope that I have represented them well enough to capture the intensity of a runaway wildfire, honor those lost to its fury, and celebrate the God-given ability of the human spirit to rebound, even from ashes.

Sandra Millers Younger
Lakeside, California
February 2013

Suggested Reading

California Department of Forestry and Fire Protection. *Engine Crew Entrapment, Fatality, and Burn Injuries, October 29, 2003, Cedar Fire.*

California Department of Forestry and Fire Protection, California Governor's Office of Emergency Services and USDA Forest Service, *California Fire Siege 2003: The Story.*

California Department of Forestry and Fire Protection and USDA Forest Service, *The 2003 San Diego Fire Siege Fire Safety Review*, 2004.

City of San Diego Fire-Rescue Department. *Cedar Fire 2003 After-Action Report.* 2004.

Egan, Timothy. *The Big Burn: Teddy Roosevelt and the Fire That Saved America.* Boston: Mariner Books. 2009.

Frankl, Viktor E. *Man's Search for Meaning.* Boston: Beacon Press, 2006.

Garvey, Megan; Jack Leonard; Christine Hanley; and Stuart Pfeifer. "Night of Fire," *Los Angeles Times,* December 28, 2003.

Gess, Denise, and William Lutz. *Firestorm at Peshtigo: A Town, Its People, and the Deadliest Fire in American History.* New York: Henry Holt and Company, 2002.

Governor's Blue Ribbon Fire Commission. *Report to the Governor.* April 5, 2004.

Halsey, Richard W. *Fire, Chaparral and Survival in Southern California.* San Diego: Sunbelt Publications, 2005.

Mutch, Robert W. *FACES: The Story of the Victims of Southern California's 2003 Fire Siege.* Tucson, Arizona: Wildland Fire Lessons Learned Center, July 2007.

National Institute for Occupational Safety and Health. *A Career Firefighter Was Killed and a Career Captain Was Severely Injured During a Wildland/Urban Interface Operation—California.* July 15, 2005.

Novato Fire Protection District. *Investigation Analysis of the Cedar Fire Incident: Engine 6162 Crew Entrapment, Fatality, and Burn Injuries, October 29, 2003.* May 26, 2004.

Perry, Tony; Stuart Pfeifer; and Jennifer Oldham. "San Diego Was in No Shape for This Fight," *Los Angeles Times,* October 31, 2003.

Pyne, Stephen J. *Fire in America: A Cultural History of Wildland and Rural Fire.* Seattle, Wash.: The University of Washington Press, 1997.

———. *Year of the Fires: The Story of the Great Fires of 1910.* New York: Penguin Books, 2001.

San Diego Regional Fire Prevention and Emergency Preparedness Task Force. *Final Report.* August 10, 2004.

Dave Downey, "Firestorm 2003: The story of a catastrophe," *The San Diego Union-Tribune,* November 16, 2003.

US Department of Agriculture Forest Service and the California Department of Forestry and Fire Protection. *The Inaja Forest Fire Disaster: Cleveland National Forest, California.* January 1957.

The White House. "President Bush Visits California—Talks to Victims of Fires: Remarks by the President to the Travel Pool. Harbison Canyon, California," November 4, 2003.

Index

About The Author

Sandra Younger lost her home and nearly her life in California's historic 2003 Cedar Fire, a bellwether of today's extreme, climate-driven wildfire catastrophes. A powerful storyteller and veteran magazine journalist, Sandra is an acclaimed author, international speaker, and certified professional coach dedicated to inspiring resilience and potential. Visit her online at sandrayounger.com.

A Gift for You

THANK YOU FOR READING *The Fire Outside My Window*. I hope the Cedar Fire story expanded your understanding of catastrophic wildfires and inspired you to live with courage, resilience, and hope, even in the face of loss and uncertainty.

If you, too, have been affected by wildfire or some other natural disaster, or if you know someone who has, please visit www.sandrayounger.com and download a complimentary copy of *The ComeBACK Formula™ Guidebook,* my summary of proven resilience-building practices for disaster survivors. If you'd like, feel free to share your story with me directly at sandra@sandrayounger.com. Sharing our stories helps us heal and grow, while encouraging others.

Also at my website, you can see color versions of the photos included here in the book, invite me to speak at your next event, and explore the possibilities of leadership coaching. While you're there, please join my mailing list so we can stay in touch.

Follow your bobcat!
Sandra

Everything can be taken from a [person] but one thing: the last of the human freedoms—to choose one's attitude in any given set of circumstances, to choose one's own way.

—Viktor E. Frankl, *Man's Search for Meaning*

www.ingramcontent.com/pod-product-compliance
Lightning Source LLC
Chambersburg PA
CBHW020432130626
46549CB00001B/108